A BIBLIOGRAPHY OF LATIN AMERICAN THEATER CRITICISM 1940–1974

Guides and Bibliographies Series: 10

A Bibliography of Latin American Theater Criticism 1940-1974

by LEON F. LYDAY and GEORGE W. WOODYARD

INSTITUTE OF LATIN AMERICAN STUDIES
THE UNIVERSITY OF TEXAS AT AUSTIN
AUSTIN * 1976

COVER ILLUSTRATION: Interior of the Teatro Municipal General San Martín in Buenos Aires, Argentina.

International Standard Book Number 0–292–70717–7
Library of Congress Card Catalogue Number 76–45126

PRINTED BY THE INSTITUTE OF LATIN AMERICAN STUDIES
MANUFACTURED IN THE UNITED STATES OF AMERICA

The Guides and Bibliographies Series is distributed for the Institute of Latin American Studies by:
University of Texas Press
P. O. Box 7819
Austin, Texas 78712

Contents

Acknowledgements

The preparation of this bibliography was made possible through extensive support provided by the Office for Graduate Research of the College of Liberal Arts at the Pennsylvania State University and the Office of Research Administration at the University of Kansas. Several graduate assistants also contributed significantly to its compilation, specifically Clare Bretz and Alice Miller at Penn State and Bonnie Reynolds and Cynthia Gouzie at Kansas. In particular, we express our appreciation to Jacqueline Eyring, who cheerfully endured the exacting demands of preparing the camera-ready manuscript copy.

Even with this invaluable assistance, the project could not have been completed without the moral support and tolerance of our wives and the magnificent seven: Shana, Lance, Devon, Kenda, Andrew, Rachel and John. To them our special thanks.

Introduction

A few years ago we completed a critical bibliography of theatrical activity in Latin America during the 1960s. Shortly thereafter, it became apparent to us that an expanded version would be useful to scholars, critics, and students in the field. The following bibliographical guide is the result of our efforts to update our work through 1974 while simultaneously collecting references back to 1940. This thirty-five year period (1940-1974) corresponds to the establishment and development of a truly national theater movement in most areas of Latin America.

Although the break with the old-style theater came about in Mexico and Argentina as early as the late 1920s and early 1930s, the so-called experimental or independent theater movement did not affect most other areas of the hemisphere until the late 1930s (Puerto Rico, Cuba) or the early 1940s (Chile and Brazil). With some few exceptions, the growth of activity since has been both constant and varied. Especially after World War II the theater movement gains new vitality and becomes increasingly more sophisticated in form and technique. The Latin American theater of this period also grows more conscious of social inequities and oppressive political and/or religious systems, and becomes more militant in dealing with them.

Creative activity generally increases in stature as it is tempered by serious critical reaction, and the theater in Latin America has elicited and profited from a growing number of histories and critical studies. The pioneer work of Carlos Solórzano in the early 1960s is the first attempt to provide a comprehensive view of the principal dramatists and theater movements in Spanish America during the twentieth century. In 1966-1967, Ediciones de Andrea published two signal studies: Frank Dauster's history covering the period from 1800 to the present (republished in 1973 in an expanded version), and José Juan Arrom's companion volume for the colonial period. Also in 1966 the University of Texas Press published Willis Knapp Jones's *Behind Spanish American Footlights*, a volume important primarily as a mine of historical and bibliographical information. Other significant histories with a national focus rather than the global viewpoint of those previously mentioned should also be consulted: José Juan Arrom (Cuba), Carlos Solórzano and Antonio Magaña Esquivel (Mexico), Sábato Magaldi, Décio de Almeida Prado, and J. Galante de Sousa (Brazil), Walter Rela (Uruguay), Orlando Rodríguez, Domingo Piga, and Julio Durán Cerda (Chile), Ricardo Descalzi (Ecuador), Guillermo Lohmann Villena and Guillermo Ugarte Chamorro (Peru), Arturo Berenguer Carisomo, Raúl Castagnino, and Luis Ordaz (Argentina), Francisco Arriví (Puerto Rico), and others.

A good deal of theatrical criticism appears in newspapers but it is seldom of high quality or transcendent importance. For this reason, few references to daily newspapers or even Sunday supplements appear in this bibliography, although in some cases the quality was sufficiently good to warrant making an exception. Most serious criticism and consequently most of the material listed here has appeared either in book form or in literary periodicals. A few journals are devoted exclusively to the theater in Latin America, but most of these are either erratic or short-lived. Two are easily accessible: *Conjunto* (Cuba) and the *Latin American Theatre Review* (Kansas). The interested critic should also consult *Talía*, the *Boletín de Estudios de Teatro* and the *Revista de Estudios de Teatro* (Buenos Aires), the *Revista Teatro* (Medellín), and *Palco e Platéia* (defunct, São Paulo). Occasionally a literary journal general in scope will devote a complete issue to the theater in Latin America, as in the case of *The Drama Review* (14, No. 2); many other major literary journals such as *Revista Iberoamericana, Sur, Revista Civilização Brasileira, Cuadernos Hispanoamericanos,* and *Hispania* also carry articles on theater.

It is superfluous to point out that for Latin American drama as well as for all other literary genres and areas a great deal of criticism of poor quality exists. With the exceptions noted, however, we have tried to be as comprehensive as possible, and many items included here may in fact shed very little light on the subject. We hasten to add, on the other hand, that a number of studies contribute greatly to our understanding and appreciation, not only of the theater in Latin America, but of principles of dramatic structure and meaning. We especially direct our readers' attention to Donald Shaw's analysis of René Marqués's *La muerte no entrará en palacio,* to René de Costa's study of Florencio Sánchez's *Barranca abajo*, to Silviano Santiago's discussion of Jorge Andrade's *A Moratória*, to Anatol Rosenfeld's introduction to the theater of Alfredo Dias Gomes, and to Tamara Holzapfel's essay on the drama of Griselda Gambaro. In addition to these close readings of specific plays and perceptive commentaries on individual playwrights, the reader is also directed to three items which, since they are post-1974, do not appear in the bibliography. The first, *Ensayos sobre teatro hispanoamericano* (Mexico: SepSetentas, 1975), is a collection of studies by Frank Dauster on Spanish American playwrights; the second, *Teatro hispanoamericano de crítica social* (Madrid: Playor, 1975) by Pedro Bravo-Elizondo includes close studies of eight contemporary plays; and the third, *Dramatists in Revolt* (Austin: University of Texas Press, 1976), is a volume of essays dealing with the dramatic trajectories of fifteen contemporary Latin American dramatists and is under the general editorship of Leon Lyday and George Woodyard.

A word about using this bibliography, which in a sense could serve as a companion volume to the above collections. Despite its length, we have decided upon the following organization for its unity versus the fragmentation produced by any other approach: numbered entries listed alphabetically by critical author, a national or regional reference in the right margin, and annotation when needed. The subject and topic appendix, listing entry numbers from the main corpus, is relatively complete but not exhaustive. Osvaldo Dragún, for example, will appear with the numbers of those studies where the focus is on his plays, but not normally with an article or book-length study on the Argentine theater. Topically, we have included those aspects or features we considered to be of greatest interest or value, as, for example, censorship, children, language, puppets, and scenography. Books and reviews are cross-listed. Anthologies of plays are included only if they contain a critical introduction. A separate section on other bibliographies of Latin American theater is also included at the beginning.

Although this bibliography was compiled, in large part, on the basis of our investigations in the libraries of the University of Kansas, the Pennsylvania State University, the University of Illinois, and various Spanish American libraries, we did make use of several major reference sources, chiefly the MLA annual bibliographies, Frank Hebblethwaite's *A Bibliographical Guide to the Spanish American Theater*, and the *Handbook of Latin American Studies*. Sins of omission and commission are inevitable in this kind of study; we hope they are few in number and that the more than 2,300 entries listed here will serve to facilitate and encourage the study of the theater of Latin America.

Leon F. Lyday
Pennsylvania State University

George W. Woodyard
University of Kansas

Bibliographies

Antuña, María Luisa y Josefina García Carranza. "Bibliografía de teatro cubano," *Revista de la Biblioteca Nacional José Martí*, Año 62, 3ª época, XIII, No. 3 (set-dic 1971), 87-154. CUBA

A bibliography of all primary sources contained in the theater collection of the Biblioteca Nacional José Martí in Havana. See Rine Leal for commentary.

Arrom, José Juan. "Bibliografía dramática venezolana," *Anuario bibliográfico venezolano*, 1946. Caracas: Tipografía Americana, 1949, pp. 197-209. VEN

Christensen, George K. "A Bibliography of Latin American Plays in English Translation," *Latin American Theatre Review*, 6/2 (Spring 1973), 29-39. GEN

La crítica teatral argentina (1880-1962). Buenos Aires: Fondo Nacional de las Artes, 1966. 78 p. ARG

Foppa, Tito Livio. *Diccionario teatral del Rio de la Plata*. Buenos Aires: Argentores, Ediciones del Carro de Tespis, 1961. 1046 p. RIVER PLATE

Forster, Merlin H. *An Index to Mexican Literary Periodicals*. New York and London: The Scarecrow Press, 1966. 276 p. MEX

A complete bibliography of 16 Mexican journals, containing seven of the post-1940 period.

____. *Letras de México (1937-1947)*. México: Universidad Iberoamericana, 1972. 200 p. MEX

Annotated index of the journal.

Foster, Virginia R. "Contemporary Argentine Dramatists: A Bibliography," *Theatre Documentation*, 4, No. 1 (1971-72), 13-20. ARG

Grismer, Raymond L. *Bibliography of the Drama of Spain and Spanish America*. 2 vol. Minneapolis: Burgess-Beckwith (s.f.), 231, 231 p. GEN

Oriented more toward Spain than toward Spanish America.

Hebblethwaite, Frank B. *A Bibliographical Guide to the Spanish American Theater*. Washington: Pan American Union, 1969. 84 p. GEN

An extremely useful annotated guide.
Reviewed: Bravo-Villarroel, Roberto.

Huerta, Jorge A. *A Bibliography of Chicano and Mexican Dance, Drama and Music*. Oxnard, California: Colegio Quetzalcoatl, 1972. 59 p. U.S. MEX

Reviewed: González de Garfinkel, Lila.

Jones, Willis Knapp. "Latin America through Drama in English: a Bibliography," *Hispania*, XXVIII, No. 2 (May 1945), 220-227. GEN

Revised and published as a monograph by the Pan American Union in 1950.

Lamb, Ruth S. *Bibliografía del teatro mexicano del siglo XX*. México: Ediciones de Andrea, 1962. 143 p. MEX

Reviewed: Dauster, Frank.

Martí de Cid, Dolores. "Sugerencias para una bibliografía del teatro iberoamericano," *Memoria* (Cuarto Congreso del Instituto Internacional de Literatura Iberoamericana, La Habana, abril de 1949). La Habana: Ministerio de Educación, Dirección de Cultura, 1949, pp. 285-288. GEN

Monterde, Francisco. *Bibliografía del teatro en México*. New York: B. Franklin, 1970. Theatre and Drama Series, 11. MEX

A reprint of the 1933 edition.

Ocampo de Gómez, Maura. *Literatura mexicana contemporánea: Bibliografía crítica*. México: Universidad Nacional Autónoma de México, Facultad de Filosofía y Letras, 1965. 329 p. MEX

Ordaz, Luis and Erminio G. Neglia. *Repertorio selecto del teatro hispanoamericano contemporáneo*. Caracas: Editorial Giannelli [1974?], s.p. GEN

A bibliography of plays by 138 Spanish American writers.

Orjuela, Héctor H. *Bibliografía del teatro colombiano*. Bogotá: Instituto Caro y Cuervo, 1974. 313 p. COL

____. *Fuentes para el estudio de la literatura colombiana: Guía bibliográfica*. Bogotá: Imprenta Patriótica del Instituto Caro y Cuervo, 1968. 863 p. [Drama, pp. 648-670.] COL

Rela, Walter. "Contribución a la bibliografía del teatro brasileño," *Cebela*, No. 1 (1965), 109-129. BRAZ

____. *Contribución a la bibliografía del teatro chileno, 1804-1960.* Noticia preliminar de Ricardo A. Latcham. Montevideo: Universidad de la República, 1960. 51 p. CHILE

Reviewed: Dauster, Frank.

____. *Fuentes para el estudio de la literatura uruguaya (1835-1968).* Montevideo: Ediciones de la Banda Oriental, 1969. 134 p. URUG

____. *Repertorio bibliográfico del teatro uruguayo 1816-1964.* Montevideo: Editorial Síntesis, 1965. 35 p. URUG

Rivero Muñiz, José. *Bibliografía del teatro cubano.* Prólogo de Lilia Castro de Morales. La Habana: Publicaciones de la Biblioteca Nacional, 1957. 120 p. CUBA

Skinner, Eugene R. "Research Guide to Post-Revolutionary Cuban Drama," *Latin American Theatre Review*, 7/2 (Spring 1974), 59-68. CUBA

Woodyard, George W. and Leon F. Lyday, "Studies on the Latin American Theatre, 1960-1969," *Theatre Documentation*, II, No. 1-2 (Fall 1969-Spring 1970), 49-84. GEN

All entries incorporated into present work.

A BIBLIOGRAPHY OF LATIN AMERICAN THEATER CRITICISM
1940–1974

1 Abascal Brunet, Manuel. *Apuntes para la historia del teatro en Chile. La zarzuela grande.* Santiago: Imprenta Universitaria, 1940. CHILE

Reviewed: Jones, Willis Knapp; Latcham, Ricardo; Mérimée, P.

2 ____ and Eugenio Pereira Salas. *Pepe Vila; la zarzuela chica en Chile.* Santiago: Imprenta Universitaria, Valenzuela Basterrica y Cía., 1952. 225 p. CHILE

3 Abdo, Ada. "Seis meses de teatro habanero," *Casa de las Américas*, III, No. 17-18 (mar-jun 1963), 89-92. CUBA

Report on II Latin American Theatre Festival in Havana.

4 Abreu, Modesto de. "Morre Oduvaldo Vianna," *Revista de Teatro* (Brazil), No. 387 (maio-jun 1972), 1-5. BRAZ

5 Abreu Gómez, Ermilo. "Celestino Gorostiza y la innovación teatral," *Nación* (30 junio 1963), p. 10. MEX

6 Acchiardi, Pablo. "Juan Aurelio Casacuberta y el arte del actor," *Cuadernos de Cultura Teatral*, No. 14 (1940), 57-100. RIVER PLATE

7 Acosta Saignes, Miguel. "El teatro primitivo en Venezuela," *400 años de valores teatrales*, ed. Aquiles Nazoa [Edición especial, No. 6] Caracas: Círculo Musical, 1967, pp. 3-7. VEN

Record with text.

8 Acuña, Manuel. *Teatro de títeres.* Buenos Aires: 1960. GEN

9 Acuña, René. "El *Rabinal Achí*: historia, estructura y significado." Unpub. Ph.D. diss., UCLA, 1973. GUAT

10 ____. "*Rabinal Achí*, teatro sacral prehispánico," in *El teatro en Iberoamérica* (Memoria del duodécimo congreso del Instituto Internacional de Literatura Iberoamericana). México: IILI (1966), pp. 39-46. GUAT

11 Acuña Paredes, Jorge. "El artista, para ser tal,

debe estar siempre en función del hombre," *Conjunto*, No. 21 (jul-set 1974), 85-94. PERU

"Recopilación de textos sobre el mimo peruano de la Plaza San Martín."

12 Acuña Paredes, Jorge. "En la calle, más libertad que en cualquier parte," *Textual*, No. 2 (set 1971), 39-41. PERU

13 Adams, Mildred. "The Drama of Brazil," in *A History of Modern Drama*, ed. Barrett Clark and George Freedley. New York: 1947, pp. 596-600. BRAZ

14 Adán, Martín. "De lo barroco en el Perú: Segura," *Mercurio Peruano*, 17, No. 187 (oct 1942), 493-503. PERU

15 Adellach, Alberto. "Chau," *Teatro'70*, No. 34-35 (oct-nov 1972), 21-37. ARG

Commentary on and analysis of his own play, Chau, papá.

16 ____. "Notas sobre *Homo dramaticus*," *Teatro'70*, No. 8-9 (abr-mayo 1971), 23-28. ARG

17 ____. "¿Qué pasó con el teatro?" *Ensayos Argentinos*. Buenos Aires: Centro Editor de América Latina, 1971, pp. 9-29. (La Historia Popular, No. 68.) ARG

Brief overview of the Argentine theater from Moreira to the present.

18 Afanador Soto, Hugo. "Algo sobre Brecht," *Conjunto*, No. 20 (abr-jun 1974), 135-136. GEN

19 Agilda, Enrique. *El alma del teatro independiente: su trayectoria emocional*. Buenos Aires: Ediciones Intercoop, 1960. 154 p. ARG

20 ____. "Comprensión popular del arte," *Revista de Estudios de Teatro*, 1, No. 3 (1960), 47-49. ARG

21 ____. "Labor escénica en la zona rural," *Revista de Estudios de Teatro*, 3, No. 8 (1964), 60-62. ARG

22 Agudiez, Juan V. "Louis Verneuil, Armando Moock, y la comedia de dos personajes," *Comparative Literature Studies* (Univ. of Maryland, College Park, Md.), 5, No. 1 (Mar 1968), 55-67. CHILE

23 Aguero, Luis. "Pasec por un festival," *Cuba*, VII, No. 69 (ene 1968), 23-24. CUBA

Interview with José Triana, Vicente Revuelta and Miriam Acevedo.

24 ____, Emilio Nogales and Marcos Pinares. "Lo que ve La Habana," *Cuba*, III, No. 22 (feb 1964), 52-57. CUBA

Report on the III Latin American Theatre Festival, activities of the Teatro Musical de La Habana, and the Teatro Nacional de Guiñol.

25 Aguilera Malta, Demetrio. "A propósito del teatro en la República Dominicana," *Boletín de la Unión Panamericana*, 81, No. 12 (dic 1947), 679-683. DOM REP

26 Aguirre, Isidora. "Teatro indio en la América india," *Conjunto*, 3, No. 7 (s.f.), 103-104. PERU

Teatro quechua, en quechua.

27 ____, Eugenio Guzmán y Rine Leal. "Recoger la hazaña de los muertos y entregarla a los vivos," *Conjunto*, 3, No. 8 (s.f.), 50-60. CHILE

Mesa redonda de Isidora Aguirre, Eugenio Guzmán y Rine Leal.

28 Aguirre, Magdalena. "Heiremans, hombre de teatro," *Cuadernos del Sur*, II, No. 9 (abr 1965), 345-346. CHILE

29 Aguirre, Yolanda. *Apuntes sobre el teatro colonial (1790-1833).* La Habana: Universidad de la Habana, 1968. CUBA

30 Albatrós. "Cachencho, el teatro y la dignidad," *Conjunto*, 3, No. 10 (s.f.), 48-50. CHILE

On the Chilean actor Fernando Gallardo, alias Cachencho.

31 Alcalde, Ramón. "Teoría y práctica de un teatro argentino," *Buenos Aires Literaria*, 2, No. 17 (feb 1954), 1-22. ARG

32 Aldao, A. *Teatro infantil. Dramatizaciones efemérides patrióticas y varios títeres.* Buenos Aires: 1960. ARG

33 Alegría, Alonso. "El teatro chicano en California: un teatro necesario," *Amaru*, No.12 (jun 1970), 29-30. U.S.

34 Alegría, Alonso. "El teatro es una infección," *Textual*, No. 2 (set 1971), 3-5. PERU

35 Alegría, Fernando. "Chile's Experimental Theater," *The Inter-American*, 4, No. 10 (Oct 1945), 24-25, 44-45. CHILE

36 Alfonso, Paco. *Inquietudes escénicas*. La Habana: Ediciones Teatro Popular, 1944. 22 p. GEN

37 Alfonzo, Rafael José. "El advenimiento de la historia y el sentido trágico del mito en *Todos los gatos son pardos*," *Revista de Literatura Hispanoamericana* (Universidad del Zulia), No. 4 (ene-jun 1973), 107-125. GEN

On Carlos Fuentes's play, Todos los gatos son pardos.

38 Alinsky, Marvin. "Fábregas' Broadway-to-Mexico Theater," *Christian Science Monitor*, 62, No. 261 (2 Oct 1970), 4. MEX

39 Alippi, Elías. "Mis experiencias como director artístico," *Boletín de Estudios de Teatro*, VII, No. 26 (jul-set 1949), 68-76. ARG

40 Allen, Richard F. "La obra literaria de Demetrio Aguilera Malta," *Mundo Nuevo*, No. 41 (nov 1969), 52-62. ECUAD

41 Almeida Prado, Décio de. *Apresentação do Teatro Brasileiro Moderno, Crítica Teatral, 1947-1955*. São Paulo: 1956. BRAZ

42 ____. "Dramatic Renaissance, The Theatre and Drama Come to Life," *Atlantic*, No. 197 (Feb 1956), 157-160. BRAZ

43 ____. *João Caetano* [O Ator, o Empresário, o Repertório]. São Paulo: Editora da Universidade de São Paulo, 1972. BRAZ

44 ____. "Noticia sobre el teatro brasileño," *Ficción*, No. 11 (ene-feb 1958), 113-118. BRAZ

Traducción de Raúl Navarro.

45 ____. *Teatro em Progresso. Crítica Teatral (1955-1964)*. São Paulo: Martins, 1964. 314 p. BRAZ

46 Almirón, David. Review: "Domingo F. Casadevall. *El tema de la mala vida en el teatro nacional.* Buenos Aires: Editorial Kraft, 1957." *Ficción*, No. 11 (ene-feb 1958), 202. ARG

47 Aloisi, Enzo. "Argentines Behind the Footlights: Twenty Years of Independent Theaters," *Américas*, 4, No. 2 (Feb 1952), 21-23, 44-45. ARG

48 Alonso, Alejandro G. "Y que las masas sean creadoras," *Conjunto*, No. 21 (jul-set 1974), 113-115. CUBA

Commentary on Amante y penol *by Herminia Sánchez and the Grupo Teatro de Participación Popular.*

49 Alonso, Amado. "Biografía de Fernán González de Eslava," *Revista de Filología Hispánica*, II, No. 3 (1940), 213-321. MEX

50 Alonso, Eduardo H. "Nuestra larga crisis teatral," *Informaciones Culturales* (La Habana), 1, No. 2 (mar-abr 1947), 29-30. CUBA

51 Alpern, Hymen, and José Martel, eds. *Teatro hispanoamericano.* New York: The Odyssey Press, 1956. GEN

Anthology includes: Arturo Alsina, La marca de fuego; *Florencio Sánchez,* Los derechos de la salud; *Samuel Eichelbaum,* Divorcio nupcial; *Armando Moock,* La serpiente; *Ricardo Rojas,* Ollantay; *Manuel Ascensio Segura,* Ña Catita. Reviewed: Dauster, Frank; Pasquariello, Anthony.

52 Alvarez, Baldomero. "Teatro universitario," *Tiempo* (La Habana), 7, No. 70 (ago 1944), 24. CUBA

53 Alvarez, José S. "Sobre Martiniano Leguizamón," *Boletín de Estudios de Teatro*, VIII, No. 28 (ene-mar 1950). ARG

54 Alves Pinto, Paulo F. "*Eles não usam Black-Tie*," *Revista Brasiliense*, No. 16 (mar-abr 1958), 179-182. BRAZ

55 "La América Latina en el IV festival internacional del teatro de las naciones," *Revista Nacional de Teatro* (La Habana), 1 (1961). GEN

56 Amora, Antônio Soares. "Gonçalves Dias: Dramaturgo," *Comentário*, VI (1965), 366-368. BRAZ

57 Amuchástegui, Aldo. "Córdoba y su comedia," *Revista*

de Teatro (Buenos Aires), 1, No. 1 (nov-dic 1960), 58-60. ARG

58 Analista (pseud. of Francisco Miró Quesada C.). *La mazorca* de Solari Swayne," *El Comercio* (Lima) (16 mayo 1965). PERU

59 Anderson-Imbert, Enrique. Review: "Carlos Solórzano. *Teatro hispanoamericano contemporáneo.* 2 vol. México: 1964." *Sur*, No. 301 (1966), 102-104. GEN

60 ____. "Tres notas sobre el teatro de Rodolfo Usigli," *Sur*, No. 244 (1957), 55-59. MEX

61 Andrade, Jorge. "Conversa com Rubem Rocha Filho," *Cadernos Brasileiros*, 7, No. 32 (nov-dez 1965), 43-56. BRAZ

62 Andrea, Pedro F. de. *Carlos Solórzano: Bibliografía.* México: Siete Hojas Volante de la CLE, 1970. 37 p. GUAT

63 Antillano, Sergio. "Ideas actuales en el teatro venezolano," *El Farol*, 23, No. 196 (set-oct 1961), 3-11. VEN

64 Antolínez, Gilberto. "El teatro institución de los Muku y Jirajara," *Revista Nacional de Cultura*, No. 56 (mayo-jun 1946), 113-129. VEN

65 *Anuario del teatro argentino.* Buenos Aires: Fondo Nacional de las Artes, 1965-71. ARG

Multiple volumes, one for each year, including photos.

66 Apstein, Theodore. "The Contemporary Argentine Theater." Unpub. Ph.D. diss., Texas, 1945. ARG

67 ____. "Letters on the Latin American Theatre: General Problems in the Theatre of Latin America," *Players Magazine* (Jan-Feb 1946), pp. 3-4, 24. GEN

68 ____. "New Aspects of the Theater in Latin America," in *Proceedings of the Conference on Latin American Fine Arts, June 14-17, 1951.* Austin: University of Texas Press, 1952, pp. 27-41. GEN

69 Ara, Guillermo. "Función y sentido de la farsa moderna argentina," in *El teatro en Iberoamérica*

(Memoria del duodécimo congreso del Instituto Internacional de Literatura Iberoamericana). México: IILI (1966). ARG

70 Aramburu, Julio. "Salta y Jujuy: temas para nuestro teatro," *Cuadernos de Cultura Teatral*, No. 16 (1942), 63-76. ARG

71 Araneda Bravo, Fidel. "Orrego Vicuña y su obra," *Anales de la Universidad de Chile*, No. 83-84 (1951), 167-184. CHILE

72 Arellano, Jesús. Review: "Antonio Magaña Esquivel y Ruth S. Lamb. *Breve historia del teatro mexicano*. México: Ediciones de Andrea, 1958." *Revista Iberoamericana*, No. 47 (ene-jun 1959), 186-188. MEX

73 Arellano Belloc, Francisco. "En torno de un problema de expresión teatral," *Nueva América*, No. 1 (set 1967), 28-29, 33. GEN

74 "Argentina: último verano castrense," *Conjunto*, No. 16 (abr-jun 1973), 20-27. ARG

A review of recent productions in Argentina.

75 Arguedas, José María. "El *Ollantay*. Lo autóctono y lo occidental en el estilo de los dramas coloniales quechuas," *Letras Peruanas* (Lima), II, No. 8 (1952), 139-140. PERU

76 Arias, Ramón. "¿Por qué debemos crear el teatro nacional?" *Nuevo Suceso*, VII, No. 77 (abr 1969), 30-35. ECUAD

77 ____. "Un teatro para Guayaquil," *Nuevo Suceso*, VII, No. 76 (mar 1969), 60-63. ECUAD

78 Arias Larreta, Abraham. *Literaturas aborígenes de América*. Kansas City: Editorial Indoamérica, 1968. 304 p. Reviewed: Irving, Thomas B. GEN

79 Aristu, Jesús. "Dürrenmatt en Lima," *Correo* (Lima) (6 mar 1964). PERU

80 Arlt, Mirta. "Recuerdos de mi padre," *Ficción*, No. 15 (set-oct 1958), 21-26. ARG

81 Arredondo, Inés. "*Diálogo entre el Amor y un viejo*," *Revista de la Universidad de México*, XIX, No. 10

(jun 1965), 30-31. MEX

On Rodrigo Cota's play, Diálogo entre el Amor y un viejo.

82 Arredondo, Inés. "Una de las tragedias de México y una tragedia mexicana," *Revista Mexicana de Literatura*, No. 9-12 (set-dic 1961), 53-55. MEX

On Usigli's play, Corona de fuego.

83 Arriví, Francisco. *Conciencia puertorriqueña del teatro contemporáneo, 1937-1956.* San Juan: Instituto de Cultura Puertorriqueña, 1967. 207 p. PTO. RICO

84 ____. "El Cuarto Festival de Teatro Puertorriqueño," *Revista del Instituto de Cultura Puertorriqueña*, 4, No. 11 (abr-jun 1961), 12-20. PTO. RICO

85 ____. *Entrada por las raíces, 1940-1961.* San Juan: 1964. 224 p. PTO. RICO

A collection of addresses and articles, several of which pertain to the Puerto Rican theater.

86 ____. *La generación del treinta: el teatro.* San Juan: Instituto de Cultura Puertorriqueña, 1960. 26 p. PTO. RICO

87 ____. *Informe de la Oficina de Fomento Teatral: año fiscal 1967-1968.* San Juan: Instituto de Cultura Puertorriqueña, 1968. 21 p. PTO. RICO

88 ____. "El Noveno Festival de Teatro del Instituto de Cultura Puertorriqueña," *Revista del Instituto de Cultura Puertorriqueña*, X, No. 36 (jul-set 1967), 12-17. PTO. RICO

89 ____. "El Octavo Festival," *Revista del Instituto de Cultura Puertorriqueña*, VIII, No. 28 (jul-set 1965), 55-63. PTO. RICO

90 ____. "Perspectiva de una generación teatral puertorriqueña, 1938-1956," *Revista del Instituto de Cultura Puertorriqueña*, I, No. 1 (oct-dic 1958), 41-47. PTO. RICO

91 ____. "El Primer Festival de Teatro Puertorriqueño," *Revista del Instituto de Cultura Puertorriqueña*, II, No. 2 (ene-mar 1959), 10-14. PTO. RICO

92 Arriví, Francisco. "El Quinto Festival," *Revista del Instituto de Cultura Puertorriqueña*, V, No. 15 (abr-jun 1962), 41-48. PTO. RICO

93 ____. "Segundo Festival de Teatro Puertorriqueño," *Revista del Instituto de Cultura Puertorriqueña*, II, No. 4 (jul-set 1959), 10-14. PTO. RICO

94 ____. "El Séptimo Festival," *Revista del Instituto de Cultura Puertorriqueña*, VII, No. 23 (abr-jun 1964), 30-40. PTO. RICO

95 ____. "El Sexto Festival," *Revista del Instituto de Cultura Puertorriqueña*, VI, No. 20 (jul-set 1963), 46-55. PTO. RICO

96 ____. "Teatros del Borinkén," *Revista del Instituto de Cultura Puertorriqueña*, XIII, No. 49 (oct-dic 1970), 7-9. PTO. RICO

97 ____. "El Tercer Festival de Teatro Puertorriqueño," *Revista del Instituto de Cultura Puertorriqueña*, No. 7 (abr-jun 1960), 37-44. PTO. RICO

98 ____, et al. *Areyto mayor*. San Juan: Instituto de Cultura Puertorriqueña, 1966. 324 p. PTO. RICO

Collection of essays by Arriví, Belaval and Piri Fernández on the Puerto Rican theater.

99 Arrom, José Juan. "Bosquejo histórico del teatro en Cuba." Unpub. Ph.D. diss., Yale, 1941. CUBA

100 ____. "Consideraciones sobre *El príncipe jardinero y fingido Cloridano*," in *Anales de la Academia Nacional de Artes y Letras* (La Habana), XXVII (1947-1948), 217-246. CUBA

On a play by the Cuban Santiago de Pita. Also in Arrom's Estudios de literatura hispanoamericana. *La Habana: Ucar García y Cía, 1950.*

101 ____. "Una desconocida comedia mexicana del siglo XVII," *Revista Iberoamericana*, XIX, No. 37 (oct 1953 - mar 1954), 79-103. MEX

Matías de Bocanegra's Canción a la vista de un desengaño. *Also in Arrom's* Certidumbre de América: estudios de letras, folklore y cultura. *La Habana: Anuario Bibliográfico Cubano, 1959 (2d. ed. Madrid: Editorial Gredos, 1971.*

102 ____. "Documentos relativos al teatro colonial de Venezuela," *Universidad de la Habana*, XXI-XXII,

No. 64-69 (ene-dic 1946), 80-101. VEN

Also in Boletín de la Academia Nacional de la Historia *(Caracas), XXIX, No. 114 (abr-jun 1946), 168-183; and* Boletín de Estudios de Teatro, *Año 4, 4, No. 15 (dic 1946), 211-223.*

103 Arrom, José Juan. "Drama de los antiguos," *Américas*, 4, No. 4 (abr 1952), 16-19. GEN

Includes Rabinal Achí, El Güegüence, *and* Ollantay.

104 ____. "En torno a la historia de la literatura dramática cubana," *Anales de la Academia Nacional de Artes y Letras* (La Habana), XXV (1944), 8-23. CUBA

105 ____. "En torno al teatro venezolano," *Revista Nacional de Cultura*, 7, No. 48 (ene-feb 1945), 3-10. VEN

106 ____. "Entremeses coloniales," in his *Estudios de literatura hispanoamericana.* La Habana: Ucar García y Cía., 1950, 71-91. GEN

107 ____. *Historia de la literatura dramática cubana.* New Haven, Conn.: Yale University Press, 1944. vii+132 p.
Reviewed: Green, Otis H. CUBA

108 ____. *Historia del teatro hispanoamericano (Epoca colonial).* México: Ediciones de Andrea, 1967. 151 p.
Reviewed: Forster, Merlin H. GEN

109 ____. "Perfil del teatro contemporáneo en Hispanoamérica," *Hispania*, XXXVI, No. 1 (Feb 1953), 26-31. GEN

Also in Bolívar *(Bogotá), No. 21 (jul 1953), 69-78; and in Arrom's* Certidumbre de América: estudios de letras, folklore y cultura. *La Habana: Anuario Bibliográfico Cubano, 1959; and as "Perfil del teatro hispanoamericano, 1939-1953," in the 2d. ed. (Madrid: Editorial Gredos, 1971) of this latter volume.*

110 ____. "Primeras manifestaciones dramáticas en Cuba, 1512-1776," *Revista Bimestre Cubana*, XLVIII (set-oct 1941), 274-284. CUBA

111 ____, ed. *El príncipe jardinero y fingido Cloridano, comedia sin fama del capitán don Santiago*

de Pita, natural de la Habana. La Habana: Sociedad Económica de Amigos del País, 1951. 113 p. CUBA

Includes introductory study and notes by Arrom. Reviewed: Aubrun, Charles V.

112 Arrom, José Juan. "Raíces indígenas del teatro americano," *Revista Bimestre Cubana*, LXIII (1949), 27-42. GEN

113 ____. "Representaciones teatrales en Cuba a fines del siglo XVIII," *Hispanic Review*, XI, No. 1 (Jan 1943), 64-71. CUBA

114 ____. Review: "Antonio Magaña Esquivel y Ruth S. Lamb. *Breve historia del teatro mexicano.* México: Ediciones de Andrea, 1958." *Revista Interamericana de Bibliografía*, IX, No. 3 (jul-set 1959), 278-279. MEX

115 ____. Review: "Carlos Solórzano. *El teatro latinoamericano en el siglo XX.* México: Editorial Pormaca, 1964." *Revista Interamericana de Bibliografía*, XVI, No. 3 (jul-set 1966), 314-315. GEN

Also discusses Solórzano's anthology, El teatro hispanoamericano contemporáneo.

116 ____. "Sainetes y sainetistas coloniales," *Memoria del Cuarto Congreso del Instituto Internacional de Literatura Iberoamericana.* La Habana: Ministerio de Educación, Dirección de Cultura, 1949, 255-267. GEN

117 ____. *El teatro de Hispanoamérica en la época colonial.* La Habana: Anuario Bibliográfico Cubano, 1956. ix+237 p. GEN
Reviewed: Aubrun, Charles V.; Dauster, Frank; Florit, Eugenio; Lohmann Villena, Guillermo; Olivera, Otto; Osorio, María Luisa; Percas, Helena.

118 ____. "El teatro de José Antonio Ramos," *Revista Iberoamericana*, XII, No. 24 (jun 1947), 263-271. CUBA

Also in Revista Cubana, *XXIII (ene-dic 1948), 164-175; and in Arrom's* Estudios de literatura hispanoamericana. *La Habana: Ucar García y Cía, 1950.*

119 Arrom, José Juan. "Voltaire y la literatura dramática cubana," *Romanic Review*, XXXIV (1943), 228-234. CUBA

Also in Promoteo *(La Habana), Año I, No. 4 (1948), 13-15.*

120 ____, and José Manuel Rivas Sacconi, eds. *La* "Laurea crítica" *de Fernando Fernández de Valenzuela, primera obra teatral colombiana*. Bogotá: Instituto Caro y Cuervo, 1960. 27 p. COL

Contains preliminary study and paleographic edition.

121 Arroyo [de Hernández], Anita. "Instantáneas del teatro en Puerto Rico," *Revista del Instituto de Cultura Puertorriqueña*, IX, No. 32 (jul-set 1966), 17-22. PTO. RICO

122 ____. "La mexicanidad en el estilo de Sor Juana," *Revista Iberoamericana*, XVII, No. 33 (1952), 53-59. MEX

123 ____. *Razón y pasión de Sor Juana*. México: Porrúa y Obregón, 1952. MEX

124 Arrufat, Antón. "Función de la crítica literaria," *Casa de las Américas*, Año III, No. 17-18 (mar-jun 1963), 78-80. GEN

Intervention in the UNEAC Forum on Criticism, Sept., 1962.

125 ____. Review: "Florencio Sánchez. *La de anoche* y *En familia*. Buenos Aires: Ediciones del Carro de Tespis, 1961." *Casa de las Américas*, II, No. 15-16 (nov 1962 - feb 1963), 44-47. URUG

126 ____. "El teatro bufo," *Revista Unión* (La Habana), I, No. 3-4 (set-dic 1962), 61-72. CUBA

127 ____, et al. "Charla sobre teatro," *Casa de las Américas*, II, No. 9 (nov-dic 1961), 88-102. GEN

Discussion during I Latin American Theatre Festival, including Ramón Chalbaud, Osvaldo Dragún, and Ugo Ulive. Published in translation as "An Interview on the Theatre in Cuba and in Latin America," Odyssey Review, *II, No. 4 (1962), 248-263.*

128 Artacho, Manuel. *Indice cronológico de datos contenidos en la* Historia del teatro en Buenos Aires *de Mariano G. Bosch.* Buenos Aires: Imprenta de la Universidad, 1940. ARG

129 Artiles, Freddy. "Teatro popular: nuevo héroe, nuevo conflicto," *Conjunto*, No. 17 (jul-set 1973), 3-7. CUBA

130 "Aspectos del teatro paraguayo contemporáneo," *Guía Quincenal de la Actividad Intelectual y Artística Argentina* (Buenos Aires), 2, No. 29 (oct 1948), 79-80. PARA

131 "*La Atlántida* (de Levy Rossell)," *Imagen*, No. 97-98 (set 1974), 139-146. VEN

132 Aubele, Luis Angel. "*Estela de madrugada* [de Ricardo Halac]," *Estudios* (Buenos Aires), No. 565 (jul 1965), 381-383. ARG

133 Aubrun, Charles V. Review: "José Juan Arrom, ed. *El príncipe jardinero y fingido Cloridano, comedia sin fama del capitán don Santiago Pita, natural de La Habana.* La Habana: Sociedad Económica de Amigos del País, 1951." *Bulletin Hispanique*, 54, No. 1 (1952), 100-101. CUBA

134 ____. Review: "José Juan Arrom. *El teatro en Hispanoamérica en la época colonial.* La Habana: Anuario Bibliográfico Cubano, 1956; Willis Knapp Jones. *Breve historia del teatro latinoamericano.* México: Ediciones de Andrea, 1956." *Bulletin Hispanique*, 59, No. 3 (1957), 340-341. GEN

135 *El autor dramático: primer seminario de dramaturgia.* San Juan: Instituto de Cultura Puertorriqueña, 1963. 242 p. PTO. RICO

Collection of essays.

136 "El autor en su tinta," *Revista de Teatro* (Buenos Aires), No. 1 (nov-dic 1960), 61-62. ARG

Questions directed to Argentine dramatists about their work and the current (1960) theater season. Includes Enzo Aloisi, Alejandro Berruti, Marco Denevi, Osvaldo Dragún, Blas Raúl Gallo, Juan Carlos Ghiano, Félix M. Pelayo, and Francisco J. Rodríguez.

137 Autran, Margarida. "Maria Clara Machado," *Revista de Teatro* (Brasil), No. 388 (jul-ago 1972), 13-14. BRAZ

138 Aúz, Víctor. "*Auto de la Compadecida*: Teatro Popular," *Revista de Cultura Brasileña*, IV (1965), 350-355. BRAZ

139 Avalos Ficacci, Rafael. "Entrevista a Salvador Novo," *Nación* (17 mar 1963), pp. 1-2. MEX

140 ____. "El teatro mexicano y Celestino Gorostiza," *Nación* (14 abr 1963), p. 1. MEX

141 Avecilla, Ceferino R. "El 'Teatro de México'," *Hemisferio, la Revista de América* (México), 3, No. 8 (jun 1944), 30, 72. MEX

142 Avila, Pablo. "*La cisne de Inglaterra* y *Ana Bolena*," *Revista Iberoamericana*, No. 27 (jun 1948), 91-96. MEX

143 ____. "Fuentes del drama romántico *El torneo*, de Fernando Calderón," *Revista Iberoamericana*, No. 30 (ago 1949/ene 1950), 253-273. MEX

144 ____. "Influencias del romanticismo europeo en *Ana Bolena*, de Fernando Calderón," *Revista Iberoamericana*, No. 25 (oct 1947), 123-134. MEX

145 Ayala, Walmir. "Brasil: Teatro de Hoje," *Cadernos Brasileiros*, IV, No. 2 (abr-jun 1962), 82-89. BRAZ

146 ____. "A crise no teatro," *Cadernos Brasileiros*, V, No. 1 (ene-fev 1963), 33-35. BRAZ

147 ____. "Teatro brasileño: Crisis y Modernidad," *Primer Acto*, No. 75 (1966), 15-18. BRAZ

148 Ayestarán, Lauro. "La Casa de la Comedia," *Boletín de Estudios de Teatro*, 2, No. 5 (abr 1944), 3-8. URUG

149 ____. *El centenario del Teatro Solís* (1856-1956). Montevideo: Comisión de Teatros Municipales, 1956. URUG

150 Ayora, Jorge. Review: "Ricardo Descalzi. *Historia crítica del teatro ecuatoriano*. Quito: Editorial Casa de la Cultura Ecuatoriana, 1968. 6 vol."

Revista Interamericana de Bibliografía, XX, No. 4 (oct-dic 1970), 477-479. ECUAD

151 Azar, Héctor. *Una proposición teatral: El espacio.* México: Universidad Nacional Autónoma de México, 1972. GEN
Reviewed: Pereira, Teresinha Alves.

152 ____. "¿Qué pasa con el teatro en México?," *Revista de Bellas Artes* (México), No. 11 (set-oct 1966), 61-67. MEX

Also in Conjunto, *No. 5 (oct-dic 1967), 94-100. In this theoretical piece, Azar talks about the "teatro oficial," "teatro comercial," and "teatro experimental."*

153 ____. "El teatro universitario en Manizales," *Conjunto*, 3, No. 10 (s.f.), 2-6. GEN
Reprinted from El Gallo Ilustrado *(15 nov 1970).*

154 Azevedo Sobrinho, Aluízio. "Dom Pedro II e o teatro," *Revista do Instituto Histórico e Geográfico Brasileiro*, No. 257 (1962), 166-173. BRAZ

155 Azparren Jiménez, Leonardo. "*Asia y el lejano oriente*," *Revista Nacional de Cultura*, No. 176 (jul-ago 1966), 101-102. VEN

On Isaac Chocrón's Asia y el lejano oriente.

156 ____. *El teatro venezolano.* Caracas: Departamento de Literatura del Instituto Nacional de Cultura y Bellas Artes, 1967. 53 p. VEN

157 ____. "El teatro venezolano no ha muerto," *Imagen*, No. 81 (15/30 jun 1973), 14. VEN

158 ____. "Theatre and Playwrights in Venezuela," *World Theatre*, 16, No. 4 (1967), 369-376. VEN

159 Azzario, Esther A. M. "Estado actual de las investigaciones sobre *Siripo*," *Revista de Estudios de Teatro*, II, No. 4 (1962), 20-28. ARG

160 B., R. "El Teatro Nacional de la Habana a Santiago," *INRA*, I, No. 5 (mayo 1960), 66-69. CUBA

161 Babín, María Teresa. "Un autor dramático puertorriqueño," *Revista Hispánica Moderna*, 11, No. 4 (jul-oct 1945), 239-240. PTO. RICO

On Manuel Méndez Ballester.

162 ____. "Veinte años de teatro puertorriqueño (1945-1964)," *Asomante*, XX, No. 4 (oct-dic 1964), 7-20. PTO. RICO

163 Babruskinas, Julio. "Brecht y el problema de la emoción en el teatro," *Conjunto*, No. 20 (abr-jun 1974), 137-140. GEN

164 ____. "Comentario a lo popular y el realismo," *Conjunto*, No. 22 (oct-dic 1974), 98. GEN

Prologue to "Lo popular y el realismo" by Bertolt Brecht in Schriften zur Literatur und Kunst.

165 Badía, Nora. "Notes: Cuba," *World Theatre*, XIV, No. 1 (Jan-Feb 1965), 60. CUBA

Cuban theater, 1959-1963.

166 Bagby, Beth. "El teatro campesino: entrevista con Luis Valdés," *Conjunto*, 3, No. 8 (s.f.), 17-25. U.S.

167 Baguer, François. "Florencio Sánchez y el teatro argentino," *Voz Gráfica* (La Habana) (mayo 1945), 24-25. RIVER PLATE

168 Bailey, Dale S. "*Pagador de Promessas*: A Brazilian Morality," *Latin American Theatre Review*, 6/1 (Fall 1972), 35-39. BRAZ

169 Baker, Philip R. "Carlos Solórzano: The Man and his Creative Works." Unpub. Ph.D. diss., Florida State, 1973. GUAT

170 Ballerini, Alberto. "Tres galanes del teatro nacional," *Boletín de Estudios de Teatro*, III, No. 8 (ene 1945), 40-46. ARG

171 Ballinger, Rex Edward. *Los orígenes del teatro español y sus primeras manifestaciones en la Nueva España*. México: Universidad Nacional Autónoma de México, Facultad de Filosofía y Letras, 1951. 156 p. MEX

172 Balmori, Clemente H. "Teatro aborigen americano," *Estudios Americanos* (Sevilla), 9, No. 45 (jun 1955), 577-601. GEN

173 Balzán, Fredy. "El teatro tiene que entrañarse con nuestras realidades," *Conjunto*, No. 14 (set-dic 1973), 34-37. BOL

An interview with Fernando Medina Ferrada.

174 Bancroft, Robert L. "The Problem of Marcela's Future in Cantón's *Inolvidable*," *Romance Notes*, XIV, No. 2 (Winter 1972), 269-274. MEX

175 Banner, J. Worth. "The Dramatic Works of Manuel Eduardo de Gorostiza." Unpub. Ph.D. diss., North Carolina, 1948. MEX

176 ____. "Ildefonso Antonio Bermejo, iniciador del teatro en el Paraguay," *Revista Iberoamericana*, No. 33 (feb-jul 1951), 97-107. PARA

177 Baralt, Luis Alejandro. "The Theatre in Latin America," *Lectures delivered at the Hispanic American Institute*. ed. J. Riis Owre. Coral Gables, Fla.: University of Miami, 1948, pp. 9-26. GEN

178 Barbero, Edmundo. "El teatro universal en la época presente y el teatro en El Salvador," *Cultura* (San Salvador), No. 3 (mayo-jun 1955), 33-40. EL SAL

179 Barisani, Blas. "Ciclo teatro nacional en Buenos Aires," *Cuadernos del Sur*, IV, No. 37 (ago 1967), 657-661. ARG

180 Barletta, Leónidas. "Sobre un teatro del pueblo," *Casa de las Américas*, II, No. 10 (ene-feb 1962), 87-107. GEN

181 ____. *Viejo y nuevo teatro (Crítica y teoría)*. Buenos Aires: Editorial Futuro, 1960. 66 p. GEN

182 Baroffio, Eugenio P. "El Teatro Solís," *Revista Histórica* (Montevideo), 28, No. 82/84 (jul 1958), 238-312. URUG

183 Barreda-Tomás, Pedro M. "El teatro de José Jacinto Milanés," *Literatura de la emancipación hispanoamericana y otros ensayos*. Lima: Universidad Nacional Mayor de San Marcos, Dirección Universitaria de Biblioteca y Publicaciones, 1972, pp. 319-345. CUBA

184 Barreda-Tomás, Pedro M. "Lo universal, lo nacional y lo personal en el teatro de René Marqués," *El teatro en Iberoamérica* (Memoria del duodécimo congreso del Instituto Internacional de Literatura Iberoamericana). México: IILI (1966). PTO. RICO

185 Barrera, Ernesto M. "Algunos aspectos en el arte dramático de Luis Enrique Osorio," *Latin American Theatre Review*, 4/2 (Spring 1971), 21-27. COL

186 ____. *Realidad y fantasía en el drama social de Luis Enrique Osorio*. Madrid: Ediciones Plaza Mayor, 1971. Reviewed: Dial, John E. COL

As Ph.D. diss., "El teatro de Luis Enrique Osorio," Southern California, 1970.

187 ____. Review: "Carlos Miguel Suárez Radillo. *13 autores del nuevo teatro venezolano*. Caracas: Monte Avila Editores, 1971." *Latin American Theatre Review*, 5/2 (Spring 1972), 81. VEN

188 ____. Review: "Carlos Solórzano. *Teatro breve hispanoamericano*. Madrid: Aguilar, 1970." *Latin American Theatre Review*, 6/1 (Fall 1972), 99-100. GEN

189 "La voluntad rebelde en *Carnaval afuera, carnaval adentro* de René Marqués," *Latin American Theatre Review*, 8/1 (Fall 1974), 11-19. PTO. RICO

190 Barro, Karla and Fabio Alonso. "B + CC + 2 pe =PP," *Conjunto*, No. 20 (abr-jun 1974), 141-147. GEN

Translation: Brecht + Creación Colectiva + 2 puestas en escena = Punto de Partida.

191 Barros, Daniel. Review: "Arturo Carril. *Nuestro hermano Florencio*. Buenos Aires: Editorial Mecenas, 1959." *Ficción*, No. 22 (nov-dic 1959), 104. URUG

192 Bastardi, Francisco. *Yo también con mis memorias: Cincuenta años de teatro argentino*. Buenos Aires: Editorial Ancora, 1963. 89 p. ARG

193 Basurto, Luis G. "Libertad moral en la obra de Usigli," *México en la Cultura* (31 ago 1952), pp. 5-6. MEX

194 ____. "El teatro y la amistad en Xavier Villaurrutia," *Cuadernos de Bellas Artes*, I, No. 5 (1960), 11-20. MEX

195 Batchelor, C. Malcolm. "Alvares de Azevedo: A Transitional Figure in Brazilian Literature," *Hispania*, XXXIX, No. 2 (May 1956), 149-156. BRAZ

196 ____. "Arthur Azevedo e a 'Comedia Carioca'," *Revista Iberoamericana*, No. 43 (ene-jun 1957), 61-69. BRAZ

197 Bayle, Constantino. "Notas acerca del teatro religioso en la América colonial," *Razón y Fe* (Madrid), 47, No. 590 (mar 1947), 220-234, and No. 591 (abr 1947), 335-348. GEN

198 Bayma, Ernesto, comp. *Consejos para un comediante; ética y metamorfosis*. Buenos Aires: Siglo Veinte, 1958. 79 p. (Colección Panorama, 19) GEN

Summary of the thoughts of actors, critics, essayists, writers, philosophers, etc. with regard to two fundamental aspects of the life of an actor.

199 Becco, Horacio Jorge. "Bibliografía de don Conrado Nalé Roxlo (1898-1971)," *Academia Argentina de Letras. Boletín*, XXXVI, No. 141-142 (jul-dic 1971), 263-268. ARG

200 Beck, Vera F. "La fuerza motriz en la obra dramática de Rodolfo Usigli," *Revista Iberoamericana*, No. 36 (ene-set 1953), 369-384. MEX

201 ____. "Observaciones sobre el teatro argentino contemporáneo," *Revista Iberoamericana*, No. 34 (ago 1951/ene 1952), 339-343. ARG

202 ____. "Xavier Villaurrutia, dramaturgo moderno," *Revista Iberoamericana*, No. 35 (feb-dic 1952), 27-39. MEX

203 Belaval, Emilio S. *Areyto*. San Juan: Biblioteca de Autores Puertorriqueños, 1948. 164 p. PTO. RICO

204 ____. "Dramaturgia, ser y realidad," *Boletín de la Academia de Artes y Ciencias de Puerto Rico*, 2, No. 2 (abr-jun 1966), 191-202. PTO. RICO

205 ____. "El teatro puertorriqueño," *Prensa Literaria* (San Juan), I, No. 1 (1963), 1-37. PTO. RICO

206 Bellini, Giuseppe. *Teatro messicano del novecento*. Milano: Instituto Editoriale Cisalpin, 1959. MEX

207 Bellini, Giuseppe. "El teatro profano de Sor Juana," *Anuario de Letras* (México), No. 5 (1965), 107-122. MEX

208 Bello, Andrés. "Revista de teatro," *Cuaderno*. Dirección de Cultura, Centro de Investigación y Desarrollo del Teatro, No. 2. Caracas: Universidad Central de Venezuela (nov 1966), 1-4. VEN

209 ____. "Teatro," *Cuaderno*. Dirección de Cultura, Centro de Investigación y Desarrollo del Teatro, No. 2. Caracas: Universidad Central de Venezuela (nov 1966), 5-9. VEN

210 Bello, Enrique. "Telón de fondo de una gran aventura dramática: el ITUCH cumple 1/4 de siglo," *Boletín de la Universidad de Chile*, No. 66 (jun 1966), 4-25. CHILE

211 Beltrán, Alejo. "Estrenos en la Habana, 3 de teatro, 1 de cine," *Cuba*, II, No. 11 (1963), 20-27. CUBA

Includes Piñera's Aire frío.

212 ____. "Festival de Teatro Hispanoamericano," *INRA*, II, No. 12 (dic 1961), 4-9. GEN

Report on I Latin American Theatre Festival in Havana.

213 ____. "Nuestra escena," *Cuba*, I, No. 1 (abr 1962), 26-29. CUBA

Report on the end of the cycle of Brechtian theater.

214 ____. "Sexto festival de teatro," *Unión*, VI, No. 1 (ene-mar 1967), 166-172. CUBA

215 ____. "Teatro de Bertolt Brecht," *INRA*, II, No. 11 (nov 1961), 84-89. CUBA

Report on the cycle of Brechtian theater in Havana.

216 Beltrán, Oscar Rafael. "Los orígenes del teatro argentino," *Anales del Instituto Popular de Conferencias; vigésimosexto ciclo, año 1940, tomo XXVI*. Buenos Aires: Publicidad Vaecaro, 1941, pp. 146-154. ARG

217 Beltrán, Oscar Rafael. "Orígenes del teatro argentino," *Cuadernos de Cultura Teatral*, No. 10 (1940), 31-52. ARG

218 ____. *Los orígenes del teatro argentino desde el virreinato hasta el estreno de* Juan Moreira *(1884)*. 2a. ed. Buenos Aires: Editorial Sopena, 1941. 155 p. ARG

219 Benavento, Gaspar Lucilo. *Títeres del mundo nuestro*. Buenos Aires: Instituto Amigos del Libro Argentino, 1955. 154 p. ARG

220 Benedetti, Mario. "Carlos Maggi y su meridiano de vida," *La Palabra y el Hombre*, No. 45 (ene-mayo 1963), 133-146. URUG

221 Benítez, Rubén A. *Una histórica función de circo*. Buenos Aires: Universidad de Buenos Aires, 1956. ARG

222 Benmussa, Simone. "Entretien avec Eduardo Manet sur le théâtre cubain," *Cahiers Renaud-Barrault*, No. 75 (1° trimestre 1971), 23-26. CUBA

223 "O berço da arte dramática do Rio de Janeiro: o teatro de Manuel Luiz," *Revista do Instituto Histórico e Geográfico Brasileiro*, No. 255 (1962), 366-375. BRAZ

Includes a bibliography.

224 Berdiales, Germán. "Algunas consideraciones sobre teatro infantil rioplatense," *Revista de Estudios de Teatro*, I, No. 2 (1959), 35-39. RIVER PLATE

225 Berenguer Carisomo, Arturo. "La crisis del teatro argentino," *Cuadernos Hispanoamericanos*, LVI, No. 167 (nov 1963), 313-327. ARG

Also in Cuadernos del Sur, *3, No. 25 (ago 1966), 681-690.*

226 ____. "La dramática realista-naturalista (1900-1918)," *Boletín de Estudios de Teatro*, I, No. 2 (jun 1943), 21-23. ARG

227 ____. *Las ideas estéticas en el teatro argentino*. Buenos Aires: Comisión Nacional de Cultura, Instituto de Estudios de Teatro, 1947. 439 p. ARG

228 ____. "Una intérprete de Coronado; Rita Carbajo

la protagonista de *Luz de luna y luz de incendio*," *Boletín de Estudios de Teatro*, VIII, No. 29-30 (mayo-set 1950), 87-90. ARG

229 Berenguer Carisomo, Arturo. "Juan Cruz Varela y el neoclasicismo," *Cuadernos de Cultura Teatral*, No. 10 (1940), 9-26. ARG

230 ____. "Martín Coronado: Su tiempo y su obra," *Cuadernos de Cultura Teatral*, No. 15 (1940), 5-24. ARG

231 ____. "La poesía dramática," *Literatura argentina*. Barcelona: Editorial Labor, 1970, pp. 113-144. ARG

232 ____. "Un teatro comprometido argentino del año 1920," *Revista de Estudios de Teatro*, V, No. 12 (1972), 28-45. ARG

233 Bermúdez Franco, Antonio. "De lo regional a lo universal: Impresiones cuyanas para el teatro argentino," *Cuadernos de Cultura Teatral*, No. 16 (1942), 81-100. ARG

234 Bernard, Jean-Jacques. "El autor dramático en 1953," *Talía*, I, No. 2 (nov 1953), 39. ARG

235 Bernardo, Mané. *Guiñol y su mundo*. México: Instituto Nacional de Bellas Artes, Departamento de Teatro, 1966. 160 p. ARG

Includes 11 of the author's plays.

236 ____. "La literatura teatral para el teatro de títeres en Latinoamérica," *El teatro en Iberoamérica* (Memoria del duodécimo congreso del Instituto Internacional de Literatura Iberoamericana). México: IILI (1966). GEN

237 ____. "El teatro independiente en la Argentina," *Lyra*, IV, No. 35-36 (jun-jul 1964). ARG

238 ____. "Teatro para títeres," *Boletín de Estudios de Teatro*, III, No. 9 (jun 1945), 87-90. ARG

239 Berrutti, Alejandro E. "El autor en el momento actual del teatro argentino," *Revista de Estudios de Teatro*, No. 2 (1959), 15-23. ARG

240 ____. Influencia del teatro gauchesco en la

evolución del teatro argentino," *Lyra*, 17, No. 174-176 (1959). ARG

Número extraordinario dedicado al teatro.

241 Berrutti, Alejandro E. "El teatro breve nacional," *Revista de Estudios de Teatro*, 2, No. 5 (1962). ARG

242 Bethencourt, João. "Nota sôbre humor no teatro contemporâneo brasileiro," *Cadernos Brasileiros*, V, No. 2 (1963), 32-36. BRAZ

243 Betti, Atilio. "Autor, actor y disponibilidad," *Revista de Estudios de Teatro*, 3, No. 8 (1964), 43-45. GEN

244 Beverido Duhalt, Francisco. "Mantener su verdad entre nosotros," *Conjunto*, No. 19 (ene-mar 1974), 105-108. MEX

In the section "Brecht en América Latina." Some commentary on Leñero's El juicio.

245 Bischoff, Efraín U. *Tres siglos de teatro en Córdoba, 1600-1900.* Córdoba: Universidad Nacional de Córdoba, Facultad de Filosofía y Humanidades, 1961. 382 p. ARG
Reviewed: Garcés, Julián.

246 Bittencourt, Djalma. "Eurico Silva," *Revista de Teatro*, (Brazil), No. 386 (mar-abr 1972), 33-34. BRAZ

Followed by the text of his Pense alto! *Silva was born in Portugal, but came to Brazil at the age of 16.*

247 Blackie [pseud. of Paloma Effrom de Olivari]. "Teatro vocacional en la Argentina," *Lyra*, X, No. 113-115 (abr 1953). ARG

248 Blaine, John A. "Studies on Sor Juana Inés de la Cruz; 1920-1972 (A Bibliography)." Unpub. M.A. essay, Penn State, 1972. 76 p. MEX

249 Blanco Amores de Pagella, Angela. "Conflictos del trabajo reflejados en el teatro de comienzos de siglo," in *Actas de las terceras jornadas de investigación de la historia y literatura rioplatense y de los Estados Unidos*. Mendoza: Universidad Nacional de Cuyo, 1968, pp. 23-33. ARG

250 Blanco Amores de Pagella, Angela. "El gran trágico y el drama nacional," *Boletín de Estudios de Teatro*, VI, No. 20-21 (mar-jun 1948), 19-29. ARG

The career of Pablo Podestá, with special attention to his role as don Zoilo in Barranca abajo.

251 ____. "El 'grotesco' en la Argentina," *Universidad* (Santa Fe, Arg.), No. 49 (jul-set 1961), 161-175. ARG

252 ____. "Influencia del teatro europeo en la temática nacional," *Cursos y Conferencias*, Año XXIX, LV, No. 287 (ene-jun 1960), 33-49. ARG

253 ____. *Iniciadores del teatro argentino.* Buenos Aires: Ediciones Culturales Argentinas, 1972. 322 p. ARG

A 114-page introduction followed by several 18th and 19th century texts.

254 ____. "Manifestaciones del teatro del absurdo en Argentina," *Latin American Theatre Review*, 8/1 (Fall 1974), 21-24. ARG

On Eduardo Pavlovsky, Griselda Gambaro, Julio Ardiles Gray, Carlos Traffic.

255 ____. *Nuevos temas en el teatro argentino; la influencia europea.* Buenos Aires: Editorial Huemul, 1965. 185 p. ARG

256 ____. "Pablo Podestá," *Boletín de Estudios de Teatro*, No. 20-21 (mar-jun 1948); 24-25 (ene-jun 1949); 26 (jul-set 1949); and 27 (oct-dic 1949). ARG

257 ____. *Pablo Podestá.* Buenos Aires: Ediciones Culturales Argentinas, 1967. 83 p. ARG

258 ____. "El problema del ser en el teatro nacional," *Universidad* (Santa Fe, Arg.), No. 57 (jul-set 1963), 171-190. ARG

259 ____. "El tema de la independencia en nuestras primeras manifestaciones teatrales," *Universidad* (Santa Fe, Arg.), No. 67 (ene-jun 1966), 9-42. ARG

260 Blanco Amores de Pagella, Angela, and Rosa Rosemblat. "Diez años de actividad teatral en Buenos Aires (1852-1862)," *Cursos y Conferencias*, XXVI, Nos. 181-183 (abr-jun 1947), 153-162. ARG

261 Bledsoe, Robert Lamar. "The Expressionism of Nelson Rodrigues: A Revolution in Brazilian Drama." Unpub. Ph.D. diss., Wisconsin, 1971. BRAZ

262 Blexen Ramírez, José Pedro. *Treinta recuerdos de teatro*. Montevideo: Editorial Florensa y Lafón, 1946. 98 p. URUG

263 Bloch, Pedro. "O espectáculo não pode parar," *Comentário*, III (1962), 67-72. GEN

264 Bloy, Red. "El teatro gesticula, baila, canta, ríe, llora," *INRA*, I, No. 3 (mar 1960), 12-21. CUBA

Report on the activities of the Teatro Nacional.

265 B[oal], A[ugusto]. "Caminos del teatro latinoamericano," *Conjunto*, No. 16 (abr-jun 1973), 77-78. GEN

The prologue to a collection of the same title, published by Casa de las Américas.

266 ____. *Categorías de teatro popular*. Buenos Aires: Ediciones CEPE, 1972. GEN

Also in Conjunto, *No. 14 (set-dic 1972), 14-33.*

267 ____. "The Joker System: An Experiment by the Arena Theatre of São Paulo," *The Drama Review*, 14, No. 2 (Winter 1970), 91-96. BRAZ

268 ____. "Que Pensa Você da Arte de Esquerda?" *Latin American Theatre Review*, 3/2 (Spring 1970), 45-53. BRAZ

269 ____. "Teatro Jornal: Primeira Edição," *Latin American Theatre Review*, 4/2 (Spring 1971), 57-60. BRAZ

270 ____. "El teatro popular en Brasil," *Revista Teatro* (Medellín), No. 7 (1971), 37-41. BRAZ

271 ____ y José Celso Martínez Correa. "El teatro brasileño de hoy," *Conjunto*, No. 9 (s.f.), 57-72. BRAZ

Reprinted from Aparte, *publication of the TUSP (Teatro de los Universitarios de São Paulo), No. 1.*

272 Boccanera Júnior, Sílio. *O Teatro na Bahia da Colonia á República (1800-1923)*. Bahia: Imprensa Official do Estado. BRAZ

273 Bolet Peraza, Nicanor. "El teatro del Maderero," *Crónica de Caracas*, 4, No. 19 (ago-dic 1954), 606-617. VEN

274 Borba Filho, Hermilo. "Um Teatro Brasileiro," *Revista Brasiliense*, No. 12 (jul-ago 1957), 180-188. BRAZ

275 ____. "O Teatro na Argentina," *História do espetáculo*. Rio de Janeiro: Edições O Cruzeiro, 1968, pp. 272-278. ARG

276 Borges Pérez, Fernando. *Historia del teatro en Costa Rica (una monografía)*. San José: Imprenta Española, 1942. 106 p. COSTA RICA

277 Bosch, Mariano G. "1830-1880: Panorama del teatro," *Cuadernos de Cultura Teatral*, No. 14 (1940), 23-56. ARG

278 ____. *Historia de los orígenes del teatro nacional argentino y la época de Pablo Podestá*. 2a. ed. Buenos Aires: Solar-Hachette, 1969. 322 p. ARG

See Artacho, Manuel, for an index to this history.

279 ____. *Manuel de Lavardén*. Buenos Aires: Edición de la Sociedad General de Autores de la Argentina, 1944. ARG

280 ____. "Orígenes del teatro nacional argentino," *Boletín de Estudios de Teatro*, 5, No. 18-19 (set-dic 1947), 175-184. ARG

281 ____. "1700-1810: Panorama del teatro," *Cuadernos de Cultura Teatral*, No. 13 (1940), 9-32. ARG

282 ____. "Viejos circos porteños; los bailes pantomímicos," *Boletín de Estudios de Teatro*, 2, No. 6 (jul 1944), 157-161. ARG

283 Bossío, Jorge Alberto. *Nemesio Trejo: de la trova popular al sainete nacional*. Buenos Aires: A. Peña Lillo Editor, 1966. 87 p. ARG

284 Boudet, Rosa Ileana. "La panadería tomada por

asalto," *Conjunto*, No. 19 (ene-mar 1974), 122-125. GEN

Brecht's play, directed by the Argentine Julio Babruskinas.

285 Boudet, Rosa Ileana. "Teatro Campesino del Tío Javier," *Conjunto*, No. 21 (jul-set 1974), 95-96. PERU

On the Peruvian theater group named in honor of the "poeta guerrillero" Javier Heraud. Followed by Tres obras de títeres, *pp. 98-110.*

286 Boudoux, Augusto. "Entrevista com Ariano Suassuna," *Revista do Globo*, No. 815 (3 mar a 16 mar 1962), 30-33. BRAZ

287 Bourgeois, Louis C. "Augusto D'Halmar, el Loti hispanoamericano," *Hispanófila*, 39, No. 3 (mayo 1970), 43-54. CHILE

288 ____. "Augusto D'Halmar en el teatro," *Duquesne Hispanic Review*, 5, No. 2 (1966), 99-111. CHILE

289 Bowman, Ned A. *Indice colectivo de obras teatrales en seis bibliotecas de Bogotá, Colombia.* Pittsburgh: University of Pittsburgh, Department of Speech and Theatre Arts and the Center for Latin American Studies, 1968. n.p. COL
Reviewed: Lyday, Leon.

290 Braschi, Wilfredo. *Apuntes sobre el teatro puertorriqueño.* San Juan: Editorial Coqui, 1970. 111 p. PTO. RICO

Originally as M.A. thesis, University of Puerto Rico, 1952.

291 ____. "Treinta años de teatro en Puerto Rico," *Asomante*, No. 1 (ene-mar 1955), 95-101. PTO. RICO

292 Brann, Sylvia J. "El arte literario de Luisa Josefina Hernández." Unpub. Ph.D. diss., Illinois, 1969. MEX

293 ____. "El fracaso de la voluntad en las comedias de Luisa Josefina Hernández," *Latin American Theatre Review*, 7/1 (Fall 1973), 25-31. MEX

294 Bravo-Elizondo, Pedro J. "Constantes del teatro

hispanoamericano de protesta social (1950-1970)." Unpub. Ph.D. diss., Iowa, 1973. GEN

295 Bravo-Elizondo, Pedro J. "El teatro chicano," *Revista Chicano-Riqueña*, I, 2 (Otoño 1973), 36-42. U.S.

296 Bravo-Villarroel, Roberto. Review: "Frank P. Hebblethwaite. *A Bibliographical Guide to the Spanish American Theater*. Washington: The Pan American Union, 1969." *Latin American Theatre Review*, 3/1 (Fall 1969), 81-83. GEN

297 Brene, José R. "Brene habla de Brene," *La Gaceta de Cuba*, IX, No. 89 (ene 1971), 10. CUBA

298 Brenes C., Gonzalo. "El cincuentenario del Teatro Nacional: el Teatro Nacional, Casa de la Cultura, 1908-1958," *Lotería* (Panamá) (2a. época), 3, No. 35 (oct 1958), 40-56. PAN

299 Bridwell, James H. "The Theater of the Anti-Absurd." Unpub. Ph.D. diss., Florida State, 1971. U.S.-MEX

Mostly U.S., but includes one chapter on Emilio Carballido.

300 "Las Brigadas de teatro de la Coordinación Provincial de Cultura de la Habana," *Conjunto*, No. 2 (1964), 59-64. CUBA

301 "Brillante desarrollo del VII Festival Regional dramático del sureste de México," *Revista de la Universidad de Yucatán*, No. 34 (jul-ago 1964), 159-163. MEX

302 Brinckmann, Bärbel. *Quellenkritische Untersuchungen zum mexicanischen Missionschauspiel, 1533-1732.* München: Renner, 1969. 246 p. MEX

303 Brncic, Zlatko. "Historia del teatro en Chile (primera parte)," *Anales de la Universidad de Chile*, Nos. 85-86 (primero y segundo semestre de 1952), 113-168. CHILE

304 ____. "El teatro chileno a través de cincuenta años, 1900-1950," *Desarrollo de Chile en la primera mitad del siglo XX*. Santiago: Editorial Universitaria, 1953. II, 385-416. CHILE

305 Bro, Luro. "Visita a Guilherme Figueiredo," *Mundo Nuevo*, No. 4 (oct 1966), 71-73. BRAZ

306 Brokaw, John W. "A Nineteenth-Century Acting Company--Teatro de Iturbide: 1856-57," *Latin American Theatre Review*, 6/1 (Fall 1972), 5-18. MEX

307 ____. "The Repertory of a Mexican-American Theatrical Troupe: 1849-1924," *Latin American Theatre Review*, 8/1 (Fall 1974), 25-35. MEX

308 Bromley, Juan. "Como nació la censura teatral en Lima," *Escena* (Lima), 1, No. 2 (dic 1953), 8, 26. PERU

309 Brower, Gary. "Fuentes de Fuentes: Paz y las raíces de *Todos los gatos son pardos*," *Latin American Theatre Review*, 5/1 (Fall 1971), 59-68. MEX

310 Bruce-Novoa. "Abolición de la propiedad: Mexican Experimental Theatre," *Latin American Theatre Review*, 8/1 (Fall 1974), 5-9. MEX

311 Brunet, Luis. "Mauricio Rosencof brinda un panorama sobre el teatro uruguayo," *Revista Nacional de Teatro*, No. 2 (1961). URUG

312 Bryant, William C. "Estudio métrico sobre las dos comedias profanas de Sor Juana Inés de la Cruz," *Hispanófila*, No. 19 (1963), 37-48. MEX

313 Buenaventura, Enrique. "Birds-Eye View of the Latin American Theatre," *World Theatre*, IX, No. 3 (Autumn 1960), 265-271. GEN

314 ____. "Cómo se monta una obra de teatro en el TEC," *Letras Nacionales*, II, No. 8 (mayo-jun 1966), 28-32. COL

315 ____. "In Colombia: An Invisible Theatre," *International Theatre Information* (Summer 1972), pp. 18-19. COL

316 ____. "Teatro y política," *Conjunto*, No. 22 (oct-dic 1974), 90-96. GEN

317 ____. "Theatre and Culture," *The Drama Review*, 14, No. 2 (Winter 1970), 151-156. GEN

318 Bueno, Salvador. "Diez años de literatura y revolución en Cuba," *Revista de la Biblioteca Nacional*

José Martí, Año 60, 3a. época, XI, No. 1 (ene-abr 1969), 161-194. CUBA

Section on dramatic literature, pp. 185-189.

319 Butler, Ross E., Jr. "Artistic Exploitation of Unifying Themes in Contemporary Brazilian Protest Theatre." Unpub. Ph.D. diss., Arizona, 1971. BRAZ

320 ____. "Social Themes in Selected Contemporary Brazilian Dramas," *Romance Notes*, XV, No. 1 (Autumn 1973), 52-60. BRAZ

321 C., C. "11 autores cubanos," *Primer Acto*, No. 108 (mayo 1969), 31-32. CUBA

Bibliography on 11 Cuban playwrights: Antón Arrufat, José R. Brene, Nicolás Dorr, Abelardo Estorino, Carlos Felipe, Rolando Ferrer, Ignacio Gutiérrez, Virgilio Piñera, Manuel Reguera Saumell, José Triana.

322 Caballero, Juan A. "La preocupación social en el teatro de Sebastián Salazar Bondy." Unpub. Ph. D. diss., Rutgers, 1971. PERU

323 Caballero y Lastres, Daniel. "Consideraciones teatrales sobre la obra de Enrique Solari Swayne," *Boletín Cultural Peruano* (Lima), No. 18 (dic 1965), 17-18. PERU

324 Cáceres Carenzo, Raúl. "El teatro de Carlos Fuentes," *Revista de la Universidad de México*, XXVI, No. 5 (ene 1972), 41-42. MEX

325 Caillet-Bois, Julio. "Las primeras representaciones teatrales mexicanas," *Revista de Filología Hispánica*, Año 1, No. 4 (1940), 376-378. MEX

326 ____. "El teatro en la Asunción a mediados del siglo XVI," *Revista de Filología Hispánica*, IV, No. 1 (1942), 72-76. PARA

327 Cajiao Salas, Teresa. "Actividades teatrales en las provincias argentinas," *Latin American Theatre Review*, 7/1 (Fall 1973), 87-90. ARG

328 Cajiao Salas, Teresa. "Balance de la temporada teatral bonaerense 1972," *Latin American Theatre Review*, 7/1 (Fall 1973), 71-86. ARG

329 ____. "Balance del Año Teatral 1972 en Lima," *Latin American Theatre Review*, 8/1 (Fall 1974), 67-73. PERU

330 ____. *Temas y símbolos en la obra de Luis Alberto Heiremans*. Santiago: Editorial Universitaria, 1970. 256 p. CHILE
Reviewed: Morris, Robert J.

331 Calderón Soria, Raúl. "Primer Congreso Panamericano de Teatro," *Cordillera* (La Paz), 2, No. 7 (oct-dic 1957), 55-57. GEN

332 Calhoun, Gloria D. "Un triángulo mitológico, idólatra y cristiano en el *Divino Narciso* de Sor Juana," *Abside* (México), XXXIV, No. 4 (oct-dic 1970), 373-401. MEX

333 Callan, Richard J. "La base jungiana de *Chantaje* por Miguel Angel Asturias," *Norte* (Amsterdam), X, No. 4 (jul-ago 1969), 88-92. GUAT

334 ____. *Miguel Angel Asturias*. New York: Twayne Publishers, 1970. 182 p. GUAT

Section on theater, pp. 120-151.
Reviewed: Cypess, Sandra; Fraser, Howard: Martin, Gerald; Menton, Seymour.

335 ____. "Teatro psicoanalítico de Miguel Angel Asturias," *Reseña de Literatura, Arte y Espectáculos* (Madrid), No. 28 (1969), 169-174. GUAT

Centers on Asturias's Soluna.

336 Calvo, Alberto. "El teatro nacional y algo de su historia," *Lotería*, 2ª época, 3, No. 35 (oct 1958), 57-60. PAN

337 Calvo Hernando, Manuel. "Cuarenta años de teatro en Méjico," *Cuadernos Hispanoamericanos*, No. 84 (dic 1956), 400-402. MEX

338 Camejo, Carucha. "El teatro de títeres en Cuba," *Conjunto*, No. 2 (1964), 3-6. CUBA

339 *Caminos del teatro latinoamericano*. La Habana:

Casa de las Américas, (1973?). GEN

Prologue by Augusto Boal. Includes Agustin del Rosario (Panama), A veces esa palabra libertad; *Osvaldo Dragún (Argentina),* Historias con cárcel; *Julio Mauricio (Argentina),* Un despido corriente; *and Víctor Torres (Chile),* Una casa en Lota Alta.

340 Campanella, Hebe. "El hoy y el aquí en el teatro argentino de los últimos veinte años," *Cuadernos Hispanoamericanos*, 78, No. 234 (jun 1969), 673-693. ARG

341 Campbell, Margaret V. "Camilo Henríquez: Aliases Quirino Limáchez and Cayo Horacio," *Romance Notes*, V, No. 3-4 (1961-1963), 26-29. CHILE

342 ____. *The Development of the National Theater in Chile to 1842*. Gainesville: University of Florida Press, 1958. 78 p. CHILE
Reviewed: Dauster, Frank.

343 Campbell, Thelma."'Satanás Diablo Demonio Lucifer,' Hero of *Los Pastores*," *Hispania*, XXVI, No. 4 (Dec 1943), 387-396. U.S.

A study of the devil in 6 versions of a play in Texan Mexican communities.

344 Campbell, Trini. "*La orgástula* en Indiana," *Latin American Theatre Review*, 8/1 (Fall 1974), 94-95. COL

345 Campos, Eduardo. "Inspiração popular e as elites no teatro brasileiro," *Clã* (Fortaleza), 10, No. 19 (maio 1960), 30-33. BRAZ

346 Campos, Jorge. Review: "Edwin T. Tolón y Jorge A. González. *Historia del teatro en la Habana*. Santa Clara: Universidad Central de las Villas, 1961." *Insula*, XVI, No. 181 (1961), 14. CUBA

347 Campra, Rosalba. "Participación de la mujer en el teatro," *Revista de la Universidad Nacional de Córdoba*, X, No. 1-2 (mar-jun 1969), 427-457. ARG

348 Camps, David. "Puppets in Cuba," *World Theatre*, No. 14 (1965), 458-459. CUBA

349 Canal Feijóo, Bernardo. "En el principio era el

teatro," *Cuadernos de Cultura Teatral*, No. 18 (1944), 63-83. GEN

350 Canal Feijóo, Bernardo. *La expresión popular dramática*. Tucumán: Universidad de Tucumán, Facultad de Filosofía y Letras, 1943. 68 p. ARG

351 ____. "La fiesta sacramental americana; fiesta y espectáculo dramático," *Boletín de Estudios de Teatro*, II, No. 7 (oct 1944), 203-208. ARG

352 ____. "Historia y teatro," *Revista de Estudios de Teatro*, II, No. 5 (1962), 5-12. GEN

353 ____. *Una teoría teatral argentina*. Buenos Aires: Centro de Estudios de Arte Dramático, Ariadna, 1956. 30 p. (Cuadernos de Estudio, 1) ARG

354 Cánepa Guzmán, Mario. *Gente de teatro: desde Camilo Henríquez hasta Jorge Díaz*. Santiago: Arancibia Hermanos, 1969. 244 p. CHILE

355 ____. *El teatro en Chile: desde los indios hasta los teatros universitarios*. Santiago: Arancibia Hermanos, 1966. 135 p. CHILE

356 ____. *El teatro obrero y social en Chile*. [Santiago]: Ediciones Cultura y Publicaciones, Ministerio de Educación, 1971. CHILE

357 Cano, Ricardo. "El teatro, una tarea para realizar," *Letras Nacionales* (Bogotá), III, No. 12 (ene-feb 1967), 53-61. GEN

358 Cantón, Wilberto. "Homenaje a Rodolfo Usigli," *Cuadernos de Bellas Artes*, II, No. 9 (1961), 22-24. MEX

359 ____. "Problemas de un teatro popular," *Nueva América*, 15 (ago 1968), 15-16. GEN

360 ____. "Teatro mexicano de la Revolución," *El Libro y el Pueblo* (México), 6, No. 10 (nov 1965), 21-24. MEX

361 Capablanca, Enrique. "*Juan Palmieri*," *Conjunto*, No. 13 (mayo-ago 1972), 14-17. URUG

362 Capdevila, Arturo. *La Trinidad Guevara y su tiempo: la vida del teatro--el yerno de la Guevara--*

el teatro de la vida. Buenos Aires: Editorial Guillermo Kraft, Limitada, 1951. 184 p. URUG

363 Capella Segreda, Yolanda. "Las varias muertes y la verdadera defunción de Trinidad Guevara," *Cuadernos de Cultura Teatral*, No. 19 (1943), 9-22. ARG

364 ____. "El teatro en Costa Rica," *Memoria de la Academia de Geografía e Historia de Costa Rica*, I, No. 3 (jun 1949), 11-17. COSTA RICA

365 Caporale Scelta, Julio. "¿Qué hubo en nuestro teatro en 1946?," *Mundo Uruguayo* (26 dic 1946), pp. 10-11. URUG

366 Carballido, Emilio. "Crónica de un estreno remoto," *Revista Iberoamericana*, XXXVII, No. 74 (ene-mar 1971), 233-237. MEX

Commentary on and analysis of Octavio Paz's La hija de Rappaccini.

367 ____. "Entrevista a Seki Sano," *Conjunto*, No. 3. MEX

368 ____. "Griselda Gambaro o modos de hacernos pensar en la manzana," *Revista Iberoamericana*, XXXVI, No. 73 (oct-dic 1970), 629-634.

369 Cárdenas de Monner Sans, María Inés. "Algo sobre nuestro teatro de hace cincuenta años," *Universidad* (Santa Fe), No. 46 (oct-dic 1960), 79-86. ARG

370 ____. "Apuntes sobre nuestro sainete y la evolución político-social argentina," *Universidad* (Santa Fe), No. 49 (1961). ARG

371 Cardona, Iván. "La pasión del teatro puertorriqueño según Luis Rafael Sánchez," *La Hora* (Puerto Rico), Año 3, Edición 79 (2 al 8 de agosto 1973), 12. PTO. RICO

372 Carella, Tulio. Review: "Luis Ordaz. *Siete sainetes porteños*. Buenos Aires: Losange, 1958." *Ficción*, No. 21 (1959), 138-139. ARG

373 ____. *El sainete*. Buenos Aires: Centro Editor de América Latina, 1967. 50 p. ARG

374 ____. *El sainete criollo*. Buenos Aires: Hachette, "El pasado argentino," 1957. ARG

375 Carilla, Emilio. "Géneros y temas: el teatro," in *El romanticismo en la América Hispánica.* Madrid: Editorial Gredos, 1958, 282-307. GEN

Also as "El teatro romántico en Hispanoamérica," Thesaurus, *No. 13 (1958), 35-56; also as* El teatro romántico en Hispanoamérica. *Bogotá: Instituto Caro y Cuervo, 1959. 24 p.*

376 ____. "El teatro independiente en la Argentina (posibilidades y limitaciones)," *Universidad* (Santa Fe, Arg.), No. 37 (ene-jun 1958), 53-82. ARG

Also published as a "separata" by the Universidad Nacional del Litoral (1958).

377 Carlino, Carlos. "Teatro y poesía," *Revista de Estudios de Teatro*, 4, No. 10 (1966), 39-54. ARG

378 Carlo, Omar del. "Autores y teatro nacional," *Ficción*, No. 8 (jul-ago 1957), 77-79. ARG

379 ____. "Breves reflexiones en torno a los teatros oficiales," *Ficción*, No. 6 (mar-abr 1957), 85-89. ARG

Includes: "Facundo en la ciudadela *de Vicente Barbieri en el Teatro Nacional Cervantes.*"

380 ____. "Buenos Aires en la encrucijada teatral," *Ficción*, No. 4 (nov-dic 1956), 128-130. GEN

381 ____. "Corrientes de la literatura dramática contemporánea," *Revista de la Universidad* (La Plata), No. 5 (jul-set 1958), 25-40. GEN

382 ____. "Cuatro obras y cuatro jóvenes dramaturgos uruguayos," *Ficción*, No. 5 (ene-feb 1957), 259-263. URUG

Antonio Larreta, Jacobo Langsner, Héctor Plaza Noblía, and Sergio Oscar Otermin.

383 ____. "El Festival Internacional de Teatro de París y la participación argentina," *Ficción*, No. 13 (mayo-jun 1958), 124-125. ARG

384 ____. "El teatro argentino y sus autores," *Cuadernos* (Paris), No. 76 (Sept 1963), 44-48. ARG

385 ____. "El teatro San Telmo y una pieza de Juan

Carlos Gené," *Ficción*, No. 11 (ene-feb 1958), 183-184. ARG

On Gené's El herrero y el diablo.

386 Carlo, Omar del. "Teatro universal y actores nacionales," *Ficción*, No. 7 (mayo-jun 1957), 110-112. ARG

387 ____ y Tulio Carella. "Las compañías teatrales extranjeras y nuestro público," *Ficción*, No. 10 (nov-dic 1957), 104-121. ARG

388 "La carpa, el teatro popular de México," *Norte* (New York) (mayo 1945), 22-25. MEX

389 Carpio, Antonio. "Cuba: panorama teatral," *Cuba*, II, No. 9 (1963), 66-71. CUBA

Theater activities and groups, 1959-1963.

390 Carril, Arturo. *Nuestro hermano Florencio*. Buenos Aires: Editorial Mecenas, 1959. 118 p. URUG
Reviewed: Barros, Daniel.

391 Carrillo, Hugo. "Orígenes y desarrollo del teatro guatemalteco," *Latin American Theatre Review*, 5/1 (Fall 1971), 39-48. GUAT

Also in Conjunto, *No. 20 (abr-jun 1974), 72-80.*

392 Carrizo, Juan Alfonso. "Los cantares tradicionales de la Rioja en su relación con el teatro," *Cuadernos de Cultura Teatral*, No. 17 (1942), 29-38. ARG

393 Casadevall, Domingo F. *La evolución de la Argentina vista por el teatro nacional*. Buenos Aires: Ediciones Culturales Argentinas, Ministerio de Educación y Justicia, 1965. 187 p. ARG

394 ____. *El teatro nacional: sinopsis y perspectivas*. Buenos Aires: Ediciones Culturales Argentinas, Ministerio de Educación y Justicia, 1961. 63 p. ARG
Reviewed: Lafforgue, J. R.; Lena Paz, Marta.

395 ____. *El tema de la mala vida en el teatro nacional*. Buenos Aires: Editorial Kraft, 1957. 200 p. ARG
Reviewed: Almirón, David.

396 Casey, Calvert. Review: "Edwin Teurbe Tolón y Jorge A. González. *Historia del teatro en La Habana.*

La Habana: Universidad Central de las Villas, 1961. Tomo I." *Revista Nacional de Teatro* (La Habana), No. 2 (1961). CUBA

397 Casey, Calvert."Teatro/61," *Casa de las Américas*, II, No. 9 (nov-dic 1961), 103-111. CUBA

398 Caso, Alfonso. "El uso de las máscaras entre los antiguos mexicanos," *Artes de México*, 16, No. 123 (1969). MEX

399 Castagnino, Lucrecia. "Un teatro independiente del interior; el centro dramático del Litoral," *Lyra*, XV, No. 158-160 (1957). ARG

400 Castagnino, Raúl H. "Ajustes preliminares para una revolución del género chico criollo," *El teatro en Iberoamérica* (Memoria del duodécimo congreso del Instituto Internacional de Literatura Iberoamericana). México: IILI (1966). ARG

401 ____. "Antecedentes acerca de una conciencia nacional en el teatro y la literatura dramática argentina," *Lyra*, XIX, No. 183-185 (1961). ARG

402 ____. "Antecedentes y elaboración de *Elelín* de Ricardo Rojas," *Revista de la Universidad de La Plata*, No. 4 (abr-jun 1958), 22-33. ARG

403 ____. *Centurias del circo criollo*. Buenos Aires: Editorial Perrot, 1959. 68 p. *Colección Nuevo Mundo*. ARG

404 ____. *El circo criollo*. Buenos Aires: Editorial Plus Ultra, 1969. 157 p. ARG

405 ____. *El circo criollo; datos y documentos para su historia, 1757-1924*. Buenos Aires: Lajouane, 1953. 143 p. ARG

2d. ed., Buenos Aires: Editorial Plus Ultra, 1969. 157 p.

406 ____. "La comedia en la escena porteña (1800-1930)," *Artes y Letras Argentinas*, 2, No. 5-6 (1961), 64, 81-82. ARG

407 ____. *Contribución documental a la historia del teatro en Buenos Aires durante la época de Rosas (1830-1852)*. Buenos Aires: Comisión Nacional de

Cultura, Instituto Nacional de Estudios de Teatro, 1944. 728 p. ARG
Reviewed: Leslie, John K.

408 Castagnino, Raúl H. "David Peña y el teatro histórico argentino," *Revista de Teatro* (Buenos Aires), No. 1 (nov-dic 1960), 24-28. ARG

409 ____. "Ernesto Rossi; contacto del gran trágico con una generación porteña," *Cuadernos de Cultura Teatral*, No. 24, 1-64. ARG

410 ____. "La escenografía en la Argentina," *Revista de Estudios de Teatro* (Buenos Aires), No. 1 (ene-mar 1959), 29-34. ARG

411 ____. *Esquema de la literatura dramática argentina (1717-1949)*. Buenos Aires: Instituto de Historia del Teatro Americano, 1950. 125 p. ARG

412 ____. "Lo gauchesco en el teatro argentino, antes y después de *Martín Fierro*," *Revista Iberoamericana*, XL, No. 87-88 (abr-set 1974), 491-508. ARG

413 ____. *Gregorio de Laferrère*. Buenos Aires: Ministerio de Educación y Justicia, 1964. ARG

414 ____. *La iniciación teatral de Martín Coronado*. Buenos Aires: Chiesa, 1951. ARG

415 ____. "Integración del repertorio dramático de Martín Coronado," *Boletín de Estudios de Teatro*, VI, No. 20-21 (mar-jun 1948), 2-6. ARG

416 ____. *José León Pagano, monitor del* Dies Irae. Buenos Aires: Talleres Gráficos D'Accurzio, 1959. 25 p. ARG

417 ____. *Literatura dramática argentina, 1717-1967*. Buenos Aires: Editorial Pleamar, 1968. 208 p. ARG
Reviewed: Dauster, Frank.

418 ____. "¿Lugones escribió teatro?; breve noticia y reproducción de un curioso trabajo del gran escritor," *Boletín de Estudios de Teatro*, III, No. 9 (jun 1945), 57-63. ARG

419 ____. "*Martín Fierro* y el teatro gauchesco," in *Martín Fierro, un siglo*. Buenos Aires: Editorial Xerox, 1972. ARG

420 Castagnino, Raúl H. "Mayo, motivo de inspiración dramática en el siglo XIX," *Revista de Estudios de Teatro* (Buenos Aires), II, No. 4 (1962), 36-41. ARG

421 ____. "Memoria y réquiem para dos siglos de circo criollo," *Talía*, V, 3, No. 19/20 (1960), 3-5. ARG

422 ____. "Panorama de una década de estrenos nacionales en los teatros porteños (1950-1960)," *Ficción*, No. 24-25 (mar-jun 1960), 135-156. ARG

423 ____. *Semiótica, ideología y teatro hispanoamericano contemporáneo*. Buenos Aires: Editorial Nova, 1974. 270 p. GEN

424 ____. "La 'Sociedad Protectora del Teatro Nacional'," *Sociedades literarias argentinas (1864-1900)*. La Plata: Universidad Nacional de La Plata, Facultad de Humanidades y Ciencia de la Educación, [s.f.], pp. 105-124. ARG

425 ____. *Sociología del teatro argentino*. Buenos Aires: Editorial Nova, [1963]. 191 p. ARG

426 ____. "Su iniciación teatral," *Boletín de Estudios de Teatro*, VIII, No. 29-30 (mayo-set 1950), 73-80. ARG

427 ____. *Teatro argentino premoreirista*. Buenos Aires: Editorial Plus Ultra, 1969. 137 p. ARG

428 ____. *El teatro de Roberto Arlt*. La Plata: Facultad de Humanidades y Ciencia de la Educación, 1964. 96 p. ARG

2d. ed., Editorial Nova, 1970.

429 ____. *El teatro en Buenos Aires durante la época de Rosas*. Buenos Aires: Comisión Nacional de Cultura, Instituto Nacional de Estudios de Teatro, 1945. ARG

430 ____. "El teatro en la obra de Ricardo Rojas," *Revista Iberoamericana*, No. 45 (ene-jun 1958), 227-238. ARG

431 ____. "El teatro pirotécnico de Alfonsina Storni," *Boletín de Estudios de Teatro*, VI, No. 22-23 (jul-dic 1948), 101-103. ARG

432 Castagnino, Raúl H. *El teatro romántico de Martín Coronado*. Buenos Aires: Ediciones Culturales Argentinas, Ministerio de Educación y Justicia, 1962. 208 p. ARG

433 ____. "Tendencias actuales del teatro argentino," *Revista Interamericana de Bibliografía*, XX, No. 4 (oct-dic 1970), 435-452. ARG

434 ____. *Teoría del teatro*. Buenos Aires: Editorial Nova, 1965. GEN

435 ____. "El vilipendiado 'género chico' criollo," *Talía*, Año 5, No. 29 (1966), 5-7. ARG

436 Castañeda, James A. "*Los empeños de un acaso* y *Los empeños de una casa:* Calderón y Sor Juana--La diferencia de un fonema," *Revista de Estudios Hispánicos*, I, No. 1 (May 1967), 107-116. MEX

437 Castellanos, Rosario. "Festival de otoño 1965," *Revista de Bellas Artes*, I, No. 5 (set-oct 1965), 88-92. MEX

438 ____. "Obras de Emilio Carballido," *Juicios sumarios: ensayos*. Xalapa, México: Universidad Veracruzana, 1966, pp. 45-51. MEX

439 ____. "Teatro Petul," *Revista de la Universidad de México*, XIX, No. 5 (ene 1965), 30-31. MEX

"El Teatro Guiñol del Centro Coordinador Tzeltzal-Tzotzil, con sede en La Cabaña, San Cristóbal, metrópoli cultural de los Altos de Chiapas."

440 Castillo, Cátulo. *Un teatro argentino para la nueva Argentina*. Buenos Aires: 1953. ARG

441 Castillo, Homero. "*Mercaderes en el templo*, obra inédita de Eduardo Barrios," *Hispania*, XLVIII, No. 4 (Dec 1965), 833-836. CHILE

442 ____. "Procedimientos dramáticos en *La gringa*," *Duquesne Hispanic Review*, VI, No. 1 (1967), 31-36. URUG

443 ____. Review: "Carlos Monsanto. *La protesta social en la dramaturgia de Acevedo Hernández*. México: B. Costa-Amic, Editor, [1971]." *Revista*

Interamericana de Bibliografía, XXII, No. 3 (jul-set 1972), 293-294. CHILE

444 Castillo, Susana D. "Festivales de teatro en América," *Latin American Theatre Review*, 8/1 (Fall 1974), 75-89. GEN

V Festival de Teatros Chicanos y I Encuentro Latinoamericano; II Festival Internacional de Teatro en Venezuela.

445 ____. "¿Qué pasa con el teatro de Venezuela?" *Mester* (UCLA), IV, No. 1 (Nov 1973), 57-58. VEN

446 ____. "El teatro de Rodolfo Santana," *Mester* (UCLA), III, No. 2 (Apr 1973), 41. VEN

447 ____ y María Elena Sandoz Montalvo. "V Festival Latinoamericano de Teatro y I Muestra Internacional," *Latin American Theatre Review*, 7/1 (Fall 1973), 49-70. GEN

448 Castro, Rosa. "Medio siglo de teatro mexicano," *Hoy* (México), No. 696 (24 jun 1950), 26-29, 66. MEX

449 ____. "Mientras el teatro agoniza," *Hoy* (México), No. 748 (23 jun 1951), 22-25, 66. MEX

450 Castro Herrera, Guillermo. "Algunos elementos constantes en la obra de Sor Juana, latentes en el *Divino Narciso*," *Lotería* (Panamá), (ene 1973), p. 63. MEX

451 Castro Leal, Antonio. "Prólogo," *Poesía, Teatro y Prosa* [de] *Sor Juana Inés de la Cruz*. Colección de Escritores Mexicanos, 1, 3a. ed. México: Editorial Porrúa, 1968. MEX

452 *Catálogo del teatro mexicano contemporáneo*. 2a. ed. México: Instituto Nacional de Bellas Artes, 1960. 245 p. MEX

453 Catania, Carlos. "El escritor y el teatro," *Universidad*, No. 55 (ene-mar 1963), 85-98.

454 Cavazzana, Rosanna. "*Defensa y triunfo del Tucumán*," *Revista de Estudios de Teatro*, IV, No. 10 (1966), 5-11. ARG

An anonymous play, possibly by Luis Ambrosio Morante.

455 Cavazzana, Rosanna. "Dramaturgia en la época de Mayo," *Revista de Estudios de Teatro*, I, No. 3 (1960), 30-37.

456 ____. "Una pieza olvidada: *Tupac Amarú* de Luis Ambrosio Morante," *Revista de Estudios de Teatro*, I, No. 1 (ene-mar 1959), 13-18. ARG

457 ____. "Teatralización de *Las noches lúgubres* de Cadalso por Luis A. Morante," *Revista de Estudios de Teatro*, I, No. 2 (abr-jun 1959), 5-14. ARG

458 Ceide-Echevarría, Gloria. Review: "Jordan B. Phillips. *Contemporary Puerto Rican Drama*. Madrid: Plaza Mayor, 1972." *Latin American Theatre Review*, 6/2 (Spring 1973), 78-79. PTO. RICO

459 Celedón, Jaime. "El ICTUS ha dicho: ¡Basta!" *Conjunto*, 3, No. 7 (s.f.), 82-83. CHILE

On the growing social commitment of the ICTUS group.

460 "Censura de las obras de teatro en 1841," *Crónica de Caracas*, 4, No. 19 (ago-dic 1954), 653-654. VEN

An exchange of correspondence.

461 Cerretani, Arturo. "Cómo nace el comediógrafo," *Revista de Estudios de Teatro*, III, No. 7 (1963), 18-24. ARG

On Gregorio de Laferrère.

462 ____. "Defilippis Novoa," *Contrapunto*, 1941. ARG

463 ____. "El grotesco criollo y sus intérpretes," *Lyra*, 17, No. 174-176 (1959). ARG

464 ____. "Pedro E. Pico y su pasión coloquial," *Revista de Estudios de Teatro*, II, No. 5 (1962), 25-27. ARG

465 Certad, Aquiles. "Buenos Aires y su activo mundo teatral," *Revista Shell* (Caracas), 3, No. 10 (mar 1954), 55-63. ARG

466 Cervera Andrade, Alejandro. *El teatro regional de Yucatán*. Prólogo de Ermilo Abreu Gómez. Mérida, México: Imprenta Guerra, 1947. 98 p. MEX

467 Cervera Espejo, Alberto. "Breves reflexiones sobre el teatro 'experimental'," *Revista de la Universidad de Yucatán*, 62 (mar-abr 1969), 74-82. GEN

468 Chacón y Calvo, José María. "Teatro cubano," *Revista Cubana*, XV (ene-jun 1941), 261-266. CUBA

469 Chalbaud, Román. "A los actores de *Tric-Trac*," *Revista de Teatro* (Caracas), I, No. 1 (set-nov 1967), 19. VEN

470 Chamberlin, Vernon A. "Schlegel y Milanés: Dos dramas románticos sobre el tema del Conde Alarcos," *Hispanófila*, No. 3 (mayo 1958), 27-38. CUBA

471 Chase, Gilbert. Review: "Fernando Ortiz. *Los bailes y el teatro de los negros en el folklore de Cuba*. Prólogo de Alfonso Reyes. La Habana, 1951." *Revista Interamericana de Bibliografía*, VII, No. 1 (ene-mar 1957), 85-87. CUBA

472 Chiavarino, Carlos. "Teatro y televisión, conflicto e interrelación," *Lyra*, Año 24, No. 198-200 (jun 1966). GEN

473 Chivite, Fernando Millán. "Breve introducción al teatro brasileño en España y mundo mental y sociológico de *O Pagador de Promessas*," *Revista de Cultura Brasileña*, No. 22 (1968?), 281-300. BRAZ

474 Chocrón, Isaac. *El nuevo teatro venezolano*. Caracas: Oficina Central de Información, 1966. 25 p. VEN

Serie: Temas culturales venezolanos, No. 4.

475 ____. "Shakespeare: autor para un teatro venezolano," *Revista Nacional de Cultura* (Caracas), 24, No. 154 (set-oct 1962), 28-43. VEN

476 ____. "Teatro," *Revista Nacional de Cultura*, 28, No. 174-175 (mar-jun 1966), 159-164. VEN

On contemporary Brazilian theater. Mentions various theatrical groups, and several young writers with some of their plays.

477 ____. *Tendencias del teatro contemporáneo*. Caracas: Monte Avila Editores, 1968. 122 p. GEN

478 Churión, Juan José. "Teatro nacional," *Crónica de*

Caracas, 4, No. 19 (ago-dic 1954), 621-641. VEN

A nineteenth-century account.

479 Cid Pérez, José. "Cincuenta años de teatro cubano," *Carteles* (La Habana), 33, No. 20 (18 mayo 1952), 110-113, 188, 189. CUBA

480 ____. "El teatro de América de ayer y de hoy; apuntes para la historia del teatro americano. Guatemala, I: teatro precolombino," *Boletín de Estudios de Teatro*, 5, No. 16 (mar 1947), 2-13. GUAT

481 ____ y Dolores Martí de Cid. *Teatro indio precolombino*. Madrid: Aguilar, 1964. GEN

Anthology. Includes: El Güegüense o Macho Ratón, El Varón de Rabinal, Ollantay.

482 "Cinco respuestas sobre el teatro de ayer," *Talía*, Año 5, No. 27 (1965), 6-7. ARG

Responden a un cuestionario Antonio Cunill Cabanillas, Samuel Eichelbaum, Edmundo Guibourg, Mecha Ortiz, Ignacio Quirós.

483 "Cinco tópicos con Nicolás Dorr," *Conjunto*, No. 16 (abr-jun 1973), 96-98. CUBA

An interview with Dorr conducted by Conjunto.

484 Cione, Otto Miguel. "Historia anecdótica del teatro nacional," *Mundo Uruguayo*, (12 jul 1945), 4-5. URUG

485 Cioppo, Atahualpa del. "Brecht tiene mucho que decir," *Conjunto*, No. 22 (oct-dic 1974), 88-89. GEN

Fragmento de "Hacia el teatro de la revolución latinoamericana," entrevista a Atahualpa del Cioppo realizado por Humberto Orsini.

486 ____. "Reflexiones elementales acerca del *Cruce sobre el Niágara*," *Amaru*, No. 10 (jun 1969), 80-83. PERU

487 Ciria, Alberto. "El teatro independiente de Buenos Aires," *Casa de las Américas*, IV, No. 25 (jul-ago 1964), 117-120. ARG

488 Clark, Fred M., and María A. Salgado. "Documentary Theatre in Mexico: Vicente Leñero's *Pueblo*

rechazado," *Romance Notes*, XIII, No. 1 (Autumn 1971), 54-60. MEX

489 Clark, Stella T. Review: "Gerardo Luzuriaga. *Del realismo al expresionismo: El teatro de Aguilera-Malta*. Madrid: Ediciones Plaza Mayor, 1971." *Latin American Theatre Review*, 6/1 (Fall 1972), 97-99. ECUAD

490 Cleto, Roberto de. "Teatro escolar (Consideraciones y sugestiones para su implantación)," *Revista de Cultura Brasileña* (Madrid), No. 35 (mayo 1973), 125-127. GEN

491 Cobb, Logan. "The Life and Works of Juan de Dios Peza." Unpub. Ph.D. diss., Missouri, 1947. MEX

492 Cocca, Aldo Armando. "La revolución de mayo en el teatro de Juan Bautista Alberdi," *Revista de Estudios de Teatro* (Buenos Aires), II, No. 4 (1962), 29-31. ARG

493 ____. *El teatro de Juan Bautista Alberdi*. Buenos Aires: Talía, 1960. ARG

494 Coe, Ada M. "Notes on Puppetry in Mexico," *Hispania*, XXVIII, No. 2 (May 1945), 199-207. MEX

495 Colecchia, Francesca. "Un ejemplo del diálogo angustiado en el teatro," *Espiral* (Bogotá), No. 104 (dic 1967), 5-13. ECUAD

Discussion of dialogue in the dramas of Francisco Tobar García.

496 ____. "*Luto eterno*," *Duquesne Hispanic Review*, II, No. 2 (1963), 77-83. ECUAD

On Jorge Icaza's play, Luto eterno.

497 ____. Review: "Margaret S. Peden, ed. and trans. *The Golden Thread and Other Plays*. Austin: University of Texas Press, 1970." *Revista Iberoamericana*, No. 75 (abr-jun 1971), 464. MEX

498 ____, and Julio Matas. *Selected Latin American One-Act Plays*. Pittsburgh: University of Pittsburgh Press, 1973. 204 p. GEN

Anthology includes: Xavier Villaurrutia,

Incredible Though It Seems: *Elena Garro,* A Solid Home; *Luisa J. Hernández,* Dialogues; *M. Montes Huidobro,* The Guillotine; *Julio Matas,* Ladies at Play; *Osvaldo Dragún,* The Man Who Turned Into a Dog; *Carlos Solórzano,* Crossroads; *Gustavo Andrade,* Remington 22; *Román Chalbaud,* The Forceps; *and Jorge Díaz,* Love Yourself Above all Others.

499 Collazos, Oscar. "Buenaventura: quince años de trabajo creador," *Conjunto*, 3, No. 10 [s.f.], 6-11. COL

500 ____. "Política y otras confusiones," *Revista Teatro* (Medellín), No. 7 (1971), 43-47. GEN

501 ____. "Trayectoria del Teatro Escuela de Cali," *Letras Nacionales*, II, No. 8 (mayo-jun 1966), 25-27. COL

502 Conte, Antonio. "Escambray: El teatro va a la montaña," *Cuba Internacional*, III, No. 20 (mar 1971), 62-66. CUBA

Activities of the Teatro Escambray.

503 Contreras, Félix. "Premio Casa de las Américas, 1972," *Cuba Internacional*, IV, No. 33 (mayo 1972), 28-39. GEN

Interview with judges Alfonso Sastre of Spain and Paulo Rogerio of Portugal, pp. 35-37.

504 ____. "El taller de las maravillas," *Cuba Internacional*, IV, No. 33 (mayo 1972), 72-74. CUBA

Brief history of Talleres y Almacenes Nacionales de Teatro, 1960-1972.

505 "Conversación con Osvaldo Dragún," *Primer Acto*, No. 77 (1966), 12-17. ARG

506 Conzevoy, Leonor. "Reelaboración de un tema clásico en el teatro de Sergio de Cecco," *Tropos*, III, No. 2 (Spring 1974), 34-48. ARG

507 Copelin, David. "Chicano Theatre: El Festival de los Teatros Chicanos," *The Drama Review*, T-60 (Dec 1973), 73-89. U.S.

508 Córdova Landrón, Arturo. *Salvador Brau, su vida,*

su obra, su época. Puerto Rico: Editorial Universitaria, 1949. 152 p. PTO. RICO

509 Cornejo, Edmundo V. *Poesía, prosa y teatro de Manuel Ascensio Segura.* Lima: Talleres Mimeográficos San Martín, 1961. PERU

510 Corporación Colombiano de Teatro (C. C. T.). "Primer seminario nacional de trabajadores del teatro," *Revista Teatro* (Medellín), No. 6 (s.f.), 17-55. COL

511 Correa, Gustavo. Review: "Willis Knapp Jones. *Breve historia del teatro latinoamericano.* México: Ediciones de Andrea, 1956." *Hispanic Review*, XXVI, No. 2 (Apr 1958), 154-155. GEN

512 ____, et al. *The Native Theater in Middle America.* New Orleans: Middle American Research Institute, Tulane University, 1961. 292 p. CENTR AM

Includes: Gustavo Correa and Calvin Cannon, "La loa en Guatemala," pp. 1-96; Gustavo Correa, "Texto de un Baile de Diablos," pp. 97-103; William A. Hunter, "The Calderonian Auto Sacramental, El gran teatro del mundo (Edition and translation of a Nahuatl version)," pp. 105-201; Barbara Bode, "The Dance of the Conquest of Guatemala," pp. 203-292.
Reviewed: Engelkirk, John.

513 ____ y Calvin Cannon. *La loa en Guatemala. Contribución al estudio del teatro popular hispanoamericano.* New Orleans: Middle American Research Institute, Tulane University, 1958. GUAT
Reviewed: Engelkirk, John.

514 Corrieri, Sergio. "Al pie de la letra," *Casa de las Américas*, XII, No. 68 (set-oct 1971), 189-192. CUBA

Report on activities of the Teatro Escambray group.

515 ____. "Escambray: Un teatro de la Revolución," *Caimán Barbudo*, II, No. 46 (mayo 1971), 22-25. CUBA

The director of Teatro Escambray talks about the group's activities, 1968-1971.

516 ____. "El Grupo Teatro Escambray, una experiencia de

la Revolución," *Conjunto*, No. 18 (oct-dic 1973), 2-6. CUBA

517 Cortazzo, Alberto P. "Don Gerónimo Podestá," *Cuadernos de Cultura Teatral*, No. 23 (1949). ARG

518 ____. "Guillermo Battaglia," *Cuadernos de Cultura Teatral*, No. 21 (1945), 93-123. ARG

519 ____. "El teatro de ideas, producto de nuestro medio," *Lyra*, XVII, No. 174-176 (1959). GEN

520 Cortes Camarillo, Félix. "Aquí no pasan cosas / de mayor trascendencia que las fosas," *Siempre!*, No. 1037 (mayo 1973), xvi. MEX

Critique of Willebaldo López's Cosas de muchachos.

521 ____. "¿Quién no llega a la cantina huyendo de la oficina y diciendo 'never more'?" *Siempre!*, No. 1042 (13 jun 1973), xvi. ARG

Critique of Israfel *by Abelardo Castillo.*

522 ____. "Rodolfo Usigli, dramaturgo de la Revolución Mexicana," *Siempre!*, No. 1028 (7 mar 1973), ii-iv. MEX

523 ____. "Silencio, teatros vacíos, ya les van a dar su público," *Siempre!*, No. 1040 (30 mayo 1973), xvi. MEX

Critique of Emilio Carballido's Silencio, pollos pelones...

524 Cosío, José Gabriel. "El drama quechua *Ollantay*," *Revista Universitaria* (Cuzco), Año XXX, No. 81 (2a. semestre 1941). PERU

525 Cossa, Roberto, Germán Rozenmacher y Yirair Mossian. "Diálogo a tres voces," *Teatro XX*, I, No. 2 (jun 1964), 6, 14. ARG

526 Cossier, Darío. "El teatro argentino y su valor cultural americano," *Revista de la Biblioteca Nacional* (San Salvador), 5, No. 4 (mayo-ago 1949), 38-50. ARG

527 Cossío del Pomar, Enrique. "Técnica y drama en el arte contemporáneo," *Cuadernos Americanos*, X, No. 5 (set-oct 1951), 117-125. GEN

528 Costa, René de. "The Dramaturgy of Florencio Sánchez: An Analysis of *Barranca abajo*," *Latin American Theatre Review*, 7/2 (Spring 1974), 25-37. URUG

529 Costa Alvarez de Sapin, Azul. "Un ciclo de nuestro teatro nacional," *Revista de Educación* (La Plata), 3, No. 6 (jun 1958), 398-403. ARG

530 Coutinho, Afrânio. "A Evolução da Literatura Dramática," in *A Literatura no Brasil*. 4 vol. Rio de Janeiro: Editorial Sul Americana, [1955-1970], II, pp. 249-283. BRAZ

531 Coy, Juan José. "Enrique Solari, dramaturgo peruano," *Sic* (Caracas), 28, No. 274 (abr-jun 1965), 166-171. PERU

532 Crema, Edoardo. "El drama artístico de Andrés Bello," *Revista Nacional de Cultura*, No. 1 (1938), 34-36; No. 19 (1940), 50-61; No. 22 (1940), 3-16; No. 23 (1940), 23-36; No. 24 (1940), 33-44. VEN

533 ____. "Un drama de Bello en un aditamento," *Revista Nacional de Cultura*, XXV, No. 160 (1963), 39-43. VEN

On Andrés Bello's play, Orlando enamorado.

534 ____. "Los modismos en el *Orlando enamorado* de Andrés Bello," *Cultura Universitaria*, LXXXIX (oct-dic 1965), 19-23. VEN

535 Crespo, Angel. "La literatura dramática en el Brasil," *Primer Acto*, No. 75 (1966), 12-14. BRAZ

536 Crimi, Humberto. "Sobre una historia del teatro mendocino," *Versión* (Mendoza), No. 2 (1959), 147-161. ARG

537 Cros, Edmond. "El cuerpo y el ropaje en el *Divino Narciso* de Sor Juana Inés de la Cruz," *Boletín de la Biblioteca de Menéndez y Pelayo*, Año XXXIX (1963), 73-94. MEX

538 Cruz, Diego Daniel. "Noticia sobre el teatro argentino," *Revista: Organo de la Universidad Nacional de San Agustín* (Arequipa), 27, No. 41/42 (1er y 2° semestre 1955), 205-227. ARG

539 Cruz, Jorge. "Autor como individuo, autor como generación," *Sur*, No. 302 (1966), 94-97. GEN

540 ____. "Crónica de Montevideo," *Sur*, No. 264 (mayo-jun 1960), 90-93. URUG

541 ____. "Francisco Defilippis Novoa," *Revista de Estudios de Teatro* (Buenos Aires), III, No. 9 (1965), 31-41. ARG

542 ____. *Genio y figura de Florencio Sánchez*. Buenos Aires: Eudeba, 1966. 192 p. URUG

543 ____. "La máquina profética de Agustín Cuzzani," *Sur*, No. 300 (1966), 119-121. ARG

Cuzzani's Para que se cumplan las escrituras.

544 ____. *Samuel Eichelbaum*. Buenos Aires: Ediciones Culturales Argentinas, Ministerio de Educación y Justicia, 1962. 95 p. ARG

545 ____. "El teatro de la ciudad de Montevideo," *Sur*, No. 275 (mar-abr 1962), 118-121. URUG

546 ____. "Verano y teatro," *Sur*, No. 311 (mar-abr 1968), 127-129. ARG

547 ____. "Visión optimista de la temporada de 1959," *Sur*, No. 262 (ene-feb 1960), 75-77. ARG

548 Cruz, José Raúl. "Cuba/Brecht en Teatro Estudio: una aplicación consecuente," *Conjunto*, No. 21 (jul-set 1974), 130-131. CUBA

549 Cruz, Pedro Nolasco. "Obras dramáticas chilenas," *Estudios sobre literatura chilena*. Santiago: Editorial Nascimento, 1940, II, pp. 343-361. CHILE

550 Cruz-Luis, Adolfo. "Conversatorio," *Conjunto*, No. 11-12 (ene-abr 1972), 19-25. CUBA

Dialogue among the participants in the production of Raúl Valdés Vivó's Naranjas en Saigon.

551 ____. "Cuatrotablas, teatro popular y enfrentamiento," *Conjunto*, No. 19 (ene-mar 1974), 4-14. PERU

History, orientation and goals of the Peruvian group Cuatrotablas.

552 Cruz-Luis, Adolfo. "En la ciudad dorada, no todo lo que brilla es oro," *Conjunto*, No. 20 (abr-jun 1974), 38-41. COL

On La ciudad dorada, *creación colectiva del Grupo La Candelaria, de Colombia.*

553 ____. "Para atacar la injusticia y la frustración; para promover la lucha y la esperanza," *Conjunto*, No. 21 (jul-set 1974), 61-65. CHILE

A brief history of Aleph, the Chilean theater group, from 1968-1973.

554 ____. "Teatro negro en el Tahuantinsuyo," *Conjunto*, No. 14 (set-dic 1972), 88-93. PERU

555 Cuadra, Fernando. "Alberto Blest Gana y el desarrollo del teatro chileno," *Apuntes* (Chile), No. 78 (dic 1973), 3-9. CHILE

556 ____. "Apuntes para una visión social del teatro chileno," *Revista EAC*, No. 2 (1972), 49-52. CHILE

557 Cuadros, Manuel E. *Pasaje y obra, mujer e historia: Clorinda Matto de Turner*. Cuzco: Editorial H. G. Rozas Sucesores, 1949. PERU

558 Cuba (Consejo Provincial de Cultura). *El teatro, panorama general*. La Habana: Imprenta CTC-R, 1964. 21 p. CUBA

559 "Cuba estrena," *Cuba*, I, No. 2 (mayo 1962), 51. CUBA

Report on plays of Manuel Reguera Saumell and Abelardo Estorino.

560 Cueto, Mireya. "The Puppet Theatre in Mexico," *World Theatre*, No. 14 (1965), 460-466. MEX

561 Cuevas, Fabiola Matilde. "Problemática en el drama de Florencio Sánchez," Unpub. Ph.D. diss., California at Davis, 1974. URUG

562 Cúneo, Dardo. "Internación en el teatro de Florencio Sánchez," *Teatro Completo de Florencio Sánchez*. Comp., Dardo Cúneo. 2a. ed. Buenos Aires: Editorial Claridad, 1952. URUG

563 Cunill Cabanellas, Antonio. *Función social del*

teatro. Santa Fe: Universidad Nacional del Litoral, 1939. 22 p. ARG

564 Curie Gallegos, Luis. "La primera representación del *Quijote* en España y América se realizó en el pueblo de Pausa en el año 1607," *Escena* (Lima), 1, No. 3 (mar 1954), 14-15. PERU

565 Curotto, Angel. "Carlos Brussa, 'leader' del teatro en el Uruguay," *Boletín de Estudios de Teatro*, 4, No. 12 (mar 1946), 57-62. URUG

566 "Un cursillo de dirección en Teatro Estudio," *Conjunto*, No. 10 (s.f.), 69-71. CUBA

On Buenaventura's work with the Teatro Estudio in Cuba, as told by Gloria Parrado and Luis Felipe Roca.

567 Cypess, Sandra M. "The Function of Myth in the Plays of Xavier Villaurrutia," *Hispania*, 55, No. 2 (May 1972), 256-263. MEX

568 ____. "The Influence of the French Theatre in the Plays of Xavier Villaurrutia," *Latin American Theatre Review*, 3/1 (Fall 1969), 9-15. MEX

569 ____. Review: "Richard Callan. *Miguel Angel Asturias*. New York: Twayne, 1970." *Revista Iberoamericana*, No. 75 (abr-jun 1971), 473. GUAT

570 "Dados sobre *Transe* e o autor," *Revista de Teatro* (Brazil), No. 389 (set-out 1972), 47-50. BRAZ

Includes comments by author, Ronald Radde, the text of the play, and reviews.

571 Dalton, Vane C. "The theatre: The foregone year (1961)," *Mexican Life*, 38, No. 1 (Jan 1962), 39-41. MEX

572 D'Amore, Reynaldo. "Dos experiencias personales en torno a la organización de un teatro," in *Teatro y universidad*. Tucumán: Facultad de Filosofía y Letras, Universidad Nacional, 1960, pp. 11-23. ARG

573 D'Amore, Reynaldo. "Panorama en lenta evolución," *Teatro XX*, I, No. 5 (oct 1964), 4. PERU

574 D'Angelo, Giuseppe. "Italianismos en el teatro de Florencio Sánchez," *Thesaurus* (Bogotá), XXIII, No. 3 (set-dic 1968), 480-514. URUG

575 Dantas, Paulo. "Na Compadecida Alma do Nordeste," *Revista Brasiliense*, No. 14 (nov-dez 1957), 90-97. BRAZ

On Ariano Suassuna's play, Auto da Compadecida.

576 Dauster, Frank N. "Cinco años de teatro hispanoamericano," *Asomante*, 15, No. 1 (ene-mar 1959), 54-64. GEN

577 ____. "El concepto de Puerto Rico en algunas obras de Francisco Arriví," in *Estudios de literatura hispanoamericana en honor a José J. Arrom*. Andrew P. Debicki and Enrique Pupo-Walker, eds. Chapel Hill: North Carolina Studies in the Romance Languages and Literatures, 1974, pp. 257-266. PTO. RICO

578 ____. "The Contemporary Mexican Theater," *Hispania*, XXXVIII, No. 1 (Mar 1955), 31-34. MEX

579 ____. "Cuban Drama Today," *Modern Drama*, IX, No. 2 (Sept 1966), 153-164. CUBA

580 ____. "Drama and Theater in Puerto Rico," *Modern Drama*, VI, No. 2 (Sept 1963), 177-186. PTO. RICO

Also as "Drama y teatro en Puerto Rico," Revista del Instituto de Cultura Puertorriqueña, *VII, No. 22 (ene-mar 1964), 1-7.*

581 ____. "The Drama of Carlos Solórzano," *Modern Drama*, VII, No. 1 (May 1964), 89-100. GUAT

582 ____. "La forma ritual en *Los huéspedes reales*," *El Nacional* (29 mar 1964), Suplemento, p. 7. MEX

On Luisa Josefina Hernández' play, Los huéspedes reales.

583 ____. "Francisco Arriví: The Mask and the Garden," *Hispania*, XLV, No. 4 (Dec 1962), 637-643. PTO. RICO

Also as: "Francisco Arriví: La máscara y el

jardín," Revista del Instituto de Cultura Puertorriqueña, *V, No. 14 (1962), 37-41.*

584 Dauster, Frank N. "Francisco Arriví y la entrada por las raíces," *Revista del Instituto de Cultura Puertorriqueña*, No. 50 (ene-mar 1971). PTO. RICO

585 ____. "The Game of Chance: The Theatre of José Triana," *Latin American Theatre Review*, 3/1 (Fall 1969), 3-8. CUBA

586 ____. "Hacia el teatro nuevo: Un novel autor dramático," *Hispania*, XLI, No. 2 (May 1958), 170-172. GUAT

On Carlos Solórzano. Reprinted in México en la Cultura *(jun 1958).*

587 ____. *Historia del teatro hispanoamericano, siglos XIX y XX*. México: Ediciones de Andrea, 1966. 121 p. GEN

2a.ed., muy ampliada, 1973. 167 p.
Reviewed: Debicki, Andrew P.; Forster, Merlin.

588 ____. "The Latin American Theatre," in *Latin America and the Caribbean*. London: Anthony Blond, 1968, pp. 789-794. GEN

589 ____. "The Literary Art of Xavier Villaurrutia." Unpub. Ph.D. diss., Yale, 1953. MEX

590 ____. "New Plays by René Marqués," *Hispania*, XLIII, No. 3 (Sept 1960), 451-452. PTO. RICO

591 ____. "New Values in Latin American Theatre," *Theatre Arts*, No. 43 (Feb 1959), 56-59, 62-73. GEN

Also in "Los nuevos valores del teatro latinoamericano," Cultura *(San Salvador), No. 15 (ene-mar 1959), 88-94.*

592 ____. "An Overview of the Spanish American Theater," *Hispania*, L, No. 4 (Dec 1967), 996-1000. GEN

593 ____. "Recent Research in Spanish American Theater," *Latin American Research Review*, I, No. 2 (Spring 1966), 65-76. GEN

594 ____. Review: "Carlos Miguel Suárez Radillo. *13 autores del nuevo teatro venezolano*. Caracas:

Monte Avila Editores, 1971." *Revista Interamericana de Bibliografía*, XXIII, No. 3 (jul-set 1973), 345-346. VEN

595 Dauster, Frank N. Review: "Carlos Solórzano. *El teatro hispanoamericano contemporáneo*. 2 vol. México: Fondo de Cultura Económica, 1964." *Revista Iberoamericana*, XXXI, No. 60 (jul-dic 1965), 311-312. GEN

596 ____. Review: "José Juan Arrom. *El teatro de Hispanoamérica en la época colonial*. La Habana: Anuario Bibliográfico Cubano, 1956." *Hispania*, XL, No. 1 (Mar 1957), 120-121. GEN

597 ____. Review: "Manuel Romero de Terreros. *Teatro breve*. México: Los Presentes, 1956." *Revista Iberoamericana*, XXIII, No. 45 (ene-jun 1958), 190-191. MEX

Six one-act plays by Manuel Romero de Terreros.

598 ____. Review: "Margaret V. Campbell. *The Development of the National Theater in Chile to 1842*. Gainesville: University of Florida Press, 1958." *Hispania*, XLII, No. 1 (Mar 1959), 141-142. CHILE

599 ____. Review: "Raúl H. Castagnino. *Literatura dramática argentina, 1717-1967*. Buenos Aires: Editorial Pleamar, 1968." *Revista Interamericana de Bibliografía*, XX, No. 4 (oct-dic 1970), 473-475. ARG

600 ____. Review: "Ruth S. Lamb. *Bibliografía del teatro mexicano del siglo XX*. México: Ediciones de Andrea, 1962." *Revista Iberoamericana*, XXIX, No. 55 (ene-jun 1963), 198-199. MEX

601 ____. Review: Antonio Magaña Esquivel and Ruth S. Lamb. *Breve historia del teatro mexicano*. México: Ediciones de Andrea, 1958." *Hispania*, XLII, No. 4 (Dec 1959), 643. MEX

602 ____. Review: "*Teatro hispanoamericano*. Hymen Alpern and José Martel, eds. New York: The Odyssey Press, 1956." *Hispania*, XL, No. 4 (Dec 1957), 497-499. GEN

603 ____. Review: "*Teatro mexicano del siglo XX*. Selección, prólogo y notas de Francisco Monterde,

Antonio Magaña Esquivel y Celestino Gorostiza. México: Fondo de Cultura Económica (Letras Mexicanas, 25, 26 y 27), 1956." *Revista Iberoamericana*, XXII, No. 44 (jul-dic 1957), 372-375. MEX

604 Dauster, Frank N. Review: "*Teatro puertorriqueño*. San Juan: Instituto de Cultura Puertorriqueña, 1959." *Revista Iberoamericana*, XXV, No. 49 (ene-jun 1960), 172-173. PTO. RICO

605 ____. Review: "Walter Rela. *Contribución a la bibliografía del teatro chileno, 1804-1960*. Montevideo: Universidad de la República, 1960." *Hispanic Review*, XXI, No. 1 (1963), 84-85. CHILE

606 ____. Review: "Willis Knapp Jones. *Behind Spanish American Footlights*. Austin: University of Texas Press, 1966." *Revista Iberoamericana*, XXXII, No. 62 (jul-dic 1966), 323-326. GEN

607 ____. "Social Awareness in Contemporary Spanish American Theater," *Kentucky Romance Quarterly*, XIV, No. 2 (1967), 120-125. GEN

608 ____. "El teatro de Elena Garro: Evasión e ilusión," *Revista Iberoamericana*, XXX, No. 57 (ene-jun 1964), 81-89. MEX

609 ____. "El teatro de Emilio Carballido," *La Palabra y el Hombre*, No. 23 (jul-set 1962), 369-384. MEX

610 ____, ed. *Teatro hispanoamericano: Tres piezas*. New York: Harcourt, Brace and World, 1965. GEN

Prologue "Theatre in Latin America," with three plays: Emilio Carballido, Rosalba y los Llaveros; *Francisco Arriví,* Vejigantes; *Enrique Solari Swayne,* Collacocha. GEN
Reviewed: Lyday, Leon.

611 ____. "El teatro vanguardista de Carlos Solórzano: Movimientos literarios de vanguardia en Iberoamérica," in *Memoria* (XI Congreso del Instituto Internacional de Literatura Iberoamericana, México), Austin: University of Texas Press, 1965, pp. 89-95. GUAT

612 ____. "The Theater of René Marqués," *Symposium*, XVIII, No. 1 (Spring 1964), 35-45. PTO. RICO

613 Dauster, Frank N. *Xavier Villaurrutia.* New York: Twayne Publishers, Inc., 1971. 155 p. MEX

Chapter 3, "The Theater," pp. 69-104, deals specifically with his dramatic production. Reviewed: Debicki, Andrew P.

614 ____ and Leon F. Lyday. *En un acto.* New York: D. Van Nostrand Co., 1974. 193 p. GEN

Anthology. Includes: Emilio Carballido, El censo; *Carlos Solórzano,* Los fantoches; *Wilberto Cantón,* El juego sagrado; *Sergio Vodanović,* El delantal blanco; *Antón Arrufat,* La repetición; *José de Jesús Martínez,* Juicio final; *Jorge Díaz,* El génesis fue mañana; *Demetrio Aguilera Malta,* El tigre; *José Triana,* El Mayor General hablará de teogonía.

615 D'Aversa, Alberto. "Grandeza y miseria del teatro popular," *Teatro XX* (Buenos Aires), Año 2, No. 16 (set 1965). ARG

616 Dávila, David. "The Life and Theater of Gabriela Roepke," Unpub. Ph.D. diss., Cincinnati, 1973. CHILE

617 Davison, Ned J. "The Dramatic Works of Eduardo Barrios," *Hispania*, XLI, No. 1 (Mar 1958), 60-63. CHILE

618 ____. *Eduardo Barrios.* New York: Twayne Publishers, Inc., 1970. 152 p. CHILE

"The Plays," pp. 28-32.

619 "De la comedia musical al teatro de protesta: Isidora Aguirre," *Conjunto*, No. 10 (s.f.), 45-47. CHILE

Conjunto *interviews Aguirre on her theater.*

620 Debesa, Fernando. "Apuntes sobre la obra dramática de Luis Alberto Heiremans," *Apuntes*, No. 43 (oct 1964), 22-32. CHILE

621 Debicki, Andrew P. Review: "Frank Dauster. *Historia del teatro hispanoamericano, siglos XIX y XX.* 2a. ed. México: Ediciones de Andrea, 1973." *Latin American Theatre Review*, 8/1 (Fall 1974), 95-96. GEN

622 ____. Review: "Frank Dauster. *Xavier Villaurrutia.* New York: Twayne Publishers, Inc., 1971." *Latin American Theatre Review*, 5/1 (Fall 1971), 87-88. MEX

623 Dehesa y Gómez Farías, María Teresa. *Introducción a la obra dramática de José Joaquín Fernández de Lizardi*. México: Universidad Nacional Autónoma de México, 1961. 206 p. MEX

M. A. thesis.

624 Delgado, Luis Humberto. "El teatro peruano en la colonia y en la república," *Cahuide* (Lima), 15, No. 125-126 (dic 1951-ene 1952), [75-82]. PERU

625 Delgado Nieto, Carlos. "La representación en la *Doncella del agua* de Jorge Rojas," *Revista de las Indias* (Bogotá), XXXV, No. 109 (mayo-jun 1949), 108-109. COL

626 "*O Demônio Familiar* e *Mãe* teriam sido peças abolicionistas?" *Revista de Teatro*, CCCXXXII (1963), 23-25. BRAZ

José de Alencar's treatment of slavery.

627 Depons, Francisco [Pons, François Raymond Joseph de]. "El teatro en Caracas durante la colonia," in "Viaje a la parte oriental de Tierra Firme en la América meridional," *El Universal* (5 mar 1967). VEN

628 Descalzi, Ricardo. *Historia crítica del teatro ecuatoriano*. 6 vol. Quito: Casa de la Cultura Ecuatoriana, 1968. 2,125 p. ECUAD
Reviewed: Ayora, Jorge; Luzuriaga, Gerardo.

629 Deuel, Pauline B. "The 'commedia dell'arte' in a Mexican Folk Theater," *Hispania*, XLVII, No. 3 (set 1964), 537-539. MEX

630 ____. "La técnica dramática de un Teatro Folklórico Mexicano," *El teatro en Iberoamérica* (Memoria del duodécimo congreso del Instituto Internacional de Literatura Iberoamericana). México: IILI (1966), pp. 85-90. MEX

631 Devine, George. "Carta aberta ao teatro brasileiro," *Módulo* (Rio de Janeiro), 8, No. 33 (jun 1963), 37-41. BRAZ

The British theater director makes recommendations for the improvement of Brazilian theater.

632 Dial, Eleanore M. "Alvaro Custodio and His

Continuing Dream: The Teatro Clásico de México in the 1960's," *Latin American Theatre Review*, 7/2 (Spring 1974), 45-57. MEX

633 Dial, Eleanore M. "Critical reaction to a decade of Spanish theatre in Mexico, 1952-1962." Unpub. Ph.D. diss., Missouri, 1968. MEX

634 ____. "Drama Critics in Search of an Identity in Mexico in the 1950's," *Latin American Literary Review*, II, No. 4 (Spring-Summer 1974), 113-125. MEX

635 Dial, John E. Review: "Ernesto Barrera. *Realidad y fantasía en el drama social de Luis Enrique Osorio.* Madrid: Ediciones Plaza Mayor, 1971." *Latin American Theatre Review*, 6/2 (Spring 1973), 74-75. COL

636 Dias Gomes, Alfredo. "*O Berço do Herói* e as *Armas do Carlos*," *Revista Civilização Brasileira*, No. 4 (set 1965), 257-268. BRAZ

637 ____. "Realismo ou esteticismo: um falso dilema," *Revista Civilização Brasileira*, No. 5/6 (mar 1966), 221-230. GEN

638 Díaz, Jorge. "Dos comunicaciones," *Latin American Theatre Review*, 4/1 (Fall 1970), 73-78. GEN

Includes "Itinerario" and "La erosión del lenguaje."

639 ____. "ICTUS: Algunas consideraciones," *Conjunto*, No. 7 (s.f.), 81-82. CHILE

640 ____. "Una obra documento para la televisión," *Conjunto*, No. 21 (jul-set 1974), 51-53. CHILE

Díaz comments about his Mear contra el viento.

641 ____. "Reflections on the Chilean Theatre," *The Drama Review*, 14, No. 2 (Winter 1970), 84-86. CHILE

642 Díaz Machicago, Porfirio. "Prólogo para mi antología del teatro boliviano," *Signo* (La Paz), 2a. época, No. 10 (3r. trimestre 1968), 7-9. BOL

643 Dibarboure, José Alberto. *Proceso del teatro uruguayo, 1808-1938; Significación de Florencio Sánchez en la escena rioplatense.* Montevideo: Claudio García y Cía, 1940. 162 p. RIVER PLATE

644 Diego, Jacobo A. de. "Enrique Muiño," *Talía*, III, No. 16 (jul 1956), 18. ARG

645 ____. "El silencio del teatro argentino," *Talía*, III, No. 17/18 (1957), 15. ARG

646 ____. "Tres nacimientos de autores," *Revista de Estudios de Teatro* (Buenos Aires), 4, No. 11 (1970), 7-10. ARG

Martiniano Leguizamón, Emilio Onrubia, Francisco Defilippis Novoa.

647 ____. "Ubicación de Ezequiel Soria," *Revista de Estudios de Teatro*, III, No. 9 (1965), 42-49. ARG

648 Díez Canedo, Enrique. "Florencio Sánchez y su teatro," *Revista Universidad de La Habana*, VI, No. 35 (1941), 7-17. URUG

649 Di Lullo, Orestes. "Contribución del folklore al teatro nacional," *Cuadernos de Cultura Teatral*, No. 16 (1942), 105-129. ARG

650 Dittborn, Eugenio. "Algunas consideraciones sobre el arte de la dirección teatral," *Aisthesis*, No. 1 (1966), 111-117. GEN

651 ____. "Constantes en la trilogía de Luis Alberto Heiremans," *Boletín de la Universidad de Chile*, No. 56 (mayo 1965), 70-80. CHILE

652 ____. "Fuentes y formas de la creación dramática en el teatro aficionado," *Conjunto*, No. 13 (mayo-ago 1972), 90-91. GEN

653 Domenech, Ricardo. "Actuación en Madrid del Teatro de Ensayo de la Universidad Católica de Chile," *Cuadernos Hispanoamericanos*, No. 142 (oct 1961), 118-125. CHILE

654 ____. "Crítica de *Un niño azul para esa sombra*," *Cuadernos Hispanoamericanos*, No. 128-129 (ago-set 1960), 259-263. PTO. RICO

On René Marqués's play.

655 Domínguez, Luis Arturo. "La ceremonia de 'la tura', ritos pre-colombinos como gérmenes dramáticos," *Revista de Estudios de Teatro* (Buenos Aires), II, No. 6 (1963), 61-67. GEN

656 Donahue, Francis. "Guerrilla Theatre with a Mexican Accent," *Latin American Theatre Review*, 6/1 (Fall 1972), 65-69. U.S.

657 ____. "Teatro de Guerrilla," *Cuadernos Americanos*, CXC, No. 5 (set-oct 1973), 17-33. U.S.

658 Dorr, Nelson. "Sin opiniones y sin intenciones no se puede presentar teatro," *Conjunto*, No. 11-12 (ene-abr 1972), 15-17. CUBA

On Raúl Valdés Vivó's Naranjas en Saigon.

659 Dorr, Nicolás. "Una casa en Lota Alto," *Conjunto*, No. 17 (jul-set 1973), 104-106. CHILE

Justification for awarding prize for Víctor Torres's play, Una casa en Lota Alto.

660 *Dos generaciones del teatro chileno*. Santiago: Universidad de Chile, 1963. CHILE

661 "*Dos viejos pánicos* en Colombia," *Conjunto*, No. 7 (s.f.), 69-71. CUBA

On Virgilio Piñera's play, Dos viejos pánicos.

662 Doudoroff, Michael J. "A Contribution to the Study of the Magi Theme in Hispanic Literature and Folklore." Unpub. Ph.D. diss., Stanford, 1969. GEN

663 Dowling, John. "The Mexico City Theatre, 1969," *Latin American Theatre Review*, 3/2 (Spring 1970), 55-66. MEX

664 Droguett, Iván. "Apuntes sobre *Fulgor y muerte de Joaquín Murieta* de Pablo Neruda," *Latin American Theatre Review*, 2/1 (Fall 1968), 39-48. CHILE

665 Dughera, Eduardo A. "El texto en el teatro actual," *Universidad*, 27 (dic 1954), 183-196. GEN

666 Dulsey, Bernard M. "Icaza sobre Icaza," *Modern Language Journal*, LIV, No. 4 (Apr 1970), 233-245. ECUAD

667 Durán, Diony. "Lizárraga, primer premio Casa de las Américas," *Conjunto*, No. 15 (ene-mar 1973), 93-94. ARG

Andrés Lizárraga's El torturador.

668 Durán, Manuel. "El drama intelectual de Sor Juana y el anti-clericalismo hispánico," *Cuadernos Americanos*, CXXIX, No. 4 (jul-ago 1963), 238-253. MEX

669 Durán Cerda, Julio. "Actuales tendencias del teatro chileno," *Revista Interamericana de Bibliografía*, Vol. 13 (1963), 152-175. CHILE

670 ____. "Civilización y barbarie en el desarrollo del teatro nacional rioplatense," *Revista Iberoamericana*, XXIX, No. 55 (ene-jun 1963), 89-124. RIVER PLATE

671 ____. *Panorama del teatro chileno, 1842-1959; estudio crítico y antología.* Santiago: Editorial del Pacífico, 1959. 371 p. CHILE

672 ____. *Repertorio del teatro chileno.* Santiago: Instituto de Literatura Chilena, 1962. 247 p. CHILE

673 ____. *El teatro chileno contemporáneo.* México: Aguilar, 1970. 498 p. CHILE

Anthology. Includes: María Asunción Requena, Ayayema; *Egon Wolff,* Los invasores; *Luis Alberto Heiremans,* El abanderado; *Sergio Vodanović*, Viña; *Alejandro Sieveking,* Animas de día claro; *Jorge Díaz,* El cepillo de dientes.
Reviewed: Luzuriaga, Gerardo.

674 ____. "El teatro chileno moderno," *Anales de la Universidad de Chile*, Año CXXI, 126 (ene-abr 1963), 168-203. CHILE

675 ____. "El teatro en las tareas revolucionarias de la independencia de Chile," *Anales de la Universidad de Chile*, No. 118-119 (3r trimestre 1960), 227-235. CHILE

676 Durón, Jorge Fidel. "Sobre el teatro en Honduras," *Honduras Rotaria* (Tegucigalpa), 17, No. 183 (jun 1958), 12-13. HOND

677 ____. "Teatro en Honduras," *Boletín de la Academia Hondureña* (Tegucigalpa), 10, No. 11 (nov 1965), 55-59. HOND

678 Dutra, Francis A. "The Theatre of Dias Gomes: Brazil's Social Conscience," *Cithara*, IV, No. 2 (May 1965), 3-13. BRAZ

679 Echagüe, Juan Pablo. "Enrique García Velloso: el hombre y su obra," *Cuadernos de Cultura Teatral*, No. 9 (1940), 87-104. ARG

680 ____. "Enrique Frexas," *Boletín de Estudios de Teatro*, I, No. 2 (jun 1943), 21-23. ARG

681 ____. *Escritores de la Argentina*. Buenos Aires: Emecé, 1945. 149 p. ARG

"Crítica sobre algunos autores teatrales argentinos: Roberto J. Payró y Gregorio de Laferrère."

682 ____. "Florencio Sánchez," *Revista Iberoamericana*, No. 17 (feb 1945), 9-24. URUG

683 ____. "Roberto J. Payró," *Revista de Estudios de Teatro* (Buenos Aires), III, No. 8 (1964), 52-59. ARG

684 ____. "El teatro de ideas," *Boletín de Estudios de Teatro*, III, No. 10 (set 1945), 145-154. GEN

685 Echavarren, Roberto. "Festival internacional de teatro en Uruguay," *Cuadernos del Sur*, II, No. 8 (mar 1965), 254-257. URUG

686 Echevarría, Néstor J. "Consideraciones en torno a la arquitectura y al quehacer musical del Teatro Colón de Buenos Aires," *Notas* (Buenos Aires), Año 9, No. 40 (set 1966), 10-12, 15. ARG

687 Eguren, Alicia. "Sugestiones del teatro religioso de Navidad para un teatro nuevo," *Lyra*, VII, No. 75-76 (nov-dic 1949). GEN

688 Ehrmann, Hans. "Chilean Theatre, 1970," *Latin American Theatre Review*, 4/2 (Spring 1971), 65-68. CHILE

689 ____. "Chilean Theatre: 1971-1973," *Latin American Theatre Review*, 7/2 (Spring 1974), 39-43. CHILE

690 ____. "Sinopsis del teatro chileno en 1953," *Escena* (Lima), 1, No. 3 (mar 1954), 17-20. CHILE

691 Ehrmann, Hans. "Teatro y público: de la nueva carpa al congreso latinoamericano," *Primer Acto*, No. 74 (1966), 55-57. CHILE

692 ____. "Theatre in Chile: A Middle-Class Conundrum," *The Drama Review*, 14, No. 2 (Winter 1970), 77-83. CHILE

693 Eichelbaum, Samuel. "Algo más sobre Florencio Sánchez," *Boletín de Estudios de Teatro*, III, No.11 (dic 1945), 237-241. URUG

694 ____. "Francisco Defilippis Novoa," *Ars*, Año XI, No. 50 (1950). ARG

695 ____. "Hostil posteridad para Ernesto Herrera," *Ficción*, 5 (ene-feb 1957), 208-211. URUG

696 "¿En qué punto está el teatro en Venezuela?" *Revista Nacional de Cultura* (Caracas), XXVII, No. 171 (set-oct 1965), 95-101. VEN

Panel discussion.

697 Engel, Walters, Alipio Jaramillo y Guillermo Silva Santamaría. "Teatro experimental. Primer salón de los seis," *Revista de las Indias* (Bogotá), XXXIV, No. 106 (nov-dic 1948), 109-117. COL

Small section on the Teatro Experimental de la Universidad Nacional.

698 Englekirk, John E. *De lo nuestro y lo ajeno*. México: Editorial Cultura, 1966. 260 p. MEX

699 ____. "Fernando Calderón en el teatro popular nuevomexicano," *Memoria* (Segundo Congreso del Instituto Internacional de Literatura Iberoamericana). Berkeley and Los Angeles: University of California Press, 1941, pp. 227-240. U.S.

700 ____. "La leyenda Ollantina," in *Literatura de la emancipación hispanoamericana y otros ensayos*. Lima: Universidad Nacional Mayor de San Marcos, Dirección Universitaria de Biblioteca y Publicaciones, 1972, pp. 302-308. PERU

701 ____. "Notes on the Repertoire of the New Mexican Spanish Folk Theatre," *Southern Folklore Quarterly*, No. 4 (Dec 1940), 227-237. U.S.

702 ____. "The Passion Play in New Mexico," *Western*

Folklore (Berkeley), XXV, No. 1 (Jan 1966), 17-33; No. 2 (Apr 1966), 105-121. U.S.

703 Englekirk, John E. Review: "Gustavo Correa y Calvin Cannon. *La loa en Guatemala. Contribución al estudio del teatro popular hispanoamericano.* New Orleans: Middle America Research Institute, Tulane University, 1958." *Hispanic Review*, XXVIII, No. 3 (July 1960), 288-291. GUAT

704 ____. "The Source and Dating of New Mexican-Spanish Folk Plays," *Western Folklore* (Berkeley), XVI, No. 4 (Oct 1957), 332-355. SOUTH WEST

705 ____. "El teatro folklórico hispanoamericano," *Folklore Americanas*, XVII (June 1957), 1-36. GEN

706 ____. "El teatro y el pueblo en el Caribe," in *Memoria* (VIII Congreso del Instituto Internacional de Literatura Iberoamericana, México). San Juan: Secretaría de Estado del Estado Libre Asociado de Puerto Rico, 1961, pp. 73-82. CARIB

707 ____. "El tema de la conquista en el teatro folklórico de Mesoamérica," *Actas* (XXXIII Congreso Internacional de Americanistas, San José), (jul 1958), 462-475. CENTR AM

708 ____. "'Y el Padre Eterno se ardía...' En torno al teatro popular mexicano," *Hispania*, XXXVI, No. 4 (Nov 1953), 405-411. MEX

709 "Entrevista a los miembros del 'Teatro Ensayo'," *Boletín Cultural* (Quito), 2, No. 14 (1 dic 1965), 2-4. ECUAD

710 Escalada Yriondo, Jorge. "En torno al primer coliseo argentino," *Estudios* (Buenos Aires), 77, No. 418 (mayo 1947), 213-216. ARG

711 ____. "Orígenes del teatro porteño," *Boletín de Estudios de Teatro*, III, No. 8 (ene 1945), 23-32. ARG

712 Escarpanter, José A. "El teatro de Carlos Felipe," *Revista Nacional de Teatro* (La Habana), No. 1 (1961). CUBA

713 Escudero, Alfonso M. "Apuntes sobre el teatro en Chile," *Aisthesis*, No. 1 (1966), 17-61. CHILE

Also as Apuntes sobre el teatro en Chile. *Santiago: Editorial Salesiana, 1967. 72 p.* Reviewed: Jones, Willis K.

714 Espina, Antonio, ed. *Las mejores escenas del teatro español e hispanoamericano.* Madrid, 1959. GEN

715 Espinel, Jaime. "Crónica épica sobre teatro guerrilla," *Revista Teatro* (Medellín), No. 7 (1971), 3-14. GEN

716 Espinosa, Aurelio M., and José Manuel Espinosa. "*Los Tejanos*: A New Mexican Spanish Popular Dramatic Composition of the Middle of the Nineteenth Century," *Hispania*, XXVII, No. 3 (Oct 1944), 291-314. U.S.

Includes introduction and linguistic notes, text of manuscript, and corrected Spanish text.

717 Espinosa, Pedro. "Andrés Lizárraga," *Revista de Teatro* (Buenos Aires), No. 1 (nov-dic 1960), 39-44. ARG

718 ____. "Plática con el Director del Instituto Nacional de Estudios de Teatro," *Talía*, V, No. 19/20 (nov 1960), 7. ARG

Contenido: Actos populares; Actividades en 1960; ¿La burocracia?

719 Espinosa Torres, Victoria. *El teatro de René Marqués y la escenificación de su obra:* Los soles truncos. México: Universidad Nacional Autónoma de México, Facultad de Filosofía y Letras, 1969. 579 p. PTO. RICO

720 Espinosa y Prieto, Eduardo, François Baguer, and Salvador Novo. "Tres autores y tres obras del teatro mexicano," *Cuadernos de Bellas Artes*, IV, No. 9 (set 1963), 27-36. MEX

On Usigli's El gesticulador, *Cantón's* Nosotros somos Dios, *and Sánchez Mayáns's* Las alas del pez.

721 Estelle, Patricio. "Apuntes a la obra de Luis Alberto Heiremans," in *El teatro en Iberoamérica* (Memoria del duodécimo congreso del Instituto Internacional de Literatura Iberoamericana). México: IILI (1966), 73-84. CHILE

722 Estorino, Abelardo. "Destruir los fantasmas, los mitos de las relaciones familiares. Entrevista

a Revuelta y Triana," *Conjunto*, No. 4 (ago-set 1967), 6-14. CUBA

Estorino interviews José Triana (author) and Vicente Revuelta (director) on Teatro Estudio's production of La noche de los asesinos.

723 Estrada, José. "El no teatro mexicano," *Mundo Nuevo*, No. 3 (set 1966), 60-61. MEX

The lack of theater and the director's responsibility.

724 Estrada, Pascual. "Angel poético y demonio dramático de Román Chalbaud," *Zona Franca*, 3, No. 45 (mayo 1967), 41-43. VEN

725 Estrada, Santiago. "El teatro argentino," *Boletín de Estudios de Teatro*, 1, No. 2 (jun 1943), 45-48. ARG

726 Estrella, Ezequiel. "La actualidad teatral en la Argentina," *Dinámica Social* (Buenos Aires), 10, No. 114 (mar 1960), 21. ARG

727 Estrella, Ulises. "Situación y proyecciones del teatro en el Ecuador," *Conjunto*, No. 11-12 (ene-abr 1972), 62-65. ECUAD

728 ____. "El teatro en el Ecuador," *Nivel*, No. 10 (oct 1963), 5. ECUAD

729 ____. "El teatro obrero en el Ecuador," *Conjunto*, No. 9 (s.f.), 117-120. ECUAD

730 Etchenique, Nira. *Roberto Arlt*. Buenos Aires: Editorial La Mandrágora, 1962. 120 p. ARG

731 "La exposición de títeres demuestra gracia pintoresca," *Boletín de Estudios de Teatro*, I, No. 4 (ene 1944), 48-49. GEN

732 Fábio, Paulo. "Oduvaldo Vianna," *Revista de Teatro* (Rio de Janeiro), No. 388 (jul-ago 1972), 30. BRAZ

733 Fábregat Cúneo, Roberto. "El teatro en el Uruguay," *América* (La Habana), 43, No. 1 (abr 1954), 59-65. URUG

734 Fábregat Cúneo, Roberto. "Theatre in Uruguay," *Américas*, 12, No. 11 (1960), 22-25. URUG

735 "Fábula y documentación," *Boletín de Estudios de Teatro*, I, No. 1 (ene 1943), 24-26. URUG

Discusses obscure points about Florencio Sánchez.

736 Facio, Angel. "Entrevista con Taco Larreta," *Primer Acto*, No. 157 (jun 1973), 44-50. URUG

737 ____. "Nuevo teatro del Brasil: Impresiones a primera vista de *Morte e Vida Severina*," *Primer Acto*, No. 75 (1966), 50-51. BRAZ

738 Faig, Carlos. "La parábola del teatro de Vicente Martínez Cuitiño," *Revista de Estudios de Teatro* (Buenos Aires), 4, No. 11 (1970), 17-20. ARG

739 Falino, Louis P., Jr. "Six Plays of Jorge Díaz: Theme and Structure." Unpub. Ph.D. diss., St. Louis Univ., 1969. CHILE

740 ____. "Theatre Notes from Chile," *Latin American Theatre Review*, 3/2 (Spring 1970), 67-70. CHILE

741 Farias, Javier. *Historia del teatro*. Buenos Aires: Editorial Atlántida, 1958. GEN

742 Farias Costa, Marcelo. *História do Teatro Cearense*. Fortaleza: Imprensa Universitária da Universidade Federal do Ceará, 1972. BRAZ

743 Felipe, Carlos. "Los pretextos y el nonnato teatro cubano," *Islas* (Santa Clara), 2, No. 1 (set-dic 1959), 79-81. CUBA

744 Fernández, Alvaro. "Primer Congreso Nacional de Cultura," *Cuba*, II, No. 10 (1963), 74-81. CUBA

Theater activities, 1962, p. 81.

745 Fernández, Gerardo. "Uruguay: El teatro y la conciencia revolucionaria," *Conjunto*, III, No. 8 (1969), 120-122. URUG

746 Fernández, José M. "Teatro experimental. Entrevista a Vicente Revuelta," *Conjunto*, No. 3. CUBA

747 Fernández, Oscar. "Brazil's New Social Theatre,"

Latin American Theatre Review, 2/1 (Fall 1968), 15-30. BRAZ

748 Fernández, Oscar. "Censorship and the Brazilian Theatre," *Educational Theatre Journal*, 25, No. 3 (Oct 1973), 285-298. BRAZ

749 ____. "The Contemporary Theater in Rio de Janeiro and in São Paulo, 1953-1955," *Hispania*, XXXIX, No. 4 (Dec 1956), 423-432. BRAZ

750 Fernández, Sergio. "La metáfora en el teatro de Sor Juana," *Artes de México*, 16, No. 123 (1969). MEX

751 ____. "Prólogo a Sor Juana Inés de la Cruz," in *Autos sacramentales de Sor Juana Inés de la Cruz.* México: Universidad Nacional Autónoma de México, 1970, pp. i-xxxvii. (Biblioteca del estudiante universitario.) MEX

752 Fernández de la Vega, Oscar y Juan F. Carvajal Bello. "Gertrudis Gómez de Avellaneda: significación de su lírica y su dramática," *Literatura Cubana.* 7a. ed. La Habana: Editorial Selecta, 1958, Vol. II. CUBA

753 Fernández Santos, Angel. "Entrevista con José Armando Ferrara," *Primer Acto*, No. 75 (1966), 19-20. BRAZ

Ferrara, an actor in João Cabral de Melo Neto's Morte e Vida Severina.

754 Ferrán, Jaime. "Teatro de arte popular en Bogotá," *Mundo Hispánico* (Madrid), 18, No. 213 (dic 1965), 36-37. COL

755 Ferrari, Juan Carlos. "El teatro y sus problemas," *Talía*, I, No. 9 (jul-ago 1954), 15. GEN

756 Ferrer Canales, José. "Un drama de Francisco Arriví," *Revista del Instituto de Cultura Puertorriqueña*, 8, No. 27 (abr-jun 1965), 1-4. PTO. RICO

On Arriví's Vejigantes. *Also in* El teatro en Iberoamérica *(Memoria del duodécimo congreso del Instituto Internacional de Literatura Iberoamericana). México: IILI, 1966.*

757 Fessler, Oscar. "Lo que podríamos aprender de Stanislavsky y Brecht," in *Teatro y Universidad.*

Tucumán: Facultad de Filosofía y Letras, Universidad Nacional, 1960, pp. 37-53. GEN

758 "Festival de verano; Festival de otoño," *Revista de Bellas Artes*, No. 12 (nov-dic 1966), 90-92. MEX

759 "Los Festivales de Teatro de la Casa de las Américas," *Conjunto*, No. 1 (1964), 51-53. GEN

760 Fialho, A. Veiga. "Teatro no Brasil: Balanço de 1964," *Revista Civilização Brasileira*, No. 1 (mar 1965), 218-221. BRAZ

761 Figueiredo, Guilherme. "Atuais tendências do teatro brasileiro," *Revista Interamericana de Bibliografía*, XV, No. 3 (jul-set 1965), 209-225. BRAZ

762 Filippelli, Eugenio. "El teatro en el interior del país," *Revista de Estudios de Teatro* (Buenos Aires), III, No. 7 (1963), 55-59. ARG

763 Flores, Ronald C. "The Specter of Assimilation: The Evolution of the Theme of Nationalism in the Theater of René Marqués," Unpub. Ph.D. diss., Pennsylvania State, 1974. PTO. RICO

764 Flores Arzayús, Gabriel M. "Prólogo," *Teatro de Enrique Buenaventura*. Bogotá: Ediciones Tercer Mundo, 1963. COL

765 Florit, Eugenio. Review: "José Juan Arrom. *El teatro de Hispanoamérica en la época colonial*. La Habana: Anuario Bibliográfico Cubano, 1956." *Hispanic Review*, XXVI, No. 3 (July 1958), 257-258. GEN

766 Flynn, Gerard. *Sor Juana Inés de la Cruz*. New York: Twayne Publishers, 1971. 123 p. MEX

"The Secular Theater," 35-55; "The Religious Theater," 56-81.

767 Fontova, José María. "Perfil y obra de Antonio Reynoso; un precursor del género chico nacional," *Lyra*, XVII, No. 174-176 (1959). ARG

768 Foppa, Tito Livio. "El drama en el teatro argentino," *Lyra*, XVII, No. 174-176 (1959). ARG

769 Forster, Merlin H. Review: "José Juan Arrom. *Historia del teatro hispanoamericano (época colonial)*. México: Ediciones de Andrea, 1967; and Frank N. Dauster. *Historia del teatro hispanoamericano (siglos XIX y XX)*. México: Ediciones de Andrea, 1966." *Latin American Theatre Review*, 1/1 (Fall 1967), 50-54. GEN

770 Foster, Virginia Ramos. "The Buenos Aires Theatre, 1966-67," *Latin American Theatre Review*, 1/2 (Spring 1968), 54-67. ARG

771 ____. "Mario Trejo and Griselda Gambaro: Two Voices of the Argentine Experimental Theatre," *Books Abroad*, 42, No. 4 (Autumn 1968), 534-535. ARG

772 ____. "Theatre of Dissent: Three Young Argentine Playwrights," *Latin American Theatre Review*, 4/2 (Spring 1971), 45-50. ARG

Discusses Hoy Napalm hoy *by Víctor de los Solares,* Hablemos al calzón quitado *by Guillermo Gentile, and* Una noche con el Señor Magnus e hijos *by Ricardo Monti.*

773 ____. "Variations of Latin American Third World Drama," *Latin American Literary Review*, II, No. 3 (Fall-Winter 1973), 35-43. GEN

774 Francis, Paulo. "De Górki a Nelson Rodrigues," *Revista Civilização Brasileira*, No. 3 (jul 1965), 189-198. BRAZ

775 ____. "Novo rumo para autôres," *Revista Civilização Brasileira*, No. 1 (mar 1965), 212-217. BRAZ

776 Franco, Luis. "Divagaciones sobre el teatro," *Cuadernos de Cultura Teatral*, No. 18 (1944), 9-31. GEN

777 Fraser, Howard M. Review: "Richard Callan. *Miguel Angel Asturias*. New York: Twayne Publishers, 1970." *Modern Language Journal*, LVI, No. 3 (Mar 1972), 182-183. GUAT

778 Frêches, Claude-Henri. "Le theatre du P. Anchieta: Contenu et structures," *Annali Istituto Universitario Orientale* (Napoli), III (1961), 47-70. BRAZ

779 Freire, Tabaré J. "Florencio Sánchez, sainetero,"

Revista Iberoamericana de Literatura (Montevideo), I, No. 1 (1959), 45-63. URUG

780 Freire, Tabaré J. *Ubicación de Florencio Sánchez en la literatura teatral.* Montevideo: Comisión de Teatros Municipales, 1961. 139 p. URUG

781 Freitas, Newton. "Notas sobre el teatro en el Brasil," *Revista de Cultura Brasileña* (Madrid), No. 31 (mayo 1971), 97-100. BRAZ

782 Frontura, Rafael. *Trasnochadas; recuerdos, anécdotas, crónicas y versos escritos en diversos países y épocas diferentes que van desde 1920 hasta 1955.* Santiago: Editorial Zig-Zag, 1957. 221 p. GEN

783 Frugoni de Fritzsche, Teresa. "Panorama del Teatro Argentino Actual," *El Teatro en Iberoamérica* (Memoria del duodécimo congreso del Instituto Internacional de Literatura Iberoamericana). México: IILI (1966), pp. 61-72. ARG

784 Fuente, Pablo de la. "El teatro en Chile," *Norte* (New York), (mayo 1942), 46. CHILE

785 Fuentes, Ricardo. "Alejandro Jodorowsky: Teatro pánico," *Imagen* (Caracas), No. 6 (?), 22. CHILE

786 G. R. P. [Gonzalo Rojas Pizarro?]. "Teatro experimental de la Universidad de Chile," *Antártica* (Santiago), No. 4 (dic 1944), 84-87. CHILE

787 Gac, Gustavo y Perla Valencia. "El último grupo de teatro popular que actuó en Chile: Teatro Experimental del Cobre," *Conjunto*, No. 21 (jul-set 1974), 54-58. CHILE

788 Galaos, José Antonio. "Teatro argentino contemporáneo," *Cuadernos Hispanoamericanos*, No. 147 (mar 1962), 392-400. ARG

789 Galich, Manuel. "Actores en Marcha por nuestra América," *Conjunto*, No. 18 (oct-dic 1973), 39-41. COL

On Actores en Marcha, a Colombian theater group, an outgrowth of the TEC.

790 G[alich], M[anuel]. "A veces, esa palabra libertad se ha dicho," *Conjunto*, No. 16 (abr-jun 1973), 78-82. PAN

Commentary on Agustín del Rosario's A veces esa palabra libertad.

791 ____. "Conversatorio con Teatro ICR," *Conjunto*, No. 15 (ene-mar 1973), 4-11. ARG

On Dalmiro Sáenz and Hip... Hip... Ufa.

792 ____. "Un crítico uruguayo habla de teatro latinoamericano, en Cuba," *Conjunto*, No. 9 (s.f.), 136-138. GEN

An interview with Gerardo Fernández, Uruguayan theater critic.

793 ____. "De *Amoretta* a *Historias con cárcel*," *Conjunto*, No. 16 (abr-jun 1973), 82-86. ARG

On Osvaldo Dragún's theater.

794 ____. "La denuncia: actual y continental," *Conjunto*, No. 19 (ene-mar 1974), 36-39. GEN

795 ____. "Díaz-Uriz: Proceso y condena de la ITT," *Conjunto*, No. 21 (jul-set 1974), 5-7. CHILE

Introductory commentary on Mear contra el viento, *play by Jorge Díaz and Francisco Uriz, which follows.*

796 ____. "Noticias ecuatorianas de teatro," *Conjunto*, No. 8 (1969), 116-119. ECUAD

797 ____. "Variaciones sobre un teatro en percusión," *Conjunto*, No. 15 (ene-mar 1973), 12-14. CHILE

On Jorge Díaz and Variaciones para muertos en percusión.

798 ____. "Venezuela en el teatro de César Rengifo," *Conjunto*, No. 22 (oct-dic 1974), 2-9. VEN

799 ____, et al. "Alentador despegue de la actual dramaturgia latinoamericana," *Conjunto*, No. 13 (mayo-ago 1972), 5-9. GEN

A dialogue involving Galich, Adolfo Cruz-Luis, Alfonso Sastre, Rogério Paulo and René de la Cruz.

800 Galindo, Alejandro. "Las artes dramáticas y la comunicación," *Conjunto*, No. 10 (s.f.), 72-86. GEN

801 Gallegos Valdés, Luis. "El Rabinal Achí," *Cultura* (El Salvador), No. 45 (jul-set 1967), 49-54. GUAT

802 ____. "El teatro en función cultural," *Cultura* (San Salvador), No. 38 (oct-dic 1965), 124-132. EL SAL

803 Gallo, Blas Raúl. *Historia del sainete nacional.* Buenos Aires: Editorial Quetzal, 1959. ARG

804 ____. "El sainete y la farsa," *Artes y Letras Argentinas*, No. 2, número extraordinario (1961), 83-84. ARG

805 ____. *El teatro y la política.* Buenos Aires: Centro Editor de América Latina, 1968. 78 p. GEN

806 Gambaro, Griselda. "¿Por qué y para quién hacer teatro?" *Talía*, No. 39/40 (s.f.), 4-6. GEN

807 Gamboa Garibaldi, Arturo. "La obra dramática de José Peón y Contreras," *Revista de la Universidad de Yucatán*, 5, No. 25 (ene-feb 1963), 60-83. MEX

808 Garasa, Delfín Leocadio. *Julio Sánchez Gardel.* Buenos Aires: Ediciones Culturales Argentinas, Ministerio de Educación y Justicia, 1963. 93 p. ARG

809 ____. "Reflexiones sobre el fenómeno teatral," *Cursos y Conferencias*, LVI, No. 288 (1960), 113-133. GEN

810 Garcés, Julián. Review: "Efraín Bischoff. *Tres siglos de teatro en Córdoba, 1600-1900.* Córdoba: 1961." *Revista de Historia de América*, No. 53-54 (1962), 240-241. ARG

811 ____. Review: "Tito L. Foppa. *Diccionario teatral del Río de la Plata.* Buenos Aires: 1961." *Revista de Historia de América*, No. 53-54 (1962), 258-259. RIVER PLATE

812 García, Germán. "La primera obra teatral de

Roberto J. Payró," *Boletín de Estudios de Teatro*, III, No. 11 (dic 1945), 217-231. ARG

813 García, Germán. *Roberto J. Payró; testimonio de una vida y realidad de una literatura.* Buenos Aires: Nova, 1961. 215 p. ARG

814 García Marruz, Fina. "Obras de teatro representadas en La Habana en la última década del siglo XVIII, según el *Papel Periódico*," *Revista de la Biblioteca Nacional José Martí*, Año 63, 3a. época, XIV, No. 2 (mayo-ago 1972), 95-125. CUBA

Critical commentary and a listing of plays, 1790-1805.

815 García Merou, Martín. "Los títeres," *Boletín de Estudios de Teatro*, I, No. 4 (ene 1944), 31-36. GEN

816 García Ponce, Juan. "*Los fantoches, Mea culpa,* y *El crucificado*," *Revista de la Universidad de México*, XIII, No. 3 (nov 1958), 27-29. GUAT MEX

Discusses Solórzano's three plays plus Celestino Gorostiza's La leña está verde.

817 ____. "El pequeño caso de Jorge Lívido" (Magaña), *Revista de la Universidad de México*, XII, No. 12 (ago 1958), 28-29. MEX

On Sergio Magaña's play, El pequeño caso de Jorge Lívido.

818 ____. "Teatro," *El Libro y el Pueblo*, época III, No. 2-3 (1959-1960), 115-119. MEX

Six months of the theater in Mexico (1959?). Includes discussion of Fernando Calderón's A ninguna de las tres *and comments on the director Héctor Mendoza.*

819 García Salaberry, Adela. *Florencio Parravicini; su vida y su obra; un estudio psiconeuropsiquiátrico de su personalidad.* Buenos Aires: Talleres Gráficos Argentinos L. J. Rosso, 1947. 124 p. ARG

820 García Velloso, Enrique. "Gregorio de Laferrère," *Nosotros*, 2a. época, XII, No. 46-47 (feb 1940), 7-18. ARG

821 ____. *Memorias de un hombre de teatro.* Buenos

Aires: Editorial Guillermo Kraft, 1942. ARG

Reprinted: Buenos Aires: Editorial Universitaria de Buenos Aires, 1960. 140 p.

822 García Velloso, Enrique. "Los primeros dramas en los circos criollos," *Boletín de Estudios de Teatro*, 7, No. 22-23 (jul-dic 1948), 74-86. ARG

823 Gariano, Carmelo. "El cambio repentino y la busca de lo esencial en la *Viuda difícil* de Conrado Nalé Roxlo," *El teatro en Iberoamérica* (Memoria del duodécimo congreso del Instituto Internacional de Literatura Iberoamericana). México: IILI (1966). ARG

824 Garibay K., Angel María. "Poesía dramática [prehispánica]," in *Historia de la literatura náhuatl*. Tomo I. México: Editorial Porrúa, 1953, pp. 331-384. MEX

825 ____. "El teatro catequístico," in *Historia de la literatura náhuatl*. Tomo II. México: Editorial Porrúa, 1954, pp. 121-159. MEX

826 Garzón Céspedes, Francisco. "Brigada 2506: la verdadera historia," *Conjunto*, No. 21 (jul-set 1974), 120-122. CUBA

On Raúl Macías's play, Brigada 2506.

827 ____. "*La chacota* comunica con su público," *Conjunto*, No. 21 (jul-set 1974), 115-117. CUBA

On Nicolás Dorr's play, La chacota.

828 ____. "Colombia: métodos de creación colectiva en un trabajo teatral contra el sistema," *Conjunto*, No. 20 (abr-jun 1974), 21-37. COL

An interview with Carlos José Reyes.

829 ____. "En América Latina el teatro le ha sido expropiado al pueblo," *Conjunto*, No. 20 (abr-jun 1974), 13-20. GEN

An interview with Julio Mauricio (Argentina).

830 ____. "El germen del teatro está latente en el pueblo," *Conjunto*, No. 20 (abr-jun 1974), 4-12. GEN

An interview with Julio Mauricio (Argentina), Carlos José Reyes (Colombia), and Herminia Sánchez (Cuba).

831 Garzón Céspedes, Francisco. "Hemos creado inquietudes de actores, de directores, de público," *Conjunto*, No. 18 (oct-dic 1973), 7-16. CUBA

On the Grupo Teatro Escambray.

832 Gates, Eunice Joiner. Review: "Willis Knapp Jones. *Antología del teatro hispanoamericano.* México: Ediciones de Andrea, 1959." *Hispania*, XLII, No. 3 (Dec 1959), 643-645. GEN

833 ____. "Usigli as Seen in His Prefaces and Epilogues," *Hispania*, XXXVII, No. 4 (Dec 1954), 432-439. MEX

834 Gaucher-Shultz, Jeanine, and Alfredo O. Morales. *Tres dramas mexicanos en un acto.* New York: Odyssey Press, 1971. xvi, 88 p. MEX

Includes: Carlos Solórzano, Los fantoches; *Elena Garro,* Un hogar sólido; *Sergio Magaña,* El suplicante.
Reviewed: Bravo-Villarroel, Roberto.

835 Gené, Juan Carlos. "Notas sobre folklore y teatro regional," in *Teatro y Universidad.* Tucumán: Facultad de Filosofía y Letras, Universidad Nacional, 1960, pp. 55-70. ARG

836 ____. "El pueblo es el único creador auténtico y fundamental de la cultura," *Conjunto*, No. 22 (oct-dic 1974), 78-82. GEN

On "creación colectiva."

837 ____. "El teatro y las masas," *Revista de la Universidad* (La Plata), No. 19 (ene-dic 1965), 117-123. ARG

Theoretical treatise on theater for the people.

838 ____. "Universidad y profesión teatral," *Revista de la Universidad* (La Plata), No. 10 (ene-abr 1960), 101-109. ARG

The role of the university in contemporary theater.

839 "La generación ecuatoriana del treinta y el teatro," *Comunidad Latinoamericana de Escritores Boletín*, 8, 18-24. ECUAD

840 Gentile, Guillermo. "Antecedentes y notas para la puesta en escena," *Teatro 70*, No. 4-5 (nov-dic 1970), 41-55. ARG

Notes on Guillermo Gentile's Hablemos al calzón quitado.

841 Ghiano, Juan Carlos. "Conrado Nalé Roxlo y el teatro," *Ficción*, No. 10 (nov-dic 1957), 88-94. ARG

842 ____. "Defilippis Novoa, espectador," *Revista de Estudios de Teatro* (Buenos Aires), No. 1 (ene-mar 1959), 35-38. ARG

843 ____. "La época de oro del teatro argentino," *Davar*, No. 87 (oct-dic 1960), 75-91. ARG

844 ____. *El grotesco de Armando Discépolo*. Buenos Aires: Ediciones Culturales Argentinas, Ministerio de Educación y Justicia, 1965. ARG

845 ____. "Martiniano Leguizamón y el teatro," *Buenos Aires*, I, No. 1 (set 1961), 145-154. ARG

846 ____. "Mito y realidad de Roberto Arlt," *Ficción*, No. 17 (ene-feb 1959), 96-100. ARG

847 ____. "Nuevos dramaturgos," *Ficción*, No. 21 (set-oct 1959), 76-80. ARG

Mentions: Juan Carlos Gené, Osvaldo Dragún, Marco Denevi, Agustín Cuzzani, Carlos Gorostiza, Juan Carlos Ferrari, and Rodolfo Kusch.

848 ____. "Prólogo," *Teatro gauchesco primitivo*. Buenos Aires: Losange, 1957. ARG

Anthology. Includes: El amor de la estanciera, El detalle de la acción de Maipú, Las bodas de Chivico y Pancha, *and* Juan Moreira.

849 ____. "Prólogo," *Tres grotescos de Armando Discépolo*. Buenos Aires: Losange, 1958. ARG

850 ____. "El teatro de Sánchez Gardel," *Academia*

Argentina de Letras, 20, No. 77 (jul-set 1951), 339-367. ARG

851 Gil Quesada, Maruja. "Punto de vista de una actriz," *Revista de Estudios de Teatro* (Buenos Aires), III, No. 7 (1963), 13-17. ARG

On Gregorio de Laferrère.

852 Gillespie, Ruth C. "Conrado Nalé Roxlo: Poet and Humorist," *Hispania*, XXXVI, No. 1 (Feb 1953), 71-75. ARG

853 Gillet, Joseph E. "José de Anchieta, the First Brazilian Dramatist," *Hispanic Review*, XXI, No. 2 (Apr 1953), 155-160. BRAZ

854 ____. "Valencian 'Misterios' and Mexican Missionary Plays in the Early Sixteenth Century," *Hispanic Review*, XIX, No. 1 (Jan 1951), 59-61. MEX

855 Giménez Pastor, Arturo. *Figuras a la distancia.* Buenos Aires: Losada, 1940. 331 p. ARG

On the origins of the Buenos Aires theater.

856 ____. "Nicolás Granada, el hombre y su obra," *Cuadernos de Cultura Teatral*, No. 14 (1940), 101-130. ARG

857 Girard, Rafael. "Una obra maestra del teatro maya," *Cuadernos Americanos*, VI, No. 6 (nov-dic 1947), 157-188. GUAT

Historia, *nombre que los chortís dan al* Baile de los gigantes *que él convirtió en dos episodios bíblicos, el degüello de San Juan y la lucha entre Garrite y Goliat.*

858 Gisbert, Teresa. *Teatro virreinal en Bolivia.* La Paz: Biblioteca de Arte y Cultura Boliviana, 1962. 35 p. BOL

859 Giusti, Roberto Fernando. "Un episodio desconocido de la juventud de Florencio Sánchez," *Boletín de Estudios de Teatro*, I, No. 2 (jun 1943). URUG

860 ____. "Estudio histórico-literario del teatro venezolano en el siglo XIX y apreciación de su

actualidad," *Revista del Liceo Andrés Bello* (Caracas), No. 2 (1946), 36-64. VEN

861 Giusti, Roberto Fernando. "Florencio Sánchez y el teatro rioplatense," *Revista Interamericana de Bibliografía*, XII, No. 1-2 (ene-jun 1962), 73-88. RIVER PLATE

862 ____. "El teatro rioplatense: del circo a las modernas expresiones de vanguardia," *Cuadernos Americanos*, No. 5 (set-oct 1954), 198-212. RIVER PLATE

863 ____. "Visión panorámica del teatro argentino," *Lyra*, XVII, No. 174-176 (1959). ARG

864 Glantz, Margo. "¿De cuál libertad se trata?" *Revista de la Universidad de México*, XX, No. 12 (ago 1966), 48. BRAZ

About Libertad, Libertad *by Brazil's Millor Fernández and Flávio Rangel.*

865 ____. "La higiene de los placeres y de los dolores," *Revista de la Universidad de México*, XXIII, No. 2 (oct 1968), suplemento, p. 12-13. MEX

On Héctor Azar's play, La higiene de los placeres y de los dolores.

866 Glickman, Enrica Jemma. "Italian Dramatic Companies and the Peruvian Stage in the 1870's," *Latin American Theatre Review*, Part I, 6/2 (Spring 1973), 41-54; Part II, 7/2 (Spring 1974), 69-80. PERU

867 Goico, Manuel de Jesús. "Raíz y trayectoria del teatro en la literatura nacional," *Anales de la Universidad de Santo Domingo,* IX, No. 33-36 (1945), 71-90; X, No. 37-38 (1946), 155-202. DOM REP

868 Gómez, Ulises. "En búsqueda del teatro latinoamericano," *Boletín Bibliográfico y Cultural*, X, No. 11 (1967), 213-218. GEN

869 Gómez de la Vega, Alfredo. "Origins, Influences and Trends of Acting and Directing in the Mexican Theatre," in *Proceedings of the Conference on Latin-American Fine Arts, June 14-17, 1951; cosponsored by the College of Fine Arts and the Institute of Latin American Studies, the University of Texas*. Austin: University of Texas Press, 1952, 42-57. MEX

870 Gómez Sánchez, Luis. "Chocano y el teatro. Dramas de José Chocano," *Correo* (Lima), (22 jul 1965). PERU

871 ____. "*Ollantay*," *Correo* (Lima), (27 feb 1965). PERU

872 Gonçalves, Delmiro. "Drama do café encontrou seu autor," *Visão*, 24, No. 24 (19 jun 1964), 20-23. BRAZ

On Jorge Andrade.

873 Gonçalves, Lopes. "Ao correr da pena... e do tempo," *Revista de Teatro* (Rio de Janeiro), No. 355 (jan-fev 1967), 14-16. BRAZ

Notes on: Alusio Azevedo, cenógrafo e figurinista; Palmira Bastos, atriz portuguesa; "o nosso primeiro baile público à fantasia"; Carlos Gomes, revistógrafo.

874 Gondim, Isaac. "In Recife: An Actor's Day," *World Theatre*, IV, No. 1 (1954), 50-52. BRAZ

875 González, Jorge Antonio. *Historia del teatro en la Habana.* Santa Clara: Dirección de Publicaciones de la Universidad Central de las Villas, 1961. CUBA

876 ____. "Repertorio teatro cubano (con anotaciones bibliográficas correspondientes a nuestra Biblioteca Nacional)," *Revista de la Biblioteca Nacional* (La Habana), 2a. serie, 2, No. 4 (oct-dic 1951), 69-184. CUBA

877 González, Manuel Pedro. "El *Ollantay* de Ricardo Rojas," *Revista Hispánica Moderna*, 10, No. 2 (ene-abr 1944), 34-36. ARG

878 González, Nilda. "El teatro de Salvador Brau," *Revista del Instituto de Cultura Puertorriqueña*, VI, No. 18 (ene-mar 1963), 16-24. PTO. RICO

879 González Cruz, Luis F. "Virgilio Piñera y el teatro del absurdo en Cuba," *Mester* (UCLA), V, No. 1 (nov 1974), 52-57. CUBA

880 González de Garfinkel, Lila. Review: "Jorge A. Huerta. *A Bibliography of Chicano and Mexican Dance, Drama and Music.* Oxnard, Calif.: Colegio Quetzalcoatl, 1972." *Latin American Theatre Review*, 6/1 (Fall 1972), 92-93. U.S. MEX

881 González-del-Valle, Luis and Antolín González-

del-Valle. "Visión del hombre y de la sociedad en tres dramaturgos argentinos contemporáneos," *Cuadernos Americanos*, Año XXX, 178, No. 5 (set-oct 1971), 210-228. ARG

Discusses Alberto Weiner, Néstor Kraly, and Roberto Cossa.

882 González Freire, Natividad. "Los chapuzones," *Conjunto*, No. 21 (jul-set 1974), 117-119. CUBA

Commentary on Los chapuzones *by Ignacio Gutiérrez.*

883 ____. "Cuba, un resumen del año teatral," *Conjunto*, No. 6 (ene-mar 1968), 85-89. CUBA

Discusses the year 1967.

884 ____. "Desarrollo del teatro en Cuba," *Revista Nacional de Teatro* (La Habana), 1 (1961). CUBA

885 ____. "En busca de un teatro cubano," *Nuestro Tiempo* (La Habana), 5, No. 25 (set-oct 1958), [6-7]. CUBA

886 ____. "La nueva generación teatral cubana," *Nuestro Tiempo* (La Habana), 4, No. 17 (mayo-jun 1957), [10-11]. CUBA

887 ____. "El VI Festival de Teatro Latinoamericano," *Casa de las Américas*, 7, No. 41 (mar-abr 1967), 116-120. CUBA

888 ____. "Sobre dramas y dramaturgos," *Revista Unión*, VI, No. 4 (dic 1967), 232-242. CUBA

889 ____. *Teatro cubano contemporáneo (1928-1957)*. La Habana: Sociedad Colombista Panamericana, 1958. CUBA

Segunda edición: (1927-1961). *La Habana: Ministerio de Relaciones Exteriores, 1961.*

890 González Lanuza, Eduardo. *Roberto Arlt*. Buenos Aires: Centro Editor de América Latina, 1971. 115 p. ARG

"Dramaturgo," pp. 95-112.

891 González Olaechea, María Eugenia. "Tres obras cortas en el Club del Teatro," *Expreso* (Lima), (8 mar 1964). PERU

892 González Padilla, María Enriqueta. "El teatro

gauchesco rioplatense y el teatro revolucionario mexicano," *Anuario de Letras* (UNAM), No. 5 (1965), 213-224. ARG MEX

893 González Paredes, Ramón. "Una obra simbólica," *Revista Nacional de Cultura*, 26, No. 166 (oct-dic 1964), 111-118. VEN

On Alejandro Lasser's La cueva.

894 González Peña, Carlos. *El alma y la máscara...* México: Editorial Stylo, 1948. 282 p. MEX

Theater in Mexico, 1925-1947.

895 Gordon, Fortuna L. "The Theater in Brazil Today," *Kentucky Foreign Language Quarterly*, 13, No. 4 (1966), 229-236. BRAZ

896 Gorostiza, Celestino. "Apuntes para una historia del teatro experimental," *México en el Arte*, No. 10-11 (1950), 23-30. MEX

897 ____. "Panorama del teatro en México," *Cuadernos Americanos*, Año XVI, XCVI, No. 6 (nov-dic 1957), 250-261. MEX

898 ____. "Las paradojas del teatro," *El Libro y el Pueblo*, IV, No. 10 (1964), 13-17, 30. GEN

899 ____. "El teatro de Xavier Villaurrutia," *Cuadernos Americanos*, LXII, No. 2 (mar-abr 1952), 287-290. MEX

900 Grases, Pedro. "La singular historia de un drama y de un soneto de Andrés Bello," in *Andrés Bello, El primer humanista de América.* Buenos Aires: Ediciones de Tridente, 1946, pp. 21-48. VEN

901 Green, Joan Rea. "Character and Conflict in the Contemporary Central American Theatre," *Contemporary Latin American Literature.* Houston: University of Houston, 1973, pp. 103-108. CENTR AM

902 ____. "The Hero in Contemporary Spanish American Theatre: A Case of Diminishing Returns," *Latin American Theatre Review*, 5/2 (Spring 1972), 19-27. GEN

903 Green, Otis H. Review: "José Juan Arrom. *Historia*

de la literatura dramática cubana. New Haven: Yale University Press, 1944." *Hispanic Review*, XIV, No. 3 (July 1946), 273-275. CUBA

904 Gregorio, Joaquín S. "Traven and Usigli," *Revista de la Universidad de México*, VIII, (1954), 15-16. MEX

905 Grifone, Julia. *Martiniano Leguizamón y su égloga "Calandria."* Buenos Aires: Universidad de Buenos Aires, Instituto de Literatura Argentina, 1940. ARG

906 Grunauer Herrera, E. A. "¿Existe un divorcio entre nuestro teatro nacional y el pueblo argentino?" *Lyra*, VII, No. 67-68 (mar-abr 1949). ARG

907 Grupo Libre Teatro Libre. "Popular por lo revolucionario," *Conjunto*, No. 19 (ene-mar 1974), 91-98. GEN

In section "Brecht en América Latina."

908 Grupo TEC. "Las últimas experiencias del Teatro Experimental de Cali: 'Nuestro arte será más arte cuanto más revolucionario sea'," *Conjunto*, No. 14 (set-dic 1972), 94-100. COL

909 Grupo Teatral Bambalinas. Review: "Osvaldo Dragún. *Milagro en el mercado viejo.*" *Primer Acto*, No. 85 (jun 1967), 60. ARG

910 Grupo Teatro Trashumante. "La experiencia de un teatro trashumante," *Conjunto*, No. 11-12 (ene-abr 1972), 68-70. MEX

911 Grupo Yarabey. "En la búsqueda de un teatro nacional," *Conjunto*, No. 19 (ene-mar 1974), 113-114. CUBA

In section "Brecht en América Latina."

912 Guardia, Alfredo de la. "The Argentine Modern Theatre," *Comentario* (Buenos Aires), 11, No. 40 (3a. entrega 1964), 17-22. ARG

913 ____. "Discurso," *Boletín de la Academia Argentina de Letras*, 31, No. 21 (jul-set 1966), 369-398. ARG

On Martín Coronado, dramatist.

914 Guardia, Alfredo de la. "Dos estudios de Samuel Eichelbaum," *Nosotros*, 2a. época, 14, No. 64 (jul 1941), 84-89. ARG

915 ____. "El drama," *Artes y Letras Argentinas*, II (1961), 61-63. ARG

Número extraordinario.

916 ____. "En torno a la situación del teatro nacional (Argentina)," *Comentario* (Buenos Aires), 11, No. 40 (1964), 17-22. ARG

917 ____. "*Ollantay* de Ricardo Rojas." Buenos Aires: Talleres Gráficos de la Dirección General del Boletín Oficial e Imprenta del Ministerio del Interior, 1964. 18 p. ARG

918 ____. "Raíz y espíritu del teatro de Eichelbaum," en *Imagen del drama*. Buenos Aires: Editorial Schapire, 1954. ARG

919 ____. *Rodolfo González Pacheco*. Buenos Aires: Ediciones Culturales Argentinas, Ministerio de Educación y Justicia, 1963. 136 p. ARG

920 ____. *El teatro contemporáneo*. Buenos Aires: Editorial Schapire, 1947. ARG

"En Argentina," pp. 196-204. Treats Roberto J. Payró, Florencio Sánchez and others.

921 ____. "El teatro de Ricardo Rojas," *Revista de la Universidad de Buenos Aires*, 5a. época, III, No. 3 (jul-set 1958), 377-388. ARG

922 ____. *Visión de la crítica dramática*. Buenos Aires: Editorial de la Pleyade, 1970. 360 p. GEN

923 Guardia, Miguel. "The Mexican Theater: Celestino Gorostiza," *Mexican Cultural Bulletin*, No. 15 (jul 1953), 3. MEX

924 ____. "*Yanga* by Othón Arróniz," *Revista de la Universidad de México*, XXV, No. 9 (mayo 1971), 43-44. MEX

925 Guarnieri, Gianfrancesco. "O Teatro como Expressão da Realidade Nacional," *Revista Brasiliense*, No. 25 (set-oct 1959), 121-126. BRAZ

926 Guerra, José Augusto. "El mundo mágico y poético de Ariano Suassuna," *Revista de Cultura Brasileña* (Madrid), No. 35 (mayo 1973), 56-71. BRAZ

927 Guerrero Zamora, Juan. "The Spanish Speaking Drama Astride Two Continents," *World Theatre*, XI, No. 4 (1962-1963), 345-358. GEN

928 ____. "Voz viva de América Latina," *Boletín* de CLE (México), No. 11 (1971). GEN

Study of four plays: Osvaldo Dragún's Historia de Panchito González; *Sergio Vodanović's* Las exiladas; *Sebastián Salazar Bondy's* El de la valija; *and Carlos Solórzano's* El sueño del ángel.

929 Guglielmini, Homero Mario. "Exposición de teatro argentino en Chile," *Boletín de Estudios de Teatro*, III, 3, No. 10 (set 1945), 161-165. ARG

930 Guibourg, Edmundo. "El teatro," *Artes y Letras Argentinas*, II, número extraordinario (1961), 59-60. ARG

931 Guimarães, Jorge. "Introdução à montagem de um auto de Anchieta," *Revista de Teatro* (Rio de Janeiro), No. 385 (jan-fev 1972), 15-21. BRAZ

932 Gutiérrez, H. C. "Antecedentes históricos del títere venezolano," *Revista Nacional de Cultura*, Año 25, No. 158-159 (mayo-ago 1963), 149-162. VEN

933 Gutiérrez, Juan María. "Ojeada histórica sobre el teatro de Buenos Aires desde su origen hasta la aparición de la tragedia de *Dido y Argia*," en su *Estudios histórico-literarios*. Buenos Aires: Angel Estrada y Cía., 1940, pp. 185-197. ARG

934 Gutkin, Adolfo. "*Amerindias*, una experiencia de creación colectiva," *Conjunto*, No. 16 (abr-jun 1973), 37-39. CUBA

The first work of the Conjunto Dramático de Oriente.

935 Guzik, Sergio. "A Mass Changes Me More. An Interview with Alexandro Jodorowsky," *The Drama Review*, 14, No. 2 (Winter 1970), 70-76. CHILE

936 Guzmán, Eugenio. "La violencia en el teatro de

hoy," *Textos* (Manizales), 1, No. 4 (s.f.), 1,8. GEN

Also in Conjunto, *No. 6 (ene-mar 1968), 24-35.*

937 Guzmán Esponda, Eduardo. "Los temas nacionales en el teatro colombiano," *Boletín de la Academia Colombiana*, XX, No. 83 (jun-jul 1970), 247-252. COL

938 Halac, Ricardo. "Del teatro muerto surge el teatro vivo," *La Opinión* (Buenos Aires), Suplemento Cultural (26 set 1971), p. 12. ARG

939 ____. "Desde el *Moreira* de Podestá al teatro político," *La Opinión* (Buenos Aires), Suplemento Cultural (1 jul 1973), p. 2. ARG

940 ____. "Tragedia del fin de Atahualpa," *La Opinion* (Buenos Aires), Suplemento Cultural (6 ago 1972), pp. 6-7. PERU

Comentarios sobre pieza del mismo título, muestra del teatro incaico.

941 Hamilton, Carlos D. "Notas sobre el teatro hispanoamericano actual," *Revista Hispánica Moderna*, XXXIV, No. 3-4 (jul-oct 1968), 661-670. GEN

This issue is the Homenaje a Federico de Onís (1885-1966), Vol. II.

942 Hamilton, D. Lee. "A Vida e as Obras de José de Anchieta," *Hispania*, XXVI, No. 4 (Dec 1943), 407-424. BRAZ

943 Hanrahan (S. J.), Thomas. "El 'Tocotín' expresión de identidad," *Revista Iberoamericana*, XXXVI, No. 70 (ene-mar 1970), 51-60. MEX

Traces existence of this motif in early dramatic and poetic pieces--Sor Juana and others.

944 Harmony, Olga. "Entre las mafias y la renovación, Héctor Mendoza y el teatro universitario," in "Diorama," suplemento de *Excelsior* (25 mar 1973), p. 13. MEX

945 Harth, Dorothy E. and Lewis M. Baldwin. *Voices of Aztlan, Chicano Literature of Today*. New York:

New American Library, 1974. U.S.

Includes: Luis Valdez, "The Actos", pp. 207-209.

946 Hechel, Ilse. "Los sainetes de Sor Juana Inés de la Cruz," *Revista Iberoamericana*, No. 25 (oct 1947), 135-140. MEX

947 Hecker Filho, Paulo. "O Teatro Brasileiro," *Anais do Segundo Congresso Brasileiro de Crítica e História Literaria*. São Paulo: No. 37 (1961), 191-219. BRAZ

948 ____. "Teatro Brasileiro," *Revista do Livro*, VI (1961), 109-130. BRAZ

949 Heiling, María Celina. "El tema del aislamiento en *Locos de verano*," *Revista de Estudios de Teatro*, 2, No. 6 (1963), 57-60. ARG

On Gregorio de Laferrère's play, Locos de verano.

950 Heiremans, Luis Alberto. "La creación personal y el trabajo en equipo en la dramaturgia chilena actual," *Atenea* (Concepción, Chile), 131, No. 380/381 (abr-set 1958), 199-205. CHILE

951 Heliodora, Bárbara. "O Desenvolvimento de um Teatro Brasileiro," *Revista Brasileira*, IX, No. 23-24 (jul-dez 1958), 124-136. BRAZ

952 ____. "A influência estrangeira no teatro brasileiro," *Cultura* (Brasília), No. 1 (jan-mar 1971), 42-51. BRAZ

953 ____. "El momento actual en el teatro brasileño," *Mundo Nuevo*, No. 3 (dic 1968), 79-83. BRAZ

954 ____. "Teatro em 70: Rio," *Palco e Platéia*, No. 7 (s.f.), 6-9. BRAZ

955 ____. "Theatre in Rio de Janeiro, 1968," *Latin American Theatre Review*, 3/1 (Fall 1969), 49-59. BRAZ

956 ____, Kleber Santos, Leo Gilson Ribeiro e Rubem Rocha Filho. "Teatro popular," *Cadernos Brasileiros*, VI, No. 3 (mar-jun 1964), 40-55. BRAZ

957 Helmer, Marie. *Apuntes sobre el teatro en la Villa Imperial de Potosí (1572-1636)*. Potosí:

Instituto de Investigaciones Históricas de la Universidad Tomás Frías, 1960. 9 p. BOL

Also in Revista del Instituto de Investigaciones Históricas *(Potosí), 1, No. 2 (1962), 215-223.*

958 Henríquez Ureña, Max. "Evocación de José Antonio Ramos," *Revista Iberoamericana*, No. 24 (jun 1947), 251-261. CUBA

959 ____. "Méndez Ballester y su teatro de símbolos," *La Nueva Democracia*, 42, No. 2 (abr 1962), 34-41. PTO. RICO

960 Henríquez Ureña, Pedro. "El teatro de la América española en la época colonial," en su *Obra crítica*. México--Buenos Aires: Fondo de Cultura Económica, 1960, pp. 698-718. GEN

Reprinted from Cuadernos de Cultura Teatral *(Buenos Aires), III (1936), 9-50.*

961 Hernández, José Alfredo. "Aspectos del teatro peruano," *Universidad Nacional de Colombia*, No. 9 (jun-ago 1947), 77-91. PERU

Also in Boletín de Estudios de Teatro, *5, No. 18/19 (set-dic 1947), 151-159, 190-192.*

962 Hernández, Luisa Josefina. "La censura y el teatro," *Revista Mexicana de Literatura*, No. 5-8 (mayo-ago 1961), 37-38. GEN

963 Hernando Balmori, Clemente. *"La conquista de los españoles" y el teatro indígena americano.* Tucumán: Universidad Nacional de Tucumán, 1955. 119 p. GEN

964 Herrera, Armando. "En torno al teatro peruano," *Excelsior* (Lima), (nov-dic 1947), 27, 31. PERU

965 ____. "El teatro en Moguera," *Escena* (Lima), 3, No. 6 (set 1955), 21-23. PERU

966 Herzfeld, Anita and Teresa Cajiao Salas. "El panorama teatral de Costa Rica en los últimos tres años," *Latin American Theatre Review*, 5/1 (Fall 1971), 25-38. COSTA RICA

967 ____. *El teatro de hoy en Costa Rica: Perspectiva crítica y antología.* San José: Editorial Costa Rica, 1973. 268 p. COSTA RICA

Includes: Alberto Cañas, Algo más que dos sueños; *Samuel Rovinski,* El laberinto; *Daniel Gallegos,* La colina; *Antonio Yglesias,* Las hormigas; *William Reuben,* Teófilo Amadeo; Una biografía.

968 Hill, Errol. "Calypso Drama," *Caribbean Quarterly*, 15, No. 2-3 (June-Sept 1969), 81-98. TRIN

Excerpt from his The Trinidad Carnival.

969 ____. *The Trinidad Carnival: Mandate for a National Theatre.* Austin: The University of Texas Press, 1972. 139 p. TRIN
Reviewed: Smith, Robert J.

970 Hiriart, Rosario. "La primera feminista de América," *Américas*, 25, No. 5 (mayo 1973), 2-7. MEX

On Sor Juana Inés de la Cruz.

971 "La historia de nuestro teatro en boca de una actriz de noble linaje: Blanca Podestá," *Continente* (Buenos Aires), No. 90 (set 1954), 130-132. ARG

972 Hoffman, E. Lewis. "Growing Pains in the Spanish American Theater," *Hispania*, XL, No. 2 (May 1957), 192-195. GEN

973 ____. "The Pastoral Drama of José Trinidad Reyes," *Hispania*, XLVI, No. 1 (Mar 1963), 93-101. HOND

974 Hohmann J., Carlos. "El teatro chileno en 1954," *Escena* (Lima), 2, No. 5 (mayo 1955), 19-22. CHILE

975 Holanda, Néstor de. "Telhado de vidrio: Gastão Tojeiro," *Revista de Teatro* (Rio de Janeiro), No. 350 (mar-abr 1966), 24. BRAZ

976 Holzapfel, Tamara. "Griselda Gambaro's Theatre of the Absurd," *Latin American Theatre Review*, 4/1 (Fall 1971), 5-11. ARG

977 ____. "A Mexican Medusa," *Modern Drama*, XII, No. 3 (Dec 1969), 231-237. MEX

On Emilio Carballido's play, Medusa.

978 Honegart, F. Karl. "Teatro en Quito," *Arco* (Bogotá), II, No. 8-9 (mayo-ago 1960). ECUAD

979 Horcasitas Pimentel, Fernando. "Piezas teatrales en lengua náhuatl. Bibliografía descriptiva," *Boletín Bibliográfico de Antropología*, XI (1949), 154-164. MEX

980 Horch, Hans Jurgen Wilhelm. *Bibliografía de Castro Alves*. Rio de Janeiro: Instituto Nacional do Livro, 1960. BRAZ

981 Howatt, Consuelo. "Rodolfo Usigli," *Books Abroad*, 24, No. 2 (Spring 1950), 127-130. MEX

982 Hoz, Enrique de la. "La escena lírica, la comedia y el drama en Bogotá durante cuatro meses," *Revista de la Universidad de los Andes*, III, No. 10 (jun 1960), 123-124. COL

983 Huerta, Jorge A. "Algo sobre el teatro chicano," *Revista de la Universidad de México*, XXVII, No. 6 (feb 1973), 20-24. U.S.

984 ____. "Chicano Theatre: A Background," *Aztlan*, II, No. 2 (1972). U.S.

985 ____. "Concerning Teatro Chicano," *Latin American Theatre Review*, 6/2 (Spring 1973), 13-20. U.S.

986 ____. Review: "Marilyn Ekdahl Ravicz. *Early Colonial Religious Drama in Mexico: From Tzompantli to Golgotha*. Washington: Catholic University of America Press, 1970." *Latin American Theatre Review*, 6/2 (Spring 1973), 76-78. MEX

987 Hulet, Claude L. "*A Beata Maria do Egito:* Uma Nova Tragédia por Rachel de Queiroz," en *Memoria* (X Congreso del Instituto Internacional de Literatura Iberoamericana, México). México: Universidad Nacional Autónoma de México, 1965, pp.135-141. BRAZ

988 Hunter, William A. "Unas versiones aztecas de tres comedias del Siglo de Oro," *Bulletin Hispanique* (Bordeaux), LXV (1963), 319-321. MEX

989 Hurwitt, Robert. "Teatro guerrilla," *Conjunto*, No. 8 (s.f.), 14-16. GEN

990 "ICTUS y la creación colectiva," *Revista EAC* (Santiago), No. 4 (1974), 7-18. CHILE

A conversation with Delfina Guzmán (actress), Nissim Sharim (actor and scenographer), Claudio di Girólamo (director), and Sergio Vodanović (playwright).

991 Ibáñez, José Luis. "A propósito de *Olímpica*," *Revista de Bellas Artes*, No. 1 (1965), 80. MEX

On Héctor Azar's Olímpica.

992 ____. "*Las cosas simples* y a propósito de ellas," *Revista de la Universidad de México*, XIII, No. 4 (dic 1958), 27. MEX

On Héctor Mendoza's Las cosas simples.

993 ____. "Notas sobre el mexicano en la escena," *Revista Mexicana de Literatura*, No. 9-10 (nueva época), (set-oct 1962), 39-42. MEX

994 Ibargüengoitia, Jorge. "*El gesticulador* de Rodolfo Usigli en El Teatro del Bosque," *Revista de la Universidad de México*, XV, No. 7 (mar 1961), 26. MEX

995 ____. "El Landrú degeneradón de Alfonso Reyes," *Revista de la Universidad de México*, XVIII, No. 10 (jun 1964), 26-27. MEX

On Alfonso Reyes's operetta, El Landrú.

996 "Miércoles de ceniza, jueves, ¿de qué?" *Revista de la Universidad de México*, XV, No. 10 (jun 1961), 27-28. MEX

On Luis Basurto's Miércoles de ceniza.

997 ____. "Teatro: annus mirabilis (1961)," *Revista de la Universidad de México*, 16, No. 5 (ene 1962), 26-27. MEX

999 Ichaso, Marilyn. "Theater in Mexico," *Américas*, 24, No. 9 (Sept 1972), 8-15. MEX

1000 Igo, John N. *Los Pastores*. San Antonio: San

Antonio College Library, 1967. xx + 35 p. MEX

An annotated bibliography of Mexican shepherds' plays, with introduction by Igo.

1001 Imbert, Julio. *Florencio Sánchez, su vida y creación.* Buenos Aires: Editorial Schapire, 1954. ARG

1002 ____. *Gregorio de Laferrère.* Buenos Aires: Ediciones Culturales Argentinas, Ministerio de Educación y Justicia, 1962. 142 p. ARG

1003 ____. "El teatro ríoplatense y Fernán Silva Valdés," *Revista Nacional* (Montevideo), 2° ciclo, 4, No. 199 (ene-mar 1959), 22-34. RIVER PLATE

1004 Inchauspe, Pedro. "Elementos tradicionales de la región central para nuestro teatro," *Cuadernos de Cultura Teatral*, No. 16 (1942), 29-58. ARG

1005 *Indices a la reseña histórica del teatro en México, 1539-1911 de Enrique de Olavarría y Ferrari. Indice de nombres; de obras; de asociaciones, establecimientos y teatros; geográfico; de materias, y de publicaciones.* México: Porrúa, S.A. (Bibliografía mexicana, 1968, No. 4) MEX

See Olavarría y Ferrari, Enrique de. Reseña histórica del teatro en México, 1539-1911.

1006 "Inexpressable Knots," *Times Literary Supplement* (London), (14 Nov 1968). GEN

On Jorge Díaz, Osvaldo Dragún, Dalmiro Sáenz, Virgilio Piñera.

1007 "Instituto de Estudios de Teatro; labor popular en pro del arte dramático," *Revista de Estudios de Teatro*, I, No. 1 (ene-mar 1959), 55-72. ARG

1008 "Instituto Nacional Argentino de Estudios de Teatro," *Boletín de la Unión Panamericana*, 86, No. 6 (jun 1948), 326-329. ARG

1009 "Instituto Nacional de Estudios de Teatro; su labor en 1942," *Boletín de Estudios de Teatro*, I, No. 1 (ene 1943), 51-54. ARG

1010 Insúa, Alberto. "Discordia y concordia de la novela y el teatro," *Cuadernos de Cultura Teatral*, No. 20 (1944), 39-66. GEN

1011 "Insurgencia teatral mexicana: CLETA," *Conjunto*, No. 16 (abr-jun 1973), 27-34. MEX

A brief history of the Centro Libre de Experimentación Teatral y Artística.

1012 Irving, Thomas B. Review: "Abraham Arias Larreta. *Literaturas aborígenes de América*. Buenos Aires: Editorial Indoamericana, 1968." *Latin American Theatre Review*, 5/1 (Fall 1971), 88-90. GEN

1013 Isman, Bonnie. "III National Theatre Festival (Córdoba, Argentina)," *Latin American Theatre Review*, 3/2 (Spring 1970), 73-75. ARG

1014 Jacobbi, Ruggiero. "La letteratura drammatica in Brasile," *Annali Istituto Universitario Orientale* (Napoli), III (1961), 71-78. BRAZ

1015 ____. *Teatro in Brasile*. Bologne: Cappelli, 1961. 122 p. BRAZ

1016 Jaimes-Freyre, Mireya. "La ausencia de un teatro modernista en Hispanoamérica," in *El teatro en Iberoamérica* (Memoria del duodécimo congreso del Instituto Internacional de Literatura Iberoamericana). México: IILI (1966). GEN

1017 Jaramillo, María Dolores. "Manizales de nuevo...," *Revista Teatro* (Medellín), No. 7 (1971), 49-50. COL

1018 Jiménez, Francisco. "Chicano Literature: Sources and Themes," *The Bilingual Review, La Revista Bilingüe* (New York), I, No. 1 (Jan-Apr 1974), 4-15. U.S.

1019 Jiménez, Manuel de Jesús. "Fiestas reales," en *Noticias de antaño*. San José, Costa Rica: Imprenta Nacional, 1946. COSTA RICA

1020 Jiménez Rueda, Julio. "El centenario de Manuel

Eduardo Gorostiza," *Revista Iberoamericana*, No. 34 (ago 1951/ene 1952), 221-223. MEX

1021 Jiménez Rueda, Julio. "Documentos para la historia del teatro en la Nueva España," *Boletín del Archivo General de la Nación* (México), XV, No. 1 (ene-mar 1944), 101-144. MEX

1022 ____. "La enseñanza del arte dramático en México en los últimos cincuenta años," *Revista de la Universidad de México*, XI, No. 6 (feb 1957), 20-21. MEX

1023 ____. "Misterios de Navidad en España y en México," *México en el Arte*, No. 6 (dic 1948), 33-37. MEX

1024 ____. "Nuestra próxima temporada de teatro," *Lux* (México), 30 jun 1944), 26-29. MEX

1025 ____. "Sor Juana Inés de la Cruz," *Revista Iberoamericana*, XVII, No. 33 (1951), 13-26. MEX

1026 ____. *Sor Juana Inés de la Cruz en su época (1651-1951)*. México: Porrúa, 1951. MEX

1027 "Um João Grilo em Caixa Alta," *Revista do Globo*, No. 761 (20 fev a 14 mar 1960), 16-18. BRAZ

On Ariano Suassuna's Auto da Compadecida.

1028 Jodorowsky, Alexandro. "Verso l'effimero panico ovvero estrarre il teatro dal teatro," *Sipario* (Milan), No. 275 (mar 1969), 4-6. CHILE

1029 Joffré, Sara. "Existe un teatro peruano?" *Latin American Theatre Review*, 8/1 (Fall 1974), 93. PERU

1030 ____. "El que pierde, paga," *Textual* (Lima), No. 2 (set 1971), 35-37. PERU

1031 Johnson, Harvey L. "Una compañía teatral," *Hojas de Cultura Popular Colombiana* (Bogotá), No. 28 (abr 1953). COL

1032 ____. "Una compañía teatral en Bogotá en 1618," *Nueva Revista de Filología Hispánica*, II, No. 4 (oct-dic 1948), 377-380. COL

1033 ____. "Compañías teatrales en Arequipa en 1621 y

1636," *Nueva Revista de Filología Hispánica*, VII (1953), 440-460. PERU

1034 Johnson, Harvey L. "Una contrata inédita, dos programas y noticias referentes al teatro en Bogotá entre 1838 y 1840," *Revista Iberoamericana*, No. 13 (nov 1943), 49-67. COL

1035 ____. "Disputa suscitada en la ciudad de México entre los Alcaldes del Crimen y los Ordinarios, por el Auto del año 1819 que mandó a las actrices no vestir traje de hombre en las funciones del Coliseo," *Revista Iberoamericana*, No. 19 (nov 1945), 131-168. MEX

1036 ____. *An Edition of* Triunfo de los Santos *with a Consideration of Jesuit School Plays in Mexico during the Sixteenth Century*. Philadelphia: University of Pennsylvania, 1941. MEX

Originally Ph.D. diss.

1037 ____. "Loa representada en Ibagué para la jura del Rey Fernando VI," *Revista Iberoamericana*, VII (1944), 296-303. COL

1038 ____. "Notas relativas a los corrales de la ciudad de México," *Revista Iberoamericana*, III, No. 5 (feb 1941), 133-138. MEX

1039 ____. "Noticias dadas por Tomás Gage, a propósito del Teatro en España, México y Guatemala (1624-1637). La representación de una comedia famosa de Lope de Vega, habladurías relativas a la famosa actriz Amariles, y producciones de indios y criollos," *Revista Iberoamericana*, No. 16 (nov 1944), 257-273. MEX GUAT

1040 ____. "Nuevos datos para el teatro mexicano en la primera mitad del siglo XVII: referencias a dramaturgos, comediantes, y representaciones dramáticas," *Revista de Filología Hispánica*, Año 4, No. 2 (1942), 127-151. MEX

1041 ____. "Nuevos datos sobre el teatro en la ciudad de Guatemala (1789-1820)," *Revista Iberoamericana*, No. 32 (ago 1950/ene 1951), 345-386. GUAT

1042 ____. "El primer siglo del teatro en Puebla de los Angeles y la oposición del obispo don Juan de

Palafox y Mendoza," *Revista Iberoamericana*, No. 20 (mar 1946), 295-339. MEX

1043 Johnson, Harvey L. Review: "J. Luis Trenti Rocamora. *El teatro en la América Colonial*. Buenos Aires: Editorial Huarpes, 1947." *Hispania*, XXXII, No. 4 (Nov 1949), 563-564. GEN

1044 ____. Review: "Willis Knapp Jones. *Breve historia del teatro latinoamericano*. México: Ediciones de Andrea, 1956." *Revista Iberoamericana*, No. 44 (jul-dic 1957), 386-390. GEN

1045 ____. Review: "William I. Oliver, ed. and trans. *Voices of Change in the Spanish American Theater*. Austin: University of Texas Press, 1971." *Revista Interamericana de Bibliografía*, XXIII, No. 1 (ene-mar 1973), 111-113. GEN

1046 ____. "The Staging of González de Eslava's *Coloquios*," *Hispanic Review*, VIII, No. 4 (Oct 1940), 343-346. MEX

1047 Jones, Willis Knapp. "Beginnings of River Plate Drama," *Hispania*, XXIV, No. 1 (Feb 1941), 79-90. RIVER PLATE

1048 ____. *Behind Spanish American Footlights*. Austin: University of Texas Press, 1966. 609 p. GEN
Reviewed: Dauster, Frank.

1049 ____. *Breve historia del teatro latinoamericano*. México: Ediciones de Andrea, 1956. 239 p. GEN
Reviewed: Auburn, Charles V.; Correa, Gustavo; Johnson, Harvey L.; Young, Howard T.

1050 ____. "Chile's Drama Renaissance," *Hispania*, XLIV, No. 1 (Mar 1961), 89-94. CHILE

1051 ____. "Chile Mirrored in its Theater," *The Pan American* (New York), 6, No. 2 (May 1945), 26-30. CHILE

1052 ____. "El drama en el Ecuador," *Anales de la Universidad de Guayaquil*, II, No. 2 (1950), 219-227. ECUAD

Also in América *(La Habana), XL, No. 1 (jul 1953), 15-22.*

1053 Jones, Willis Knapp. *El drama en las Américas: algunas diferencias*. Guayaquil: Imprenta de la Universidad, 1946. 23 p. ECUAD

1054 ____. "Gauchos on Stage," *The Pan American* (New York), 5, No. 8 (Jan 1945), 13, 16. RIVER PLATE

1055 ____. "'La Gringa' Theme in River Plate Drama," *Hispania*, XXV, No. 3 (Oct 1942), 326-332. RIVER PLATE

Also as "El tema de 'La Gringa' en el drama rioplatense," Boletín de Estudios de Teatro, *I, No. 3 (oct 1943), 29-35.*

1056 ____. "Immigrants on the Argentine Stage," *The Pan American* (New York), 6, No. 4 (Jul-Sept 1945), 25-28. ARG

1057 ____. "Latin American Drama--A Reading List (First Installment)," *Books Abroad*, 17, No. 1 (Winter 1943), 27-31. GEN

Second installment: 17, No. 2 (Spring 1943), 121-125.

1058 ____. "Latin American Drama: a Postscript," *Books Abroad*, 18, No. 1 (Winter 1944), 26-27. GEN

1059 ____. "A Latin American Drama Anthology," *Hispania*, XXXV, No. 3 (Aug 1952), 321-323. GEN

1060 ____. *Men and Angels: Three South American Comedies*. Carbondale: Southern Illinois University Press, 1970. 191 p. GEN

Anthology. Includes: José María Rivarola Matto, The Fate of Chipi González *(Paraguay); Miguel Frank,* Man of the Century *(Chile); and Camilo Darthés and Carlos Darnel,* The Quack Doctor *(Argentina).*
Reviewed: Morris, Robert J.

1061 ____. "New Life in Chile's Theater," *Modern Drama*, 2, No. 1 (May 1959), 57-62. CHILE

1062 ____. "Old Theatres of the New World," *The Pan American* (New York), 5, No. 7 (Dec 1944), 38-42. GEN

1063 Jones, Willis Knapp. "Paraguay's Theatre," *Books Abroad*, 15, No. 1 (Winter 1941), 40-42. PARA

1064 ____. Review: "Alfonso M. Escudero. *Apuntes sobre el teatro en Chile*. Santiago: Editorial Salesiana, 1967." *Latin American Theatre Review*, 1/1 (Fall 1967), 54-55. CHILE

1065 ____. Review: "Eugenio Pereira Salas. *El teatro en Santiago del nuevo extremo*. Santiago: Imprenta Universitaria, 1941." *Books Abroad*, 17, No. 2 (Spring 1943), 170. CHILE

1066 ____. Review: "Josefina Pla. *El teatro en el Paraguay. Primera parte: De la fundación a 1870*. Asunción: Escuela Salesiana, 1967." *Latin American Theatre Review*, 1/1 (Fall 1967), 55. PARA

1067 ____. Review: "Manuel Abascal Brunet. *Apuntes para la historia del teatro en Chile: La zarzuela grande*. Santiago: Imprenta Universitaria, 1940." *Revista Iberoamericana*, No. 10 (oct 1942), 410-411. CHILE

1068 ____. "Three Great Latin American Dramatists: Eichelbaum, Usigli and Marqués," *Specialia* (Carbondale: Southern Illinois University), No. 1, n.d. GEN

1069 ____. "Women in the Early Spanish American Theatre," *Latin American Theatre Review*, 4/1 (Fall 1970), 23-33. GEN

1070 Josseau, Fernando. "*El prestamista* camina de Santiago a París," *Cuadernos* (Paris), No. 70 (mar 1963), 29-31. CHILE

1071 Júlio, Sílvio. *Três Aspectos do Drama na Atualidade Brasileira*. Rio de Janeiro: 1957. 55 p. BRAZ

1072 Jurado, Oscar. "Santiago García y el teatro latinoamericano: En busca de un lenguaje propio," *Conjunto*, No. 15 (ene-mar 1973), 122-127. COL

An interview with the Colombian director, Santiago García.

1073 Kanellos, Nicolás. "Mexican Community Theatre in a Midwestern City," *Latin American Theatre Review*, 7/1 (Fall 1973), 43-48. U.S.

1074 Karavellas, Panos D. "La dramaturgia de Samuel Eichelbaum." Unpub. Ph.D. diss., Michigan State, 1970. ARG

1075 Karnis, Michael V. "Surviving Pre-Columbian Drama," *Educational Theatre Journal*, IV (1952), 39-45. GEN

1076 Kirschenbaum, Leo. "Has the Brazilian Drama a History?" *Theatre Annual* (1946), 9-22. BRAZ

1077 ____. "O marxismo no teatro brasileiro," *Memoria* del Sexto Congreso del Instituto Internacional de Literatura Iberoamericana. México: IILI (1954), pp. 179-185. BRAZ

1078 Klein, Eva. "Teatro de Ensayo," *Conjunto*, 3, No. 7 (s.f.), 90-91. CHILE

On the activities of the Chilean theater group, Teatro de Ensayo, in 1967.

1079 Klein, Maxine. "A Country of Cruelty and its Theatre," *Drama Survey*, 7, No. 1-2 (Winter 1968-69), 164-170. GUAT

1080 ____. "Theatre of the Ancient Maya," *Educational Theatre Journal*, XXIII, No. 3 (Oct 1971), 269-276. GUAT

1081 Knowles, John. "Luisa Josefina Hernández: A Study of Her Dramatic Theory and Practice." Unpub. Ph. D. diss., Rutgers, 1969. MEX

1082 Kolb, Glen L. "Simbolismo y universalidad en el *Ollantay* de Rojas," *Hispania*, XLVI, No. 2 (May 1963), 328-332. ARG

1083 Korn, Guillermo. *15 meses de teatro en Caracas*. Caracas: Italgráfica, 1972. VEN

1084 Korn, Jack. "Teatro para niños," *Talía*, IV, No. 23 (1962), 26. ARG

Discusses productions such as Canciones para mirar *by María Elena Walsh, and* Josefina y el ladrón *by Lucía Benedetti.*

1085 Kourilsky, Françoise. "Approaching Quetzalcoatl: The Evolution of El Teatro Campesino," *Performances*, 2, No. 1 (Fall 1973), 37-46. U.S.

1086 ____. "Entretien avec Daniel et Luis Valdez," *Travail Théâtral* (Paris), No. 7 (avr-juin 1972), 59-70. U.S.

1087 ____. "El Teatro Campesino," *Travail Théâtral* (Paris), No. 7 (avr-juin 1972), 56-59. U.S.

1088 Krynen, Jean. "Mito y teología en *El Divino Narciso* de Sor Juana," en *Actas del Tercer Congreso Internacional de Hispanistas*. Carlos H. Magis, ed. México: El Colegio de México por la Asociación Internacional de Hispanistas, 1970, pp. 501-505. MEX

1089 Kuehne, Alyce de. "The Antigone Theme in Anouilh, Marechal and Luis Rafael Sánchez," in *Papers on French-Spanish, Luso-Brazilian, Spanish American Literary Relations*. Brockport, N.Y.: SUNY, Dept. of Foreign Languages [MLA Seminar 17, December 1970], pp. 50-70. ARG PTO. RICO

1090 ____. "Hamlet y el concepto del 'personaje' pirandelliano en una farsa de Cuzzani," *Cuadernos Americanos*, XXVII, No. 1 (ene-feb 1969), 408-418. ARG

1091 ____. "Influencias de Pirandello y de Brecht en Mario Benedetti," *Hispania*, LI, No. 3 (Sept 1968), 408-415. URUG

1092 ____. "Influencias del teatro francés en el teatro poético de vanguardia de Margarita Urueta," *Revista Hispánica Moderna*, 33, No. 1-2 (1967), 75-84. MEX

1093 ____. "El mito de Pigmalión en Shaw, Pirandello y Solana," *Latin American Theatre Review*, 2/2 (Spring 1969), 31-40. MEX

1094 ____. "La realidad existencial y 'la realidad creada' en Pirandello y Salvador Novo," *Latin American Theatre Review*, 2/1 (Fall 1968), 5-14. MEX

1095 ____. *Teatro mexicano contemporáneo (1940-1962)*. México: 1962. 162 p. MEX

1096 Kuehne, Alyce de. "Xavier Villaurrutia, un alto exponente de Pirandello," *Revista Iberoamericana*, No. 66 (jul-dic 1968), 313-322. MEX

1097 Kühner, Maria Helena. *Teatro em Tempo de Síntese*. Rio de Janeiro: Editôra Paz e Terra, 1971. BRAZ

1098 Kurz, Harry. "The Americas Through the Opera Glass," *Hispania*, XXV, No. 2 (May 1942), 131-140. GEN

Brief plot review of some of the developing plays and playwrights.

1099 ____. "The 'Cuadernos' of the Instituto Nacional de Estudios de Teatro," *Hispania*, XXVIII, No. 2 (May 1945), 212-219. GEN

A discussion of the volumes, some on theater.

1100 ____. Review: "*Cuadernos de Cultura Teatral*. No. 22. Buenos Aires: Instituto Nacional de Estudios de Teatro, 1947." *Hispania*, XXXI, No. 4 (Nov 1948), 506-509. ARG

Issue contains three articles: "Mariano Galé, Benemérito del teatro argentino," by José Antonio Saldías; "Semblanza de Francisco de Ducasse," by Julio C. Viale Paz; and "La sugestión telúrica en el teatro de Julio Sánchez Gardel," by Juan Oscar Ponferrada.

1101 Lacosta, Francisco C. "El teatro misionero en la América hispana," *Cuadernos Americanos*, CXLII, No. 24 (1965), 171-178. GEN

1102 Ladra, David. "La técnica de la deshumanización (encuentro con Víctor García)," *Conjunto*, No. 9 (s.f.), 110-116. ARG

Reprinted from Sipario, *No. 275. Translated by Judith Weiss.*

1103 Lafforgue, Jorge R. *Breve panorama del teatro nacional*. Buenos Aires: Secretaría de Estado de Obras Públicas, Dirección General de Obra Social, 1967. ARG

1104 Lafforgue, Jorge R. *Florencio Sánchez*. Buenos Aires: Centro Editor de América Latina, 1967. 62 p. URUG

1105 ____. Review: "Domingo F. Casadevall. *El teatro nacional: sinopsis y perspectivas*. Buenos Aires: Ediciones Culturales Argentinas, Ministerio de Educación y Justicia, 1961." *Revista de la Universidad de Buenos Aires*, VIII, No. 3-4 (1963), 577-583. ARG

1106 Laguado, Arturo. "El gaucho en la escena argentina," *Boletín Cultural y Bibliográfico* (Bogotá), X, No. 3 (1967), 629-634. ARG

1107 ____. "La inmigración europea y el sainete criollo en la Argentina," *Boletín Cultural y Bibliográfico*, X, No. 7 (1967), 1566-1574. ARG

1108 Lamb, Ruth S. "Celestino Gorostiza y el teatro experimental en México," *Revista Iberoamericana*, No. 45 (jul-dic 1958), 141-145. MEX

1109 ____. "Elena Garro y el Teatro de lo Absurdo," in *El teatro en Iberoamérica* (Memoria del duodécimo congreso del Instituto Internacional de Literatura Iberoamericana). México: IILI (1966). MEX

1110 ____. "Influjos locales en el teatro mexicano moderno," in *Memoria* (X Congreso del Instituto Internacional de Literatura Iberoamericana, México), México: UNAM, 1965, pp. 51-57. MEX

1111 ____. Review: "Hildburg Schilling. *Teatro profano en la Nueva España (Fines del siglo XVI a mediados del siglo XVIII)*. México: Centro de Estudios Literarios, Imprenta Universitaria, 1958." *Hispania*, XLII, No. 3 (Sept 1959), 458. MEX

1112 ____. "Rubén Darío: el poeta en el teatro," *Latin American Theatre Review*, 1/1 (Fall 1967), 18-26. NIC

Also in Homenaje a Rubén Darío (1867-1967). *Los Angeles: University of California Latin American Center, pp. 190-199.*

1113 ____. "El teatro brasileño actual," *Anuario de Filología* (Maracaibo), Año VIII-IX, No. 8-9 (1969-1970), 257-268. BRAZ

1114 Lamb, Ruth S., ed. *Three Contemporary Latin-American Plays*. Waltham, Mass.: Xerox College Publishing, 1973. 184 p. GEN

Anthology. Includes: René Marqués, El apartamiento; *Egon Wolff,* Los invasores; *and Emilio Carballido,* Yo también hablo de la rosa.

1116 Landeta Rosales, Manuel. "Los teatros en Caracas en más de tres siglos," *Crónica de Caracas*, 4, No. 19 (ago-dic 1954), 642-652. VEN

Also in Cuaderno. *Dirección de Cultura, Centro de Investigación y Desarrollo del Teatro, No. 1. Caracas: Universidad Central de Venezuela (jun 1966), 1-12.*

1117 Lanuza, José Luis. "La historia a través del teatro argentino," *Lyra*, XVII, No. 174-176 (1959). ARG

1118 ____. "La historia nacional como tema de teatro," *Cuadernos de Cultura Teatral*, No. 17 (1942), 67-86. ARG

1119 ____. "Recordación de Juan B. Alberdi, autor de *La revolución de mayo*," *Revista de Estudios de Teatro* (Buenos Aires), No. 3 (1960), 5-8. ARG

1120 ____. "El teatro rioplatense: del circo a las modernas expresiones de vanguardia," *Cuadernos Americanos*, 12, No. 5 (set-oct 1954), 198-212. RIVER PLATE

1121 Lara, Jesús. "El teatro en el Tawantisuyo," *Literatura de la emancipación hispanoamericana y otros ensayos*. Lima: Universidad Nacional Mayor de San Marcos, Dirección Universitaria de Biblioteca y Publicaciones, 1972, pp. 309-313. PERU

1122 Larew, Leonor A. "The 1967-68 Chilean Theater Season," *World Theatre*, XVII, No. 5-6 (May-June 1968). CHILE

1123 ____. "Two Mexican Women Dramatists of Today: Notes," *Latin American Literary Review*, II, No. 4 (Spring-Summer 1974), 171-172. MEX

On Marcela del Río (pseudonym, Mara Reyes) and Margarita Urueta.

1124 Larraín Acuña, Hernán. "*Versos de ciego*: una obra discutida," *Apuntes*, No. 11 (mayo 1961), 1-30. CHILE

On Luis Alberto Heiremans's play, Versos de ciego.

1125 Larreta, Antonio. "El naturalismo en el teatro de Florencio Sánchez," *Número* (Montevideo), II, No. 6-8 (1950), 227-235. URUG

1126 Latcham, Ricardo A. "Curtain Time in Chile: Teatro Experimental Pioneered New Movement to Stimulate Chileans' Interest in Good Theater," *Américas*, 4, No. 9 (Sept 1952), 16-19, 41. CHILE

1127 ____. Review: "Manuel Abascal Brunet. *Apuntes para la historia del teatro en Chile: La zarzuela grande*. Santiago: Imprenta Universitaria, 1940." *Anales de la Universidad de Chile*, No. 44 (1941), 218-220. CHILE

1128 Latorre, Alfonso. "El teatro en el Perú," *Cultura y Pueblo* (Lima), 1, No. 2 (abr-jun 1964), 32-33. PERU

1129 Latorre, Mariano. "Anotaciones sobre el teatro chileno en el siglo XIX," *Atenea,* 95, No. 291/292 (set-oct 1949), 239-277. CHILE

1130 ____. "Apuntes sobre el teatro chileno contemporáneo," *Atenea*, 90, No. 278 (ago 1948), 254-272; 91, No. 281/282 (nov-dic 1948), 92-114. CHILE

1131 ____. "El teatro chileno en la colonia," *Atenea*, XCIII, No. 288 (jun 1949), 462-472; XCIV, No. 289-290 (jul-ago 1949), 138-151. CHILE

1132 Lavelli, Jorge. "El director como oficiante," *Mundo Nuevo,* No. 12 (jun 1967), 66-69. GEN

Argentine director--interview by Silvia Rudni.

1133 Laverdi, Cecilia. "Anotaciones sobre Brecht en Cuba," *Casa de las Américas*, II, No. 15-16 (mar 62-feb 63), 77-90; III, No. 17-18 (mar-jun 63), 92-98. CUBA

1134 Lázaro, Angel. "Sobre un teatro en el Palacio de

Bellas Artes," *Informaciones Culturales* (La Habana), 1, No. 3 (mayo-jun 1947), 3-4. CUBA

1135 Lazo, Raimundo. "Sor Juana Inés de la Cruz," *Anales de la Academia Nacional de Artes y Letras* (La Habana), XXXIII (1951), 165-186. MEX

1136 Leal, Luis. "El 'tocotín mestizo' de Sor Juana," *Abside* (México), XVIII, No. 1 (Jan-Mar 1954), 51-64. MEX

1137 Leal, Rine R. "Acerca de una bibliografía de teatro cubano," *Revista de la Biblioteca José Martí*, Año 63, 3ª época, XIV, No. 2 (mayo-ago 1972), 164-172. CUBA

A commentary on the María Luisa Antuña and Josefina García Carranza bibliography.

1138 ____. "Actuales corrientes en el teatro cubano," *Nueva Revista Cubana*, I, No. 1 (abr-jun 1959), 163-170. CUBA

1139 ____. "Algunas consideraciones sobre el teatro cubano," *Insula*, No. 260-261 (jul-ago 1968), 9. CUBA

1140 ____. "Charros, monólogos, y un Ionesco desconcertante," *Cuba*, VII, No. 76 (ago 1968), 42-44. MEX

Teatro Hidalgo de México en Habana, julio-agosto de 1968.

1141 ____. "Diario de viaje: Festival de Teatro Latinoamericano, Casa de las Américas," *Cuba*, III, No. 31 (nov 1964), 56-62. GEN

Leal's tour with foreign participants during the IV Latin American Theatre Festival.

1142 ____. *En primera persona*. La Habana: Instituto del Libro, 1967. 369 p. GEN

Collection of 73 newspaper reviews, 1954-1966.

1143 ____. *Introducción a Cuba. El teatro*. La Habana: Cuadernos Populares, Instituto del Libro, 1968. CUBA

Also in Portuguese; translated by Rogério Paulo. Lisboa: Cuadernos Seará Nova, 1971.

1144 ____. "Mesa redonda: Hablan directores," *Conjunto*, 3, No. 7 (s.f.), 8-25. GEN

Orlando Rodríguez (Chile), Santiago García (Colombia), Juan Vicente Melo (México), Federico Wolff (Uruguay) opinan sobre las dificultades actuales de la escena latinoamericana.

1145 Leal, Rine R. "Notas sueltas sobre el teatro de Emilio Carballido," *Casa de las Américas*, V, No. 30 (mayo-jun 1965), 96-99. MEX

1146 ____. "Los premios del premio," *Cuba*, VII, No. 76 (ago 1968), 45-46. CUBA

Interview with Héctor Quintero.

1147 ____. "Seis meses de teatro en pocas palabras," *Casa de las Américas*, II, No. 11-12 (mar-jun 1962), 46-50. CUBA

1148 ____. "Siete autores en busca de un teatro," *Conjunto*, III, No. 6 (ene-mar 1968), 7-23. GEN

Includes Aimé Césaire (Martinique), Hiber Conteris (Uruguay), Manuel Galich (Guatemala), Alvaro Menén Desleal (El Salvador), Alfonso Sastre (Spain), Francisco Urondo (Argentina), Rodolfo Walsh (Argentina).

1149 ____. "Siete días de entreacto," *Cuba*, VII, No. 69 (ene 1968), 24-25. CUBA

Report on I National Seminar on Theatre, Dec 1967.

1150 ____, ed. *Teatro cubano en un acto. Antología.* La Habana: Ediciones R, 1963. CUBA

Anthology. Includes: Antón Arrufat, El caso se investiga; *Nora Badía,* Mañana es una palabra; *Raúl de Cárdenas,* Las palanganas; *Nicolás Dorr,* Las pericas; *Abelardo Estorino,* El peine y el espejo; *Rolando Ferrer,* Los Próceres; *Ignacio Gutiérrez,* Los mendigos; *Matías Montes Huidobro,* Gas en los poros; *Virgilio Piñera,* Falsa alarma; *Manuel Reguera Saumell,* El general Antonio estuvo aquí; *José Triana,* El Mayor General hablará de teogonía.

1151 ____. "El teatro en Cuba," *Cuba*, III, No. 30 (oct 1964), 64-73. CUBA

Outline of development of Cuban theater, 1570-1964.

1152 Leal, Rine R. "El teatro en un acto en Cuba," *Revista Unión*, 5, No. 6 (ene-feb 1963), 52-75. CUBA

1153 ____. "Viaje de un largo siglo hacia el teatro," *Islas*, No. 11 (ene-abr 1970), 59-77. CUBA

1154 ____. "Virgilio Piñera o el teatro como ejercicio mental," *La Gaceta de Cuba*, III, No. 34 (5 abr 1964), 2-3. CUBA

1155 ____, et al. "Un títere es un símbolo, no tiene que repetir al hombre," *Conjunto*, No. 9 (s.f.), 126-135. GEN

An interview with the directors of the Teatro Nacional de Guiñol de Cuba.

1156 Legido, Juan Carlos. *El teatro uruguayo de Juan Moreira a los independientes, 1886-1967.* Montevideo: Ediciones Tauro, 1968. 159 p. URUG

1157 Leguizamón de Rosso Guerrero, Blanca. "Mi padre: Martiniano Leguizamón," *Revista de la Universidad de La Plata*, No. 9 (set-dic 1959), 146-147. ARG

1158 Leinaweaver, Richard E. "Mexico's Second City: The 1971-72 Season," *Latin American Theatre Review*, 6/1 (Fall 1972), 71-75. MEX

A report on the theater season in Guadalajara.

1159 ____. "*Rabinal Achí*: Commentary," *Latin American Theatre Review*, 1/2 (Spring 1968), 3-15. GUAT

1160 Leite, José, Roberto Teixera, et al. *Gente nova, nova gente; artes plásticas, teatro, música, cinema, fotografia.* Rio de Janeiro: Ed. Expressão e Cultura, 1967. 136 p. BRAZ

1161 Leite, Luiza Barreto. *A mulher no teatro brasileiro.* Rio de Janeiro: Ediciones Espetáculo, 1965. 227 p. BRAZ

1162 ____. "As mulheres no teatro brasileiro," *Comentário*, V (1964), 118-132. BRAZ

1163 Leite, Serafim. *História da Companhia de Jesus no Brasil.* 10 vol. Rio de Janeiro: Civilização

Brasileira, 1938-50. BRAZ

Includes plays and commentary.

1164 Lemos, Martín F. *El desarrollo de los teatros filodramáticos.* Buenos Aires: Ediciones Culturales Argentinas, Ministerio de Educación y Justicia, 1965. 42 p. ARG

1165 ____. "Una faz poco conocida de Pablo Podestá," *Revista de Estudios de Teatro* (Buenos Aires), III, No. 8 (1964), 39-42. ARG

1166 ____. "Florencio Sánchez y Ernesto Herrera: actores vocacionales," *Revista de Estudios de Teatro* (Buenos Aires), 4, No. 11 (1970), 26-29. URUG

1167 ____. *Nuestro teatro y sus críticos fallecidos.* Buenos Aires: Sociedad General de Autores de la Argentina, 1962. 42 p. ARG

1168 ____. "El primer cabaret no fue el de 'Los dientes del perro'," *Revista de Estudios de Teatro*, 3, No. 9 (1965), 50-53. ARG

1169 ____. "Sainetes y saineteros criollos," *Lyra*, 17, No. 174-176 (1959). (Número extraordinario dedicado al teatro.) ARG

1170 ____. "Tres figuras inolvidables del viejo sainete criollo," *Boletín de Estudios de Teatro*, 8, No. 28 (ene-mar 1950), 13-24. ARG

Discusses Nemesio Trejo, Carlos M. Pacheco, and Luis Vittone.

1171 Lena Paz, Marta. "Para una revalidación de Carlos Mauricio Pacheco," *Universidad* (Santa Fe), No. 50 (oct-dic 1961), 61-82. RIVER PLATE

1172 ____. "Prefiguraciones del grotesco criollo en Carlos Mauricio Pacheco," *Universidad* (Santa Fe), No. 54 (oct-dic 1962), 119-156. RIVER PLATE

1173 ____. "Presencia de Nicolás Granada," *Universidad* (Santa Fe), No. 76 (jul-dic 1968), 157-177. ARG

1174 ____. Review: "Domingo F. Casadevall. *El teatro nacional: Sinopsis y perspectivas.* Buenos Aires: Ediciones Culturales Argentinas, Ministerio de

Educación y Justicia, 1961." *Universidad* (Santa Fe), No. 52 (1962), 268-270. ARG

1175 Leñero, Vicente. "¿Por qué un teatro documental?" *La Vida Literaria* (México), 1, No. 4 (mayo 1970), 8-9. MEX

Leñero on why he wrote Compañero, *his play on the life of Che Guevara. Also includes bibliography on Leñero.*

1176 León, Argeliers. "Pantominas y bailes en el folklore de Cuba," *Revista Nacional de Teatro* (La Habana), 1 (1961). CUBA

1177 Leonard, Irving A. Review: "Guillermo Lohmann Villena. *El arte dramático en Lima durante el virreinato*. Madrid: Publicaciones de la Escuela de Estudios Hispanoamericanos de la Universidad de Sevilla, 1945." *Hispanic Review*, XIV, No. 4 (Oct 1946), 364-366. PERU

1178 ____. Review: "J. Luis Trenti Rocamora. *El teatro en la América colonial*. Buenos Aires: Editorial Huarpes, 1947." *Hispanic Review*, XVI, No. 4 (Oct 1948), 346-348. GEN

1179 ____. "The 1790 Theater Season of the Mexico City Coliseo," *Hispanic Review*, XIX, No. 2 (Apr 1951), 104-120. MEX

1180 ____. "El teatro en Lima, 1790-1793," *Hispanic Review*, VIII, No. 2 (Apr 1940), 93-112. PERU

1181 ____. "La temporada teatral de 1792 en el Nuevo Coliseo de México," *Nueva Revista de Filología Hispánica*, V (1951), 349-410. MEX

1182 ____. "The Theater Season of 1791-1792 in Mexico City," *The Hispanic American Historical Review*, 31, No. 2 (May 1951), 349-364. MEX

1183 Lescano Abella, Mario. "Historia sintética de los teatros habaneros," *Arquitectura* (La Habana), 10, No. 113 (dic 1942), 481-488. CUBA

1184 Leslie, John Kenneth. Review: "Raúl H. Castagnino. *Contribución documental a la historia del teatro en Buenos Aires durante la época de Rosas (1830-1852)*. Buenos Aires: Comisión Nacional de Cultura,

Instituto Nacional de Estudios de Teatro, 1944." *Hispanic Review*, XVI, No. 4 (Oct 1948), 348-349. ARG

1185 Levy, Matilde. *El extranjero en el teatro primitivo de Buenos Aires (Antecedentes hasta 1880.* Buenos Aires: Universidad de Buenos Aires, 1962. 52 p. ARG

1186 Lewis, Allen. "The Theatre in Mexico," *The Texas Quarterly*, II, No. 1 (Spring 1959), 143-155. MEX

1187 Lichtblau, Myron L. "La conciencia de Latinoamérica en tres dramas contemporáneos," *Humanitas* (Monterrey, Mexico), No. 9 (1968), 249-258. GEN

On Enrique Solari Swayne's Collacocha, *Francisco Arriví's* Vejigantes, *and Egon Wolff's* Los invasores.

1188 ____. "A Novelist Turns to Drama: Manuel Gálvez's *Calibán*," *Latin American Theatre Review*, 7/1 (Fall 1973), 13-16. ARG

1189 Linares, Joaquín. "Los poemas dramáticos de Martín Coronado; al margen de *La piedra del escándalo* y *La chacra de Don Lorenzo*," *Boletín de Estudios de Teatro*, VIII, No. 29-30 (mayo-set 1950), 81-85. ARG

1190 Linde, Jed. "Five Faces in Mexico's New Theatre," *Américas*, 20, No. 2 (Feb 1968), 16-25. MEX

Alexandro Jodorowsky, Carlos Ancira, Margarita Urueta, Juan López Moctezuma, Juan José Gurrola.

1191 ____. "Mexico's Strolling Players," *Américas*, 18, No. 11 (Nov 1966), 34-37. MEX

1192 Lindo, Hugo. "Jóvenes dramaturgos de El Salvador," *Estudios Centro Americanos* (San Salvador), 15, No. 154 (nov 1960), 584-591. EL SAL

1193 ____. "Literatura dramática en El Salvador," *Cultura Hispánica* (San Salvador), Año 1, No. 3 (jul-set 1967), 3-50. EL SAL

Also in Revista Interamericana de Bibliografía, *XVIII, No. 3 (jul-set 1968), 258-279.*

1194 Liscano, Juan. "Teatro y folklore," *Revista Nacional de Cultura*, XXXIII, No. 212-215 (ene-dic 1973), 9-25. VEN

1195 Lizarralde, Fernando. *El Ollantay argentino*. Buenos Aires: Término, 1953. ARG

Essay on Ricardo Rojas's play Ollantay.

1196 Lizondo Borda, Manuel. "Temas del norte para el teatro argentino," *Cuadernos de Cultura Teatral*, No. 16 (1942), 13-24. ARG

1197 Llanes, Ricardo M. *Teatros de Buenos Aires*. Buenos Aires: Municipalidad de la Ciudad de Buenos Aires, Cuadernos de Buenos Aires, 1968. 74 p. ARG

Historical data on the Buenos Aires theaters.

1198 Lockward, Jaime A. *Teatro dominicano: pasado y presente*. Ciudad Trujillo: Editorial La Nación, s.f. 77 p. DOM REP

Also as "Teatro dominicano: pasado y presente," Revista de Educación *(Ciudad Trujillo), 8a. época, 28, No. 3 (set-dic 1958), 13-25.*

1199 Lohmann Villena, Guillermo. "Apuntaciones sobre el arte dramático en Lima durante el virreinato," *Tres*, No. 7 (dic 1940), 28-57. PERU

1200 ____. *El arte dramático en Lima durante el virreinato*. Madrid: Publicaciones de la Escuela de Estudios Hispanoamericanos de la Universidad de Sevilla, 1945. PERU
Reviewed: Leonard, Irving A.

1201 ____. "Las comedias del Corpus Christi en Lima en 1635 y 1636," *Mar del Sur*, IV, No. 11 (mayo-jun 1950), 21-23. PERU

Also in Revista de Indias *(Madrid), 10, No. 42 (oct-dic 1950), 865-868.*

1202 ____. *Historia del arte dramático en Lima durante el virreinato, I: Siglos XVI y XVII*. Lima: Imprenta Americana, 1941. 271 p. PERU
Reviewed: Moreyra, Manuel.

1203 ____. Review: "José Juan Arrom. *El teatro de Hispanoamérica en la época colonial*. La Habana: Anuario Bibliográfico Cubano, 1956." *Revista*

Interamericana de Bibliografía, 7, No. 4 (oct-dic 1957), 422-423. GEN

1204 Lohmann Villena, Guillermo. "El teatro en el Perú virreinal: Las comedias de Corpus Christi en Lima en 1635 y 1636," *Boletín de Estudios de Teatro*, VIII, No. 31 (oct-dic 1950), 145-147. PERU

See also item #1201.

1205 ____. "El teatro en Sudamérica española hasta 1800," in Guillermo Díaz-Plaja, ed., *Historia general de las literaturas hispánicas.* IV, 1ª parte. Barcelona: 1956, pp. 373-389. GEN

1206 ____ and R. Moglia. "Repertorio de las representaciones teatrales en Lima hasta el siglo XVIII," *Revista de Filología Hispánica*, V, No. 4 (1943), 313-343. PERU

1207 López, César. "Apuntes sobre las relaciones del público y la escena," *Conjunto*, No. 3 (s.f.). GEN

1208 López, Oswaldo. "Criticism of Mexican Reality in Selected Plays of Emilio Carballido." Unpub. Ph.D. diss., Pittsburgh, 1973. MEX

1209 López Nussa, Leonel. "Releyendo a *Yarini*," *Revista Unión*, 3, No. 4 (set-dic 1962), 86-96. CUBA

Reactions to Carlos Felipe's Réquiem por Yarini.

1210 López Rosas, José Rafael. "El teatro colonial en Santa Fe: Antecedentes históricos." Santa Fe, Arg.: 1948. 21 p. ARG

Tirada aparte del Boletín del departamento de Estudios Etnográficos y Coloniales de Santa Fe.

1211 Luca, Gemma R. del. "Creativity and Revolution: Cultural Dimension of the New Cuba," in *Cuba, Castro and Revolution*, ed. Jaime Suchlicki. Coral Gables: University of Miami Press, 1972, pp. 94-118. CUBA

Section on theater, pp. 105-107.

1212 Luchting, Wolfgang A. "*El rabdomante*, o el escepticismo burgués," *Mundo Nuevo*, No. 33 (mar 1969), 38-44. PERU

Critique of Salazar Bondy's El rabdomante.

1213 ____. Review: "Julio Ramón Ribeyro. *Teatro.*

Lima: Universidad Nacional de Educación, 1972." *Books Abroad*, 47 (Autumn 1973), 734. PERU

1214 Luzuriaga, Gerardo. "El IV Festival de Manizales," *Latin American Theatre Review*, 5/1 (Fall 1971), 5-16. GEN

1215 ____. *Del realismo al expresionismo: El teatro de Aguilera Malta*. Madrid: Ediciones Plaza Mayor, 1971. 204 p. ECUAD
Reviewed: Clark, Stella T.; Lyday, Leon; Woodyard, George.

1216 ____. "La evolución estilística del teatro de Aguilera Malta," *Latin American Theatre Review*, 3/2 (Spring 1970), 39-44. ECUAD

1217 ____. "La generación ecuatoriana del treinta y el teatro," *Boletín* de la Comunidad Latinoamericana de Escritores, No. 8 (1970), 18-24. ECUAD

1218 ____. "Presencia latinoamericana en el IX Festival de Nancy," *Latin American Theatre Review*, 6/2 (Spring 1973), 65-69. GEN

1219 ____. Review: "Julio Durán Cerda. *Teatro chileno contemporáneo*. México: Aguilar, 1970." *Latin American Theatre Review*, 4/1 (Fall 1970), 84-85. CHILE

1220 ____. Review: "Ricardo Descalzi. *Historia crítica del teatro ecuatoriano*. 6 vol. Quito: Casa de la Cultura Ecuatoriana, 1968." *Latin American Theatre Review*, 3/1 (Fall 1969), 81. ECUAD

1221 ____. Review: "Ricardo Descalzi. *Historia crítica del teatro ecuatoriano*. 6 vol. Quito: Casa de la Cultura Ecuatoriana, 1968." *Revista Iberoamericana*, No. 75 (abr-jun 1971), 470. ECUAD

1222 ____. "Tercer festival de Manizales," *Latin American Theatre Review*, 4/2 (Spring 1971), 71-72. GEN

1223 ____ and Robert S. Rudder. *The Orgy, Modern One-Act Plays from Latin America*. Los Angeles: UCLA Latin American Center, 1974. 180 p. GEN

Anthology. Includes: Enrique Buenaventura, The Orgy *and* The Schoolteacher; *Osvaldo Dragún,* The Story of The Man Who Turned Into a Dog *and*

The Story of Panchito González; *José Martínez Queirolo,* R. I. P.; *Marco Denevi,* Romeo Before the Corpse of Juliet *and* You Don't Have to Complicate Happiness; *Alvaro Menén Desleal,* Black Light; *Alberto Adellach,* March; *Carlos Solórzano,* The Crucifixion; *and Jorge Díaz,* The Eve of The Execution, or Genesis was Tomorrow.

1224 Lyday, Leon F. "Antonio Alvarez Lleras and his Theatre," *Latin American Theatre Review*, 2/2 (Spring 1969), 21-30. COL

1225 ____. "The Colombian Theatre Before 1800," *Latin American Theatre Review*, 4/1 (Fall 1970), 35-50. COL

1226 ____. "The Dramatic Art of Antonio Alvarez Lleras." Unpub. Ph.D. diss., North Carolina, 1966. COL

1227 ____. "Egon Wolff's *Los invasores*: A Play Within a Dream," *Latin American Theatre Review*, 6/1 (Fall 1972), 19-26. CHILE

1228 ____. "History and Legend in *El virrey Solís* of Antonio Alvarez Lleras," *Hispania*, LII, No. 1 (Mar 1969), 13-20. COL

1229 ____. "Jorge Amado's *Tenda dos Milagres* and Dias Gomes' *O Berço do Herói*: Views of the Modern Consumer Society," *South Eastern Latin Americanist*, XVI, No. 4 (Mar 1973), 1-3. BRAZ

1230 ____. "*O Pagador de Promessas* and *O Berço de Herói:* Variations on a Theme," *Romance Notes*, XIV, No. 2 (Winter 1972), 275-282. BRAZ

1231 ____. Review: "Frank N. Dauster. *Teatro hispanoamericano: tres piezas*. New York: Harcourt, Brace and World, Inc., 1964." *Modern Language Journal*, LI, No. 7 (Nov 1967), 436. GEN

1232 ____. Review: "Gerardo Luzuriaga. *Del realismo al expresionismo: el teatro de Aguilera Malta*. Madrid: Ediciones Plaza Mayor, 1971." *Modern Language Journal*, LVII, No. 5-6 (Sept-Oct 1973), 303. ECUAD

1233 ____. Review:"Margaret S. Peden, ed. and trans. *The Golden Thread and Other Plays*. Austin: University of Texas Press, 1970." *Revista*

Interamericana de Bibliografía, XXII, No. 4 (oct-dic 1972), 425-427. MEX

1234 Lyday, Leon F. Review: "Ned A. Bowman. *Indice colectivo de obras teatrales en seis bibliotecas de Bogotá, Colombia.* Pittsburgh: Department of Speech and Theatre Arts and the Center for Latin American Studies, University of Pittsburgh, 1968." *Latin American Theatre Review*, 3/2 (Spring 1970), 81. COL

1235 ____. Review: "*Teatro chileno actual.* Santiago: Empresa Editora Zig Zag, 1966." *Hispania*, LI, No. 3 (Sept 1968), 586-587. CHILE

1236 ____. "Satire in the Comedies of Martins Pena," *Luso-Brazilian Review*, V, No. 2 (Dec 1968), 63-70. BRAZ

Also in: John B. Means, ed. Essays on Brazilian Literature. *New York: Simon and Schuster, 1971, pp. 143-150.*

1237 ____. "Structure and Theme in Dias Gomes' *O Berço do Herói*," *South Atlantic Bulletin*, XXXVII, No. 2 (May 1972), 10-15. BRAZ

1238 Lyford, Katharine van Etten. "Uruguay on Stage," *Américas*, 2, No. 3 (Mar 1950), 24-27, 43. URUG

1239 Lyon, John E. "The Argentine Theatre and the Problem of National Identity: A Critical Survey," *Latin American Theatre Review*, 5/2 (Spring 1972), 5-18. ARG

1240 McCrossan, Sister Joseph Marie. "The Role of the Church and the Folk in the Development of Early Drama in New Mexico." Unpub. Ph.D. diss., Pennsylvania, 1945. U.S.

1241 Mace, Carroll E. "Nueva y más reciente información sobre los bailes-drama de Rabinal y del descubrimiento del *Rabinal-Achí*," *Conjunto*, No. 10 (s.f.), 51-64. GUAT

Reprinted from Antropología e Historia de Guatemala, *XIX, No. 2 (jul-dic 1967).*

1242 Mace, Carroll E. "Three Quiché Dance-Dramas of Rabinal, Guatemala." Unpub. Ph.D. diss., Tulane, 1966. GUAT

1243 Machado, María Clara. "Teatro amador (Una experiencia positiva)," *Revista de Cultura Brasileña* (Madrid), No. 35 (mayo 1973), 119-124. BRAZ

1244 ____. "El teatro infantil en Río," *Américas*, 9, No. 3 (mar 1957), 7. BRAZ

1245 MacHale, Tomás P. "Introducción a *El palomar a oscuras* de Luis Alberto Heiremans," *Anales de la Universidad de Chile*, CXXV, No. 141-144 (ene-dic 1967), 146-147. CHILE

Followed by the play, El palomar a oscuras, drama en tres actos, *pp. 148-183.*

1246 ____. "Notas sobre Luis Alberto Heiremans," *Mapocho*, III, No. 7 (1965), 59-66. CHILE

1247 Maciel, Luiz Carlos. "O Bicho que o Bicho Deu," *Revista Civilização Brasileira*, No. 7 (maio 1966), 289-298. BRAZ

On Se correr o bicho pega, se ficar o bicho come *by Oduvaldo Vianna Filho e Ferreira Gullar.*

1248 ____. "Situação do Teatro Brasileiro," *Revista Civilização Brasileira*, No. 8 (jul 1966), 213-226. BRAZ

Also in Conjunto, *3, No. 8 (s.f.), 105-115. Translated by Hélio Eichbauer.*

1249 McKay, Douglas R. Review: "Sergio Vodanovik (sic). *Deja que los perros ladren; Nos tomamos la Universidad.*" *Latin American Literary Review*, I, No. 1 (Fall 1972), 115-119. CHILE

1250 ____. Review: "*Teatro contemporáneo*: Value and Limitations. [*Teatro contemporáneo: Recorded Dramatic Works in Spanish.*] Philadelphia: The Center for Curriculum Development, Inc., 1971." *Modern Language Journal*, LVI, No. 4 (Apr 1972), 243-246. GEN

1251 McLean, Malcolm D. "The Life and Works of Guillermo Prieto (1818 -1897)." Unpub. Ph.D. diss., Texas, 1951. MEX

1252 McLees, Ainslee Armstrong. "Elements of Sartrian Philosophy in *Electra Garrigó*," *Latin American Theatre Review*, 7/1 (Fall 1973), 5-11. CUBA

On Virgilio Piñera's play Electra Garrigó.

1253 Madrid, Antonieta. "Encuesta: el teatro y los jóvenes," *Imagen* (Caracas), No. 43 (15/28 feb 1969), 8, 17-18. VEN

Interview with José Gabriel Núñez, Pablo Antillano, Hermán Lejter, Antonio Briceño, Rodolfo Santana, Paul Williams, and Alberto Rodríguez Barrera.

1254 Magaldi, Sábato. *Aspectos da dramaturgia moderna.* São Paulo: Conselho Estadual de Cultura, Comissão de Literatura, 1962. GEN

1255 ____. *Panorama do teatro brasileiro.* São Paulo: Difusão Européia do Livro, 1962. 274 p. BRAZ

1256 ____. "Perspectivas do teatro brasileiro," *Comentário*, III, No. 3 (1962), 274-278. BRAZ

1257 ____. "A Procura de *Rasto Atrás*," *Comentário*, (1° trimestre 1968), 42-50. BRAZ

On Jorge Andrade's play, Rasto Atrás.

1258 ____. "Teatros oficiais de Brasília," *Habitat* (São Paulo), No. 11 (1960), 3-6. BRAZ

1259 Magalhães Júnior, Raymundo. *Artur Azevedo e sua época.* 3ª ed. rev. e aum. Rio de Janeiro: Civilização Brasileira, 1966. 360 p. BRAZ

1260 Magaña Esquivel, Antonio. "Los acuerdos del Instituto Latinoamericano de Teatro," *Nación* (mayo 1963), p. 11. GEN

1261 ____. "Balance de la Temporada de Oro del teatro mexicano," *Cuadernos de Bellas Artes*, IV, No. 1 (ene 1963), 64-67. MEX

Followed by nine pages of photos.

1262 ____. "Celestino Gorostiza, director y comediógrafo," *Letras de México*, II, No. 16 (15 abr 1940), 6. MEX

1263 Magaña Esquivel, Antonio. "González Bocanegra, poeta y dramaturgo," *Cuadernos de Bellas Artes*, II, No. 4 (abr 1961), 8-11. MEX

1264 ____. *Imagen del teatro*. México: Ediciones Letras de México, 1940. 167 p. MEX

A study of the Mexican theater of the time, including playwrights, actors, directors, and stage designers.
Reviewed: Putnam, Samuel.

1265 ____. "La madurez de Emilio Carballido como dramaturgo," *Nación* (16 feb 1964), p. 11. MEX

1266 ____. "Manuel Eduardo de Gorostiza y su obra dramática," *Estaciones* (México), I, No. 1 (1956), 85-91. MEX

1267 ____. *Medio siglo de teatro mexicano (1900-1961)*. México: Instituto Nacional de Bellas Artes, 1964. 174 p. MEX

1268 ____. "Momentos críticos sufrió el teatro mexicano en 1963," *Nación* (5 ene 1964), p. 11. MEX

1269 ____. "Notas sobre teatro peruano," *El Nacional*, Supl. 8040 (5 mayo 1963), p. 11. PERU

1270 ____. "La política en el teatro mexicano," *Revista de la Universidad de Yucatán*, 3, No. 15 (mayo-jun 1961), 18-29. MEX

1271 ____. "El problema de las ediciones. El teatro mexicano en 1963," *Nación* (12 ene 1964), p. 11. MEX

1272 ____. "Rafael Delgado en el teatro," *Cuadernos de Bellas Artes*, 4, No. 10 (nov 1963), 43-52. MEX

1273 ____. *Salvador Novo*. México: Empresas Editoriales, 1971. 318 p. MEX

1274 ____. "Son indispensables ediciones del teatro mexicano," *Nación* (13 ene 1963), p. 11. MEX

1275 ____. *Sueño y realidad del teatro*. México: Ediciones Instituto Nacional de Bellas Artes, 1949. MEX

1276 ____. "Teatro," *Buró Interamericano de Arte: Boletín* (México), No. 2 (oct 1952), 50-52. MEX

1277 Magaña Esquivel, Antonio. *El teatro: contrapunto.* México: Fondo de Cultura Económica, 1970. 111 p. MEX

Pre-Hispanic through the Revolution. Includes 50 p. of photos.

1278 ____. "El teatro mexicano contemporáneo," *Revista Interamericana de Bibliografía*, XIII, No. 4 (1963), 402-423. MEX

A brief history of 20th-century Mexican theater; includes a 4-page bibliography.

1279 ____. "El teatro mexicano reciente," *Nación* (25 set 1960), p. 11. MEX

1280 ____. "El teatro regional yucateco," *Cuadernos de Bellas Artes*, III, No. 7 (jul-ago 1962), 42-52. MEX

1281 ____. "El teatro y el cine," in *México, 50 años de revolución* (IV. *La cultura*). México: Fondo de Cultura Económica, 1962, pp. 369-411. MEX

1282 ____. "El teatro y la Revolución," *Cuadernos de Bellas Artes*, I, No. 4 (1960), 17-19. MEX

1283 ____. "Los teatros en México hasta el siglo XIX," *Revista Interamericana de Bibliografía*, XXII, No. 3 (jul-set 1972), 242-256. MEX

1284 ____ and Ruth S. Lamb. *Breve historia del teatro mexicano.* México: Ediciones de Andrea, 1958. 176 p. MEX

Manuales Studium, 8.
Reviewed: Arellano, Jesús; Arrom, José J.; Dauster, Frank.

1285 Magariños, Santiago. "*Tric-Trac* de Isaac Chocrón, juegos de hombres," *Revista de Teatro* (Caracas), I, No. 1 (set-nov 1967), 16-18. VEN

1286 Maloney, Janet E. "The Theatre of Samuel Eichelbaum." Unpub. Ph.D. diss., Northwestern, 1963. ARG

1287 Mancera, Eduardo. "El teatro que yo pretendo," *Cultura Universitaria* (Caracas), No. 87 (jul-set 1965), 48-54. VEN

1288 Mancini, Marcello. "Luigi Pirandello en América

Latina," *Imagen* (Caracas), No. 16 (15/30 ene 1968), 6-7. GEN

1289 Manet, Eduardo. "Movimiento teatral cubano desde sus orígenes hasta 1955," *Primer Acto*, No. 108 (mayo 1969), 14-21. CUBA

1290 Manjarrez, Héctor. "*La investigación* y el nuevo teatro," *Revista de la Universidad de México*, XXI, No. 9 (mayo 1967), 20-24. MEX

Theater as experience and the collective participation of spectators and actors.

1291 Mañón, Manuel. "El teatro en la colonia," *Máscara* (Buenos Aires), 7, No. 93 (jun 1948), 11-14. ARG

1292 Marchant Lazcano, Jorge. "Temporada teatral, 1973," *Apuntes* (Santiago), No. 78 (dic 1973), 29-34. CHILE

1293 Maria y Campos, Armando de. *Andanzas y picardías de Eusebio Vela (autor y comediante mexicano del siglo XVIII)*. México: Compañía de Ediciones Populares, 1944. 234 p. MEX

1294 ____. *Archivo de teatro; crónicas de enero a diciembre de 1946*. México: Compañía de Ediciones Populares, 1947. 259 p. MEX CHILE

1295 ____. "Los autores mexicanos y el INBA," *Cuadernos de Bellas Artes*, 5, No. 12 (dic 1964), 49-60. MEX

1296 ____. "Balbuceos del teatro en Chile," *Hemisferio* (México), 3, No. 5 (mar 1944), 28-29. CHILE

1297 ____. *Breve historia del teatro en Chile*. México: Compañía de Ediciones Populares, 1940. 46 p. CHILE

1298 ____. "Capítulos inéditos del teatro en México," *Romance* (México), (15 nov 1940), 11, 15. MEX

1299 ____. "Las comedias en el Corpus mexicano colonial," *Humanismo*, II, No. 11-12 (1953), 111-114. MEX

1300 ____. *Crónicas de teatro de* Hoy. México: Ediciones Botas, 1941. 249 p. MEX

1301 ____. *La dramática mexicana durante el gobierno del*

Presidente Lerdo de Tejada. México: Compañía de Ediciones Populares, 1946. 82 p. MEX

1302 Maria y Campos, Armando de. *Entre cómicos de ayer; apostillas con ilustraciones sobre el teatro en América*. México: Editorial Arriba el Telón, 1949. 206 p. GEN

1303 ____. *Guía de representaciones teatrales en la Nueva España (siglos XVI a XVIII)*. México: B. Costa-Amic, Editor, 1959. 212 p. (Colección "La Máscara.") MEX

1304 ____. "El hijo pródigo en el teatro mexicano," *El Hijo Pródigo* (México), 4, No. 13 (abr 1944), 38-43. MEX

1305 ____. "Itinerario del teatro guadalupano," *Humanismo*, 1, No. 6 (dic 1952), 57-60. MEX

1306 ____. "Laureles en la obra dramática de José Peón Contreras," *Cuadernos de Bellas Artes*, II, No. 5 (mayo 1961), 10-13. MEX

Also in Revista de la Universidad de Yucatán, *XI, No. 65 (set-oct 1969), 70-75.*

1307 ____. *Manuel Acuña en su teatro*. México: Compañía de Ediciones Populares, 1952. MEX

1308 ____. *Manuel Eduardo de Gorostiza y su tiempo*. México: Talleres Gráficos de la Nación, 1959. MEX

1309 ____. *Memoria de teatro, crónicas (1943-1945)*. México: Compañía de Ediciones Populares, 1946. 174 p. MEX

1310 ____. "Obra inédita de Manuel Eduardo de Gorostiza," *Cuadernos Americanos*, XV, No. 5 (1956), 149-178. MEX

1311 ____. "Origen del teatro en el Ecuador," *Hemisferio* (México), (ago 1944), 24-25. ECUAD

1312 ____. "Pepe Elizondo y el teatro de su tiempo," *Todo* (México), No. 1000 (6 nov 1952), 32-33. MEX

1313 ____. *El programa en cien años de teatro en México*. México: Ediciones Mexicanas, 1950. 62 p. MEX

1314 Maria y Campos, Armando de. *El teatro de género chico en la Revolución mexicana.* México: Talleres Gráficos de la Nación, 1956. 439 p. MEX

1315 ____. "El teatro de Sor Juana en Manila en 1790," *Vida Universitaria* (Nuevo León), VII, No. 353 (25 dic 1957), 7, 11. MEX

1316 ____. "El teatro en El Salvador," *Hemisferio* (México), (jul 1944), 24-25. EL SAL

1317 ____. "El teatro en México antes de Eusebio Vela," *Boletín de Estudios de Teatro* (Buenos Aires), V, No. 16 (mar 1947), 40-48. MEX

1318 ____. "El teatro en México: cómo se celebraban las obras nacionales y extranjeras a mediados del siglo pasado," *Romance* (México), (22 abr 1941), 11, 18. MEX

1319 ____. *El teatro está siempre en crisis... (Crónicas de 1946 a 1950).* México: Ediciones Arriba el Telón, 1954. 240 p. MEX

Numerous brief chronicles dealing with Mexican and European plays, playwrights and actors.

Reviewed: Valle, Rafael H.

1320 ____. "El teatro mexicano entre dos siglos," *Artes de México*, 16, No. 123 (1969). MEX

1321 ____. "El teatro nacional de Costa Rica," *Hemisferio* (México), (jun 1944), 25. COSTA RICA

1322 ____. *La virgen frente a las candilejas... o, El teatro guadalupano.* México: Compañía de Ediciones Populares, 1954. 148 p. MEX

1323 Marial, José. "Actual problemática del teatro independiente en Buenos Aires," in *Teatro y universidad.* Tucumán: Facultad de Filosofía y Letras, Universidad Nacional, 1960, pp. 89-102. ARG

1324 ____. "Etapas del teatro independiente," *Lyra*, XVII, No. 174-176 (1959). ARG

1325 ____. *El teatro independiente.* Buenos Aires: Ediciones Alpe, 1955. 260 p. ARG

1326 Marino, Rubén. "Loquepasa lleva la agitación al

escenario," *Conjunto*, No. 11-12 (ene-abr 1972), 57-62. ARG

The modus operandi of the Grupo Loquepasa.

1327 Marón, Tufic. "Problemas del teatro en México," *Etcaétera*, II, No. 5 [39], (abr 1967), 144-152. MEX

1328 Marqués, René. "La función del escritor puertorriqueño en el momento actual," *Cuadernos Americanos*, Año XXII, Vol. CXXVII, No. 2 (mar-abr 1963), 55-63. PTO. RICO

1329 ____. "Nacionalismo vs. universalismo," *Cuadernos Americanos*, XXV, No. 3 (mayo-jun 1966), 215-230. GEN

1330 Marshall, Elizabeth B. Review: "Gerald Flynn. *Sor Juana Inés de la Cruz*. New York: Twayne Publishers, Inc., 1971." *Modern Language Journal*, LVII, No. 1-2 (Jan-Feb 1973), 75-76. MEX

1331 Martí de Cid, Dolores. "Latin American Theatre," *First Stage*, VI, No. 1 (Spring 1967), 3-11. GEN

Translated by Warren S. Hubbard.

1332 ____. "Myth and Mythological Love in Giraudoux and Nalé Roxlo," *Papers on French-Spanish, Luso-Brazilian, Spanish-American Literary Relations*. Brockport, N.Y.: SUNY, Dept. of Foreign Languages [MLA Seminar 17, December 1970], 32-45. ARG

1333 Martin, Eleanor Jean. "*Carnaval afuera, carnaval adentro*: Síntesis del pensamiento social de René Marqués," *Revista Chicano-Riqueña*, II, No. 1 (invierno 1974), 39-49. PTO. RICO

1334 ____. "The Society in the Drama of René Marqués." Unpub. Ph.D. diss., N. Y. U., 1973. PTO. RICO

1335 Martin, Gerald. Review: "R. J. Callan. *Miguel Angel Asturias*. New York: Twayne Publishers, Inc., 1970." *Hispanic Review*, No. 41 (1973), 586-589. GUAT

1336 Martínez, Gilberto. "Mi experiencia directa con la obra de Bertolt Brecht," *Conjunto*, No. 20 (abr-jun 1974), 106-126. COL

By the editor of the Revista Teatro *of Medellín.*

1337 Martínez, Luis. "El mundo dramático de Gertrudis Gómez de Avellaneda," *Islas* (Santa Clara), I, No. 3 (1959), 585-591. CUBA

1338 Martínez Berrones, María Guadalupe. "En torno al teatro de don M. E. de Gorostiza," *Humanitas* (Monterrey), No. 8 (1967), 203-218. MEX

1339 Martínez Chibbaro, Emilio. "Experiencias de un actor," *Aisthesis*, No. 1 (1966), 118-124. CHILE

1340 Martínez Cuitiño, Vicente. "Elogio de Gregorio de Laferrère," *Cuadernos de Cultura Teatral*, No. 15 (1940), 65-108. ARG

1341 ____. "Imagen de Pacheco," *Revista de Cultura Teatral*, No. 20 (1944), 9-34. ARG

1342 Martínez Moreno, Luis. "Pedro de la Barra y el Teatro Experimental," *Cuadernos de Guayas* (Guayaquil), 4, No. 5 (abr 1953), 6, 14. CHILE

1343 Martínez Tamayo, María Elena. "Popular Theatre throughout the World: Mexico," *World Theatre*, V, No. 3 (Summer 1956), 215-218. MEX

Portion as "El teatro popular en México," Nuestro Tiempo *(La Habana), 5, No. 21 (ene-feb 1958), 8.*

1344 Martins, Wilson. "O teatro no Brasil," *Hispania*, XLVI, No. 2 (May 1963), 239-251. BRAZ

Also as "The Theater in Brazil," Theater Annual, *No. 20 (1963), 20-40.*

1345 ____ and Seymour Menton. *Teatro Brasileiro Contemporâneo.* New York: Appleton-Century-Crofts, 1966. 405 p. BRAZ

Anthology. Includes: Raimundo Magalhães Júnior, O Homem que Fica*; Pedro Bloch,* As Mãos de Eurídice*; Jorge Andrade,* A Moratória*; Guilherme Figueiredo,* A Rapôsa e as Uvas*; Ariano Suassuna,* Auto da Compadecida.

1346 Marulanda Morales, Octavio. "Sobre la formación del actor en Colombia," *Letras Nacionales* (Bogotá), II, No. 8 (mayo-jun 1966), 37-41. COL

1347 Marulanda Morales, Octavio. "Teatro 65: Un año de premoniciones," *Letras Nacionales* (Bogotá), II, No. 6 (ene-feb 1966), 50-58. COL

1348 Masotta, Oscar. *Sexo y traición en Roberto Arlt.* Buenos Aires: Jorge Alvarez, 1965. ARG

1349 Matas, Julio. Review: "William I. Oliver. *Voices of Change in the Spanish American Theater. An Anthology.* Austin: University of Texas Press, 1971." *Revista Iberoamericana*, No. 80 (jul-set 1972), 554-556. GEN

1350 ____. "Teatro cubano en un acto," *Revista Unión*, III, No. 1 (ene-mar 1964), 168-170. CUBA

1351 ____. "Theater and Cinematography," in *Revolutionary Change in Cuba*, ed. by Carmelo Mesa-Lago. Pittsburgh: University of Pittsburgh Press, 1971, pp. 427-445. CUBA

Section on theater, pp. 432-436.

1352 ____. "Tres antologías de teatro," *Revista Iberoamericana*, No. 79 (abr-jun 1972), 279-285. GEN

Review of Carlos Solórzano, Teatro breve hispanoamericano; *George Woodyard,* The Modern Stage in Latin America: Six Plays; *and Carlos Miguel Suárez Radillo,* 13 autores del nuevo teatro venezolano.

1353 Mayer, Edward H. "Chilean Theatre in the Sixties: A Decade of Protest." Unpub. Ph.D. diss., Missouri, 1971. CHILE

1354 Mazzara, Richard A. "Alfredo Dias Gomes, Social Commentator and Artist," *Latin American Theatre Review*, 2/2 (Spring 1969), 41-59. BRAZ

1355 ____. "Dramatic Variations on Themes of *El sombrero de tres picos, La zapatera prodigiosa,* and *Una viuda difícil*," *Hispania*, XLI, No. 2 (May 1958), 186-189. GEN

1356 ____. "From Essay to Theatre in the Northeast of Brazil," *Academics* (Oakland University), 1972/3. BRAZ

1357 ____. "Poetic Humor and Universality of Suassuna's *Compadecida*," *Ball State University Forum*, 10, No. 3 (1969), 25-30. BRAZ

1358 Mazzara, Richard A. "The Theatre of Jorge Andrade," *Latin American Theatre Review*, 1/1 (Fall 1967), 3-18. BRAZ

1359 ____. "Three Tragedies by Hermilo Borba Filho," *Hispania*, LI, No. 4 (Dec 1968), 830-838. BRAZ

1360 ____. "Two New Plays by Jorge Andrade," *Latin American Theatre Review*, 2/1 (Fall 1968), 49-52. BRAZ

1361 Mazzei, Angel. "El derecho y el teatro," *Revista de Estudios de Teatro*, 3, No. 9 (1965), 5-12. GEN

1362 ____. "La modalidad expresiva de Pedro E. Pico," *Revista de Estudios de Teatro* (Buenos Aires), 4, No. 11 (1970), 21-25. ARG

1363 Mazzeti, María. "Es la hora del teatro," *Revista de Cultura Brasileña* (Madrid), No. 35 (mayo 1973), 128-130. GEN

1364 Medina Ferrada, Fernando. "La crisis y el teatro experimental en México," *Teatro* (Madrid), No. 3 (ene 1953), 32. MEX

1365 ____. "Función educadora del teatro," *Abril* (La Paz), No. 2 (ene 1964), 67-69. BOL

1366 ____. "Venezuela y el teatro alineado," *Conjunto*, No. 17 (jul-set 1973), 8-10. VEN

1367 Mediza, Alberto. "Entrevista a Antonio Larreta," *Conjunto*, No. 13 (mayo-ago 1972), 10-13. URUG

1368 Megrini, César. "Teatro argentino: aproximación a un pecado original," *Revista de Occidente*, 34, No. 100 (jul-set 1971), 153-163. ARG

1369 Membrives, Lola. "El teatro y sus problemas," *Talía*, I, No. 8 (mayo-jun 1954), 24. GEN

1370 *Memoria del Primer Congreso Panamericano de Teatro* [Ciudad de México, 12-18 de octubre de 1957]. México: Instituto Nacional de Bellas Artes, Secretaría de Educación Pública, 1957. 230 p. GEN

1371 Mendes, Miriam G. "Marta, a Arvore e o Relógio," *Palco + Platéia*, No. 7 (s.f.), 23-25. BRAZ

On Jorge Andrade's plays.

1372 Méndez, Graziella. "Cañaveral en los bateyes," *INRA*, II, No. 5 (mayo 1961), 64-67. CUBA

Paco Alfonso's Cañaveral *in the sugar mills.*

1373 ____. "El pueblo en escena, Primer festival de aficionados," *Cuba*, I, No. 7 (nov 1962), 74-77. CUBA

Report on I Amateur Theatre Festival in Havana, Sept-Nov 1962.

1374 Méndez Plancarte, Alfonso. "Piezas teatrales en la Nueva España del siglo XVI. Siete ediciones y una supresión," *Abside*, VI, No. 2 (abr-jun 1942), 218-224. MEX

1375 Méndez y Mendoza, Eugenio. "Teatro nacional," *Cuaderno* (Caracas), No. 2 (nov 1966), 10-27. VEN

1376 Mendonça, Paulo. "Suassuna," *Anhembi*, XXVI, No. 78 (1957), 616-617. BRAZ

1377 Mendoza, Héctor. "Situación actual del teatro en México," *Diálogos* (México), 1, No. 2 (ene-feb 1965), 28-30. MEX

1378 Mendoza, María Luisa. "New Directions for Mexican Theater," *Américas*, 10, No. 4 (Apr 1958), 13-17. MEX

1379 Mendoza, Miguel Angel. "Presencia del teatro en México," *Mañana* (México), 37, No. 371 (7 oct 1950), 126-127. MEX

1380 Mendoza, Vicente. "Un teatro religioso colonial en Zumpango de la Laguna," *Anales del Instituto de Investigaciones Estéticas*, No. 16 (1948), 49-56. MEX

1381 Mendoza Gutiérrez, Alfredo. *Cómo escribir teatro rural.* Pátzcuaro, México: Centro Regional de Educación Fundamental para la América Latina, Monografías de Trabajo, I, 1956. 119 p. GEN

1382 ____. *Nuestro teatro campesino*... Pátzcuaro, México: Centro Regional de Educación Fundamental para la América Latina, 1960. 243 p. MEX

1383 Mendoza López, Margarita. "Bertolt Brecht en México," *Conjunto*, No. 19 (ene-mar 1974), 102-104. MEX

1384 ____. "El teatro mexicano: ¿Ha traspuesto las fronteras?" *Vida Literaria*, No. 14 (s.f.), 16-17. MEX

1385 Mendoza Varela, Eduardo. "Venturas y azar, logros y reveses del teatro en Santa Fé de Bogotá," *Revista del Colegio Mayor de Nuestra Señora del Rosario* (Bogotá), 70, No. 486 (nov-dic 1969/ene 1970). COL

1386 Menén Desleal, Alvaro. "Historia del teatro en El Salvador--José Emilio Aragón y Luigi Pirandello: Posibilidad de un paralelismo imposible," *Cultura* (San Salvador), No. 35 (ene-mar 1965), 31-34. EL SAL

1387 ____. "Historias de moros y cristianos," *Cultura* (San Salvador), No. 34 (oct-dic 1964), 49-52. EL SAL

1388 Menton, Seymour. "The Life and Works of Federico Gamboa." Unpub. Ph.D. diss., New York, 1952. MEX

1389 ____. Review: "Richard J. Callan. *Miguel Angel Asturias*. New York: Twayne Publishers, Inc., 1970." *Latin American Theatre Review*, 4/2 (Spring 1971), 85-86. GUAT

1390 Mérimée, P. Review: "Manuel Abascal Brunet. *Apuntes para la historia del teatro en Chile. La zarzuela grande*. Santiago: Imprenta Universitaria, 1940." *Bulletin Hispanique*, 55, No. 2 (1953), 216. CHILE

1391 Mertens, Federico. *Confidencias de un hombre de teatro; medio siglo de vida escénica. Biografías, monografías, crítica, ensayos*. Buenos Aires: NOS, 1948. 222 p. ARG

1392 ____. "Orfilia Rico," *Cuadernos de Cultura Teatral*, No. 21 (1945), 69-87. ARG

1393 "Mesa redonda: Hablan directores," *Conjunto*, III, No. 7 (abr 1968), 8-25. GEN

Orlando Rodríguez (Chile), Santiago García (Colombia), Juan Vicente Melo (México), and Federico Wolff (Uruguay).

1394 Meza, Gustavo. "Debray: *Proceso a un proceso*," *Conjunto*, 3, No. 7 (s.f.), 78-80. CUBA

Meza directed the production of Proceso a un proceso, *documentary-theater on Regis Debray.*

1395 Mibelli, Américo and Wilson Armas. *Las dependencias del teatro independiente.* Montevideo, 1960. 110 p. URUG

1396 Michalski, Ian. "Breve historia del 'Teatro nuevo' en el Brazil," *Revista de Cultura Brasileña* (Madrid), No. 33 (mayo 1971), 29-48. BRAZ

1397 ____. "Teatro carioca em 1966, ou Um Elefante que Resiste ao Caos," *Revista Civilização Brasileira*, No. 11/12 (dez 1966/mar 1967), 181-191. BRAZ

1398 Millán Chivite, Fernando. "Breve introducción al teatro brasileño en España y Mundo mental y sociológico de *O Pagador de Promessas*," *Revista de Cultura Brasileña* (Madrid), No. 22 (set 1967), 281-300. BRAZ

1399 Miller, Charlotte Elizabeth. "Florencio Sánchez: The South American Eugene O'Neill." Unpub. Ph. D. diss., Washington, 1946. URUG

1400 Miramón, Alberto. *Luis Vargas Tejada.* Bogotá: Editorial Kelly, 1970. 87 p. COL

1401 Miranda, Antonio. "El teatro brasileño contemporáneo: Gonçalves y Eichbauer," *Imagen* (Caracas), No. 29 (15/30 jul 1968), 19. BRAZ

Interview with director Martin Gonçalves and scenographer Helio Eichbauer.

1402 Miranda, Julio E. "José Triana o el conflicto," *Cuadernos Hispanoamericanos*, No. 230 (feb 1969), 439-444. CUBA

1403 ____. "El nuevo teatro cubano," *La Estafeta Literaria* (Madrid), No. 364 (feb 1967), 33-34. CUBA

1404 ____. "El nuevo teatro cubano," *Revista de Occidente*, XXXV, No. 105 (dic 1971), 336-346. CUBA

1405 ____. "Sobre el nuevo teatro cubano," in *Nueva literatura cubana*, ed. Julio E. Miranda. Madrid: Taurus, 1971, pp. 105-115. CUBA

Among others, Arrufat's Siete contra Tebas *and Triana's* Noche de los asesinos.

1406 Miranda, Nilda. "Escambray: Un teatro de la Revolución," *Caimán Barbudo*, II, No. 47 (jun 1971), 28-31. CUBA

Report on the Teatro Escambray, 1968-71.

1407 Mitchell, John D. "Theatre in Mexico Moves Ahead," *Theatre Annual*, XI (1953), 7-14. MEX

1408 "Mito, realidad y transcendencia de la escena independiente," *Teatro XX* (Buenos Aires), 1, No. 7 (dic 1964), 1-2, 6-7; 1, No. 8 (ene 1965), 2, 6; 1, No. 9 (feb 1965), 2. ARG

Discusses development and current status of the independent movement in Argentina.

1409 Mitre, Adolfo. "Facundo en el Nacional de Comedia," *Ficción*, No. 4 (nov-dic 1956), 124-127. ARG

On the presentation of Vicente Barbieri's Facundo en la Ciudadela *by the Comedia Nacional Argentina.*

1410 ____. "Laferrère, señor de una época," *Revista de Estudios de Teatro*, III, No. 7 (1963), 7-12. ARG

1411 Moglia, Raúl. "Representación escénica en Potosí en 1663," *Revista de Filología Hispánica*, V, No. 2 (abr-jun 1943), 166-167. BOL

1412 Molinari, Diego Luis. "1830-1880: Panorama histórico, social y literario," *Cuadernos de Cultura Teatral*, No. 14 (1940), 5-22. ARG

1413 Monasterios, Rubén. "Los dramaturgos venezolanos, hoy," *Conjunto*, 3, No. 8 (1969), 38-49. VEN

César Rengifo, José Ignacio Cabrujas, Gilberto Pinto, Isaac Chocrón, Manuel Trujillo, Román Chalbaud, Elizabeth Schön.

1414 ____. "Un intento fallido," *Imagen* (Caracas), No. 43 (15/28 feb 1969), 20. VEN

Theater of Rodolfo Santana, especially his Los hijos del Iris.

1415 ____. "Notas para una introducción a la dramática

de Román Chalbaud," *Revista de Teatro* (Caracas), I, No. 2 (dic 1967/feb 1968), 6-9. VEN

1416 Monasterios, Rubén. "El primer encuentro del teatro en provincia," *Cultura Universitaria* (Caracas), No. 96-97 (jul-dic 1967), 51-59. VEN

1417 ____. "¿Qué pasa con Román Chalbaud?" *Imagen* (Caracas), No. 29 (1967?), 20. VEN

1418 ____. "Recuento: Venezuela, 1970," *Latin American Theatre Review*, 4/2 (Spring 1971), 69-70. VEN

1419 ____. "68 teatral en Venezuela," *Imagen* (Caracas), No. 38-39 (1/31 dic 1968), 19. VEN

1420 ____. "Tendencias en el teatro venezolano," *Insula*, XXIV, No. 272-273 (jul-ago 1969), 29. VEN

1421 Monleón, José. "Diálogo con Jorge Díaz," *Primer Acto*, No. 69 (1965), 32-37. CHILE

1422 ____. "Entrevista con Enrique Buenaventura," *Primer Acto*, No. 145 (jun 1972), 22-32. COL

1423 ____. "Latinoamérica: orgía y revolución," *Primer Acto*, No. 157 (jun 1973). GEN

1424 Monner Sans, José María. "Un autor teatral de ayer," *Revista de Estudios de Teatro*, I, No. 1 (ene-mar 1959), 7-11. ARG

Some aspects of the life and works of Román Gómez Masía.

1425 ____. "Dos personajes de Laferrère," *Revista de Estudios de Teatro*, IV, No. 11 (1970), 11-16. ARG

1426 ____. "Estado actual del teatro," *Boletín de Estudios de Teatro*, III, No. 11 (dic 1954), 205-210. ARG

1427 ____. "La iniciación de Laferrère en el teatro," *Boletín de Estudios de Teatro*, I, No. 1 (ene 1943), 21-23. ARG

1428 ____. "El mejor teatro de Laferrère," *Nosotros*, XVIII, No. 73 (abr 1942), 37-42. ARG

1429 Monner Sans, José María."Prólogo," a *La gringa, En familia,* y *Barranca abajo* de Florenio Sánchez. Buenos Aires: Angel Estrada Editores, 1946. URUG

1430 Monsanto, Carlos H. "Antonio Acevedo Hernández: Emancipador de las masas a través de su teatro," *Literatura de la emancipación hispanoamericana y otros ensayos.* Lima: Universidad Nacional Mayor de San Marcos, Dirección Universitaria de Biblioteca y Publicaciones, 1972, pp. 314-318. CHILE

1431 ____. "*Infierno negro*: Drama de protesta social," *Duquesne Hispanic Review*, 10, No. 1 (1971), 11-22. ECUAD

On Demetrio Aguilera Malta's play.

1432 ____. "El mundo dramático de Antonio Acevedo Hernández," *Mapocho*, No. 22 (1970), 53-60. CHILE

1433 ____. *La protesta social en la dramaturgia de Acevedo Hernández.* México: B. Costa-Amic, 1971. 166 p. CHILE
Reviewed: Castillo, Homero; Rodríguez Sardiñas, Orlando.

1434 ____. "Trascendencia de Antonio Acevedo Hernández en la dramaturgia chilena," *Contemporary Latin America.* CHILE

A selection of papers presented at the Second Annual Conference on Latin America, University of Houston, Harvey L. Johnson and Richard V. Weekes, eds., (April 27-29, 1967).

1435 Monsen, Benedicta S. "Plantation Playwright, Jorge Andrade of Brazil," *Américas*, VIII, No. 8 (Aug 1956), 8-12. BRAZ

1436 Monsiváis, Carlos. "Doce y una, trece," *Revista de la Universidad de México*, XIX, No. 4 (dic 1964), 28-29. MEX

On Juan José Gurrola's production of Juan García Ponce's play, Doce y una, trece.

1437 ____. "*Landrú*, o crítica de la crítica humorística o cómo iniciar una polémica sin previo aviso," *Revista de la Universidad de México*, XVIII, No. 10 (jun 1964), 28-29. MEX

On Ibargüengoitia's critique of Reyes's operetta, Landrú.

1438 Monterde, Francisco. "Un aspecto del teatro profano de Sor Juana Inés de la Cruz," *Filosofía y Letras* (México), XI, No. 22 (1946), 247-257. MEX

1439 ____. "Autores de teatro mexicano, 1940-1950," *México en el Arte*, No. 10-11 (1951?), 39-46. MEX

1440 ____. "Una evasión romántica de Fernando Calderón," *Revista Iberoamericana*, No. 33 (feb-jul 1951), 81-89. MEX

1441 ____. "Federico Gamboa, novelista y dramaturgo," *Cuadernos del Idioma* (Buenos Aires), 2, No. 5 (jul 1966), 27-45. MEX

1442 ____. "*La hebra de oro* y otras evasiones," *Revista de la Universidad de México*, X, No. 10 (1956). MEX

On Emilio Carballido's La hebra de oro.

1443 ____. "Juárez, Maximiliano y Carlota en las obras de los dramaturgos mexicanos," *Cuadernos Americanos*, XXIII, No. 5 (set-oct 1964), 231-240. MEX

1444 ____. "El sainete en palacio, flor del tiempo profano de Sor Juana," *El Hijo Pródigo*, XI, No. 35 (15 feb 1946), 85-87. MEX

1445 ____. "*El sainete segundo* de Sor Juana y *El pregonero de Dios* de Acevedo," in *Homenaje a don Francisco Gamoneda*. México, 1946, pp. 325-333. MEX

Also in Occidente *(Santiago de Chile), No. 6 (set-oct 1945); and as a separate work, México, 1946, 13 p.*

1446 ____. "El teatro de Sor Juana," *Universidades de América*, III, No. 13 (ene 1952), 36-38. MEX

1447 Montero, Marco Arturo. "Util aportación a la dramaturgia mexicana," *El Libro y el Pueblo*, XVII, No. 20 (nov-dic 1955), 116-119. MEX

Discusses Enrique Othón Díaz's play La creciente.

1448 Montes, Jorge Roberto. "Buenos Aires, tierra de teatros experimentales," *Teatro* (Madrid), No. 4 (feb 1953), 21-25. ARG

1449 Montes Huidobro, Matías. *Persona, vida y máscara del teatro cubano*. Miami: Ediciones Universal, 1973. CUBA

Preliminary essay by Julio Matas.

1450 ____. "Técnica dramática de José Antonio Ramos," *Journal of Inter-American Studies and World Affairs*, XII, No. 2 (apr 1970), 229-241. CUBA

1451 Montoya, Angela. "Influencia de Brecht en el teatro colombiano," *Conjunto*, No. 20 (abr-jun 1974), 128-130. COL

1452 ____. "Teatro La Candelaria," *Letras Nacionales*, No. 24 (mayo-jun 1974), 82-85. COL

1453 Montoya, María Teresa. *El teatro en mi vida*. México: Ediciones Botas, 1956. 365 p. MEX

1454 Monzón, Antonio. "El teatro porteño en el histórico año de la Revolución de Mayo," *Boletín de Estudios de Teatro* (Buenos Aires), 8, No. 28 (ene-mar 1950), 3-12. ARG

1455 Moore, Ernest Richard. "Bibliografía de Ignacio Rodríguez Galván," *Revista Iberoamericana*, No. 15 (mayo 1944), 167-191. MEX

1456 ____, J. T. Reid and R. E. Warner. "Bibliografía de Santiago Argüello," *Revista Iberoamericana*, No. 10 (oct 1942), 427-437. NIC

1457 Mora, Gabriela. "Notas sobre el teatro chileno actual," *Revista Interamericana de Bibliografía*, XVIII, No. 4 (oct-dic 1968), 415-421. CHILE

1458 Mora V., Juan Miguel de. "Esquema del teatro mexicano," *Hoy* (México), (oct 1946). MEX

1459 ____. *Panorama del teatro en México*. México: Editora Latino Americana, 1970. MEX

1460 ____. "El teatro como compenetración ontológica," *Espejo*, I, No. 2 (2° trimestre 1967), 197-202. GEN

1461 Mora V., Juan Miguel de. "El teatro en México," *Espejo*, No. 1 (1° trimestre 1967), 183-192. MEX

1462 Morales, Arqueles. "Los Trashumantes, una expresión de teatro responsable en Panamá," *Conjunto*, No. 18 (oct-dic 1973), 23-24. PAN

On a Panamanian collective theater group doing documentary theater; followed by fragments of three works.

1463 Morales, Ernesto. *Historia del teatro argentino.* Buenos Aires: Lautaro, 1944. 295 p. ARG

1464 ____. "1810-1830: Panorama del teatro," *Cuadernos de Cultura Teatral*, No. 13 (1940), 65-90. ARG

1465 Morales, María Victoria. "La actividad teatral en Puerto Rico," *Horizontes*, V, No. 10 (1962), 92-102. PTO. RICO

Theater groups, plays and activities since 1958.

1466 Morán, Julio César. "Conducta humana y coherencia existencial en *Un guapo del 900* de Samuel Eichelbaum," *Estudios Literarios e Interdisciplinarios* (La Plata), (1968), pp. 71-96. ARG

1467 Morandi, Julio. "Argentina, un año muy censurado," *Conjunto*, No. 6 (ene-mar 1968), 90-95. ARG

The year 1967.

1468 Morejón, Nancy. "Si llueve, te mojas... también," *Conjunto*, No. 21 (jul-set 1974), 123-126. CUBA

Commentary on Si llueve, te mojas como los demás *by Héctor Quintero.*

1469 Moreno, Antonio. "Xavier Villaurrutia: The Development of his Theater," *Hispania*, XLIII, No. 4 (Dec 1960), 508-514. MEX

1470 ____. "Xavier Villaurrutia: The Man and his Dramas." Unpub. Ph.D. diss., Pittsburgh, 1953. MEX

1471 Moreno, Armando. "Como vi *El pagador de promesas*," *Primer Acto*, No. 75 (1966), 21. BRAZ

Comments by the director in Spain.

1472 Moreyra, Manuel. Review: "Guillermo Lohmann

Villena. *Historia del arte dramático en Lima durante el virreinato, siglos XVI y XVII.* Lima: Imprenta Universitaria, 1941." *Revista Iberoamericana*, No. 11-12 (Feb 1943), 139-140. PERU

1473 Morfi, Angelina. *Temas del teatro.* Santo Domingo: Editora del Caribe, 1969. 123 p. PTO. RICO

Includes essays on plays by Alejandro Tapia, Enrique Laguerre, René Marqués, Francisco Arriví, and Piri Fernández.

1474 ____. "Cóctel de don Nadie," *Revista del Instituto de Cultura Puertorriqueña*, XIII, No. 47 (abr-jun 1970), 12-14. PTO. RICO

1475 Morgado, Benjamín. *Eclipse parcial del teatro chileno.* Santiago: Ediciones Sendas, 1943. 21 p. CHILE

1476 Mori, Arturo. "El teatro mexicano reanuda su marcha," *Arte y Plata* (México), 3, No. 29 (jun 1947), 20. MEX

1477 ____. *Treinta años de teatro hispanoamericano.* Prólogo de José Elizondo. México: Editorial Moderna, 1941. 243 p. GEN
Reviewed: Weisinger, Nina Lee.

1478 Morris, Robert J. "The dramatic perspective in contemporary Peru," *Revista de Estudios Hispánicos*, 5, No. 1 (ene 1971), 107-117. PERU

1479 ____. "The Peruvian Theater, 1946-66." Unpub. Ph. D. diss., Kentucky, 1970. PERU

1480 ____. Review: "Teresa Cajiao Salas. *Temas y símbolos en la obra de Luis Alberto Heiremans.* Santiago de Chile: Editorial Universitaria, 1970." *Latin American Theatre Review*, 7/1 (Fall 1973), 109-110. CHILE

1481 ____. "Ricardo Palma and the Contemporary Peruvian Theatre," *Romance Notes*, XIV, No. 3 (Spring 1973), 465-468. PERU

1482 ____. "The Theatre of Juan Ríos Rey," *Latin American Theatre Review*, 7/2 (Spring 1974), 81-95. PERU

1483 Morris, Robert J. "The Theatre of Julio Ortega," *Latin American Theatre Review*, 6/1 (Fall 1972), 41-51. PERU

1484 ____. "The Theatre of Sebastián Salazar Bondy," *Latin American Theatre Review*, 4/1 (Fall 1970), 59-71. PERU

1485 Morton, Carlos. "The Teatro Chicano," *The Drama Review*, 18, No. 4 (Dec 1974), 71-76. U.S.

1486 Mosches, Julio César. "La historia, tema de teatro," *Talía*, I, No. 4 (ene 1954), 18. GEN

1487 Moser, Gerald M. "Jorge Andrade's São Paulo Cycle," *Latin American Theatre Review*, 5/1 (Fall 1971), 17-24. BRAZ

1488 Mostajo, Francisco. *El teatro en Arequipa del siglo XVI al siglo XVII*. Arequipa: Escuela Nacional de Arte Escénico, Servicio de Difusión, serie VI, 9; Estudios de Teatro Peruano, 1953. PERU

1489 "El movimiento teatral chileno," *Conjunto*, 3, No. 7 (s.f.), 75-102. CHILE

Commentary by Isidora Aguirre, Eugenio Guzmán, Jorge Díaz, Jaime Celedón, Orlando Rodríguez, Gustavo Meza, Eva Klein, Raúl Rivera, Nelson Villagra, Eugenio Dittborn, Jaime Vadell, Delfina Guzmán, José Chesta, María Asunción Requena, y Shenda Román.

1490 Moya, Ismael. "El circo y el payador," *Revista de Estudios de Teatro*, 1, No. 1 (ene-mar 1959), 19-28. ARG

1491 ____. "El teatro de Rojas," in *Ricardo Rojas*. Buenos Aires: Ediciones Culturales Argentinas, 1961, pp. 54-79. ARG

1492 Moya, Nilda Celia. "Ambrosio Morante y el drama *Tupac Amaru*," *Revista de Estudios de Teatro*, IV, No. 10 (1966), 20-34. ARG

1493 Muguercia, Magaly. "En Cuba: el teatro," *Universidad de la Habana*, No. 186-187-188 (jul-dic 1967), 71-76. CUBA

1494 ____. "¿Por qué? ¿para qué? y ¿para quién? se

escriben obras de teatro en una sociedad socialista," *Conjunto*, No. 17 (jul-set 1973), 110-111. GEN

1495 Mullen, Edward J. "A Note on the Plays of Carlos Díaz Dufóo, hijo," *Latin American Theatre Review*, 4/1 (Fall 1970), 51-58. MEX

1496 ____. "The *Revista Contemporáneos* and the Development of the Mexican Theatre," *Comparative Drama*, 4, No. 4 (1970), 272-282. MEX

1497 Muncy, Michèle. *Salvador Novo y su teatro. Estudio crítico.* Río Piedras: Ediciones Atlas, 1971. 246 p. MEX

1498 Muñoz, Mario. "Dalmiro Sáenz, ¡*Hip... hip... ufa*!" *La Palabra y el Hombre*, No. 44 (oct-dic 1967), 851-854. ARG

1499 Muñoz, Peggy. "Charles Rooner and the Mexican Theater," *Mexican-American Review* (Mexico), 23, No. 5 (May 1955), 18, 29-34. MEX

1500 ____. "Staged by Mexico," *Américas*, 5, No. 7 (jul 1953), 6-8, 41-43. MEX

1501 Murch, Anne C. "Genet - Triana - Kopit: Ritual as 'Danse Macabre'," *Modern Drama*, XV, No. 4 (Mar 1973), 369-381. CUBA

On José Triana's La noche de los asesinos.

1502 Nacci, Chris N. *Concepción del mundo en el teatro mexicano del siglo veinte, según las ideas y los sentimientos expresados por 85 autores en 252 obras, la voluntad humana y las influencias en las cuales está sujeta.* México: Impresora Económica, 1951. 115 p. MEX

1503 Nascimento, Abdias do, ed. *Dramas para Negros e Prólogo para Brancos.* Rio de Janeiro: Teatro Experimental do Negro, 1961. 419 p.

Anthology includes: Lúcio Cardoso, O Filho Pródigo; *Romeu Crusoé,* O Castigo de Oxalá; *Rosário Fusco,* Auto da Noiva; *Abdias do Nascimento,*

Sortilégio; *Agostinho Olavo,* Além do Rio (Medea); *José de Morais Pinho,* Filhos de Santo; *Joaquim Ribeiro,* Aruanda; *Nélson Rodrigues,* Anjo Negro; *Tasso da Silveira,* O Emparedado. Reviewed: O'Dwyer, Heitor.

1504 Nascimento, Abdias do. "The Negro Theatre in Brazil," *African Forum*, No. 2 (1967), 35-53. BRAZ

1505 ____. "Teatro negro del Brasil (una experiencia socio-racial)," *Conjunto*, 3, No. 9 (s.f.), 14-28. BRAZ

Reprinted from Civilização Brasileira, *Caderno esp. No. 2.*

1506 Natella, Arthur A. "Enrique Solari Swayne and *Collacocha*," *Latin American Theatre Review*, 4/2 (Spring 1971), 39-44. PERU

1507 ____. "The Major Contemporary Dramatists of Peru." Unpub. Ph.D. diss., Syracuse, 1970. PERU

1508 ____. "The New Drama of Peru," *Books Abroad*, 45, No. 2 (Spring 1971), 256-259. PERU

1509 ____. Review: "Erminio G. Neglia. *Pirandello y la dramática rioplatense*. Florence: Valmartina Editore, 1970." *Latin American Theatre Review*, 5/2 (Spring 1972), 82. RIVER PLATE

1510 "National popular theatre in Quito," *World Theatre*, 16, No. 5-6 (Sept-Dec 1967), 538-541. ECUAD

1511 Neglia, Erminio. "*Almas de ahora* de Alvarez Lleras," *El Espectador* (Bogotá), (9 ene 1966), p. 11-E. COL

1512 ____. "El grotesco criollo y el inmigrante italiano," *Boletín Argentores*, 35, No. 131 (ene-jun 1970), 1-9. ARG

1513 ____. *Pirandello y la dramática rioplatense*. Firenze: Consiglio Nazionale delle Ricerche, Valmartina Editore, 1970. 149 p. RIVER PLATE
Reviewed: Natella, Arthur A.

1514 ____. "Una recapitulación de la renovación teatral en Hispanoamérica," *Latin American Theatre Review*, 8/1 (Fall 1974), 57-66. GEN

1515 Neglia, Erminio. "Temas y rumbos del teatro rural hispanoamericano del siglo XX," *Latin American Theatre Review*, 5/1 (Fall 1971), 49-57. GEN

1516 "Nelson Rodrigues: Um Debate," *Cadernos Brasileiros*, 8, No. 35 (maio-jun 1966), 46-52. BRAZ

1517 Nichols, Madaline Wallis. "The Argentine theatre," *Bulletin Hispanique*, XLII, No. 1 (jan-mar 1940), 39-53. ARG

Also as separata: The Argentine Theatre. *Bordeaux: Feret et Fils, 1940. 14 p.*

1518 "The 1946 theatrical season in Argentina," *Argentine News* (nov-dic 1946), 21-22. ARG

1519 Niño Vela, Jorge. "Lola Membrives: Un ejemplo de vocación artística y una gloriosa carrera de actriz," *Lyra*, XVII, No. 174-176 (1959). ARG

1520 Noguera, Héctor. "Hacia un teatro auténticamente chileno," *Conjunto*, No. 13 (mayo-ago 1972), 89-90. CHILE

1521 Nogués, Germinal. "Teatro de mimo en Buenos Aires," *Américas*, 23, No. 10 (oct 1971), 25-31. ARG

1522 Nolte M., Arturo. "Cronología de los montajes de obras brechtianas en Perú," *Conjunto*, No. 21 (jul-set 1974), 128-129. PERU

1523 Nomland, John B. *Teatro mexicano contemporáneo, 1900-1950.* México: Instituto Nacional de Bellas Artes, 1967. 337 p. MEX

1524 Novaes, Maria Stella de. "O teatro no Espíritu Santo. O teatro jesuítico. O teatro popular. Propulsores do teatro no Espíritu Santo. O *Melpomene* e o Carlos Gomes," *Revista de História* (São Paulo), No. 42 (abr-jun 1960), 461-470. BRAZ

1525 Novella Marani, Alma. "Presencia de Alfieri en el teatro de Juan Cruz Varela," in *Algunos aspectos de la cultura literaria de Mayo.* La Plata: Universidad Nacional de La Plata, 1961, pp. 277-306. ARG

1526 Novo, Salvador. "A clase con el maestro Novo

(curso de dirección)," *Revista de la Escuela de Arte Teatral* (México), No. 2-3 (abr-set 1961), 13-30. MEX

1527 Novo, Salvador. "Chaos and Horizons of Mexican Drama," *Theatre Arts Monthly*, XXV (May 1941), 393-398. MEX

1528 ____. *Letras vencidas*. Xalapa: Universidad Veracruzana, 1962. 267 p. MEX

Contains: "El teatro y la Revolución mexicana," pp. 125-154; "Respuesta académica a Celestino Gorostiza," pp. 193-210; "El teatro por fuera," pp. 211-243; "El teatro en México," pp. 247-267.

1529 ____. "La metamorfosis de Ulises," *Artes de México*, 16, No. 123 (1969). MEX

1530 ____. "Mis abundantes razones para escribir *In Pipiltzintzin* o *La guerra de las gordas*," *Revista de la Universidad de México*, XVII, No. 9 (mayo 1963), 21-23. MEX

1531 ____. "Los ocho contra el teatro: Yo el primero," *La Palabra y el Hombre*, No. 39 (jul-set 1966), 355-367. MEX

1532 ____. "El teatro en México," *La Palabra y el Hombre*, No. 20 (oct-dic 1961), 649-660. MEX

Also in Cuadernos de Bellas Artes, *II, No. 10 (oct 1961), 61-71.*

1533 ____. "El teatro mexicano en 1950," *Boletín Bibliográfico Mexicano*, 11, No. 131-132 (nov-dic 1950), 11-14. MEX

1534 ____. *Toda la prosa*. México: Empresas Editoriales, 1964. 819 p. MEX

Includes several essays on theater, some of them published earlier in his Letras vencidas.

1535 Novoa, Mario E. "Virgilio Piñera: Premio al pánico," *Exilio* (New York), 4, No. 4 to 5, No. 1 (invierno-primavera 1971), 127-141. CUBA

On Virgilio Piñera's Dos viejos pánicos.

1536 Nucete-Sardi, José María. "Momentos del teatro

venezolano," *Revista de Estudios de Teatro* (Buenos Aires), 1, No. 1 (ene-mar 1959), 5-6. VEN

1537 Nuevo Teatro Cooperativo de Trabajo Limitado. *Los primeros diez años de Nuevo Teatro.* Buenos Aires: Nuevo Teatro, 1960. ARG

1538 Nunes, Cassiano. "Algumas Reflexões sobre o Teatro de Martins Pena," *Latin American Theatre Review*, 2/1 (Fall 1968), 53-57. BRAZ

1539 Núñez, Carlos. "Un mes de teatro," *INRA*, II, No. 3 (mar 1961), 32-35. CUBA

1540 ____. "El pueblo en escena, Festival del Teatro," *INRA*, II, No. 4 (abr 1961), 86-91. CUBA

Report on Festival de Teatro Obrero-Campesino, Mar 1961.

1541 Núñez, Enrique Bernardo. "El teatro del Coliseo," *Crónica de Caracas*, 4, No. 19 (ago-dic 1954), 588-605. VEN

1542 Núñez, Estuardo. "Literatura peruana reciente (1964-1965)," *Journal of Inter-American Studies*, 8, No. 1 (1966), 34-43. PERU

Section on theater, pp. 36-37.

1543 ____. "El teatro," in *La literatura peruana en el siglo XX, 1900-1965.* México: Editorial Pormaca, 1965, pp. 60-70. PERU

1544 Núñez y Domínguez, José de J. "La literatura contemporánea de México: el teatro a fines del siglo XIX," *Bulletin de L'I.F.A.L.* (México), No. 10 (nov 1945), 20-24. MEX

1545 Núñez y Domínguez, Roberto. *Descorriendo el telón; cuarenta años de teatro en México.* Madrid: Gráficas Editorial Rollán, 1956. 616 p. MEX

1546 Oberdoerffer, Marianne. "Contemporary Mexican Theatre, 1923-59." Unpub. Ph.D. diss., Texas, 1960. MEX

1547 Obino, Aldo. "A obra fabulosa de Suassuna," *Revista de Teatro* (Brazil), No. 385 (jan-fev 1972), 26. BRAZ

1548 "Obras de Florencio Sánchez en el Brasil," *Revista de Estudios de Teatro*, I, No. 2 (1959), 24. URUG

1549 Obry, Olga. "Brazil in the Melting Pot," *World Theatre*, XI, No. 3 (1962), 255. BRAZ

1550 ____. "The Haps and Mishaps of the Brazilian Puppet," *World Theatre*, XIV (1965), 452-457. BRAZ

1551 Ocampo, María Luisa. "Recuerdo de José Antonio Ramos," *Revista Iberoamericana*, No. 24 (jun 1947), 301-308. CUBA

1552 "Ocho preguntas. Entrevista," *Conjunto*, 3, No. 7 (s.f.), 96-98. CHILE

Interview with the Chilean director, Orlando Rodríguez.

1553 O'Connell, Richard B. "Gorostiza's *Contigo pan y cebolla* and Sheridan's *The Rivals*," *Hispania*, XLIII, No. 3 (Sept 1960), 384-387. MEX

1554 Odena, Isidro J. "Elementos para la formación de un teatro nacional," *Cuadernos de Cultura Teatral*, No. 17 (1942), 43-62. ARG

1555 O'Dwyer, Heitor. "Dramas para Negros e Prólogo para Brancos," *Leitura*, No. 61 (1962), 54-56. BRAZ

Review article on Abdias do Nascimento's book.

1556 Oenslager, Donald. "Theatre Horizons of South America," *The Record*, 6, No. 5 (Sept-Oct 1950), 12-21. GEN

1557 Oeste de Bopp, Marianne. "Autos mexicanos del siglo XVI," *Historia Mexicana*, III, No. 1 (jul-ago 1953), 112-123. MEX

1558 ____. *Influencia de los misterios y autos europeos en los de México (anteriores al barroco)*. México, 1952. 282 p. MEX

1559 O'Gorman, Edmundo. "Dos documentos de nuestra historia literaria (siglo XVI)," *Boletín del*

Archivo General de la Nación (México), XI (1940), 591-616. MEX

1560 "Una ojeada al teatro viejo: lo que puede verse en un museo local," *Boletín de Estudios de Teatro* (Buenos Aires), 2, No. 5 (abr 1944), 53-56. ARG

1561 Ojeda, Jorge Arturo. "Teatro lúcido y didáctico," *Revista de Bellas Artes*, No. 24 (nov-dic 1968), 57-62. GEN

Deals briefly with Cuzzani's Sempronio, *Wolff's* Los invasores, *Arreola's* La hora de todos, *Salazar Bondy's* El fabricante de deudas, *and Marqués's* Un niño azul para esa sombra.

1562 Olavarría y Ferrari, Enrique de. *Reseña histórica del teatro en México, 1539-1911.* México: Porrúa, 1961. 5 vols., 3680 p. MEX

Also see: Indices a la reseña histórica del teatro en México. *México: Porrúa, 1968.*

1563 Olea, Héctor R. "Breve historia del Teatro Apolo," *Letras de Sinaloa* (Culiacán), 4, No. 20 (15 set 1950), 32-39. MEX

1564 Olguín, Manuel. "La filosofía de José Antonio Ramos y su afinidad con la del pueblo y los pensadores de los Estados Unidos," *Revista Iberoamericana*, No. 24 (jun 1947), 291-299. CUBA

1565 Oliveira, Waldemar de. "A propósito... sobre direitos autorais," *Revista de Teatro* (Rio), No. 349 (jan-fev 1966), 26-29. BRAZ

1566 Oliver, Manuel María. "Material para la historia del teatro argentino," *Argentores*, 10, No. 43 (jul 1944), 51-52. ARG

1567 ____. "Para la historia del teatro argentino," *Boletín de Estudios de Teatro* (Buenos Aires), 2, No. 6 (jul 1944), 122-124. ARG

1568 Oliver, William I. *Voices of Change in the Spanish American Theater.* Austin and London: The University of Texas Press, 1971. 294 p. GEN

Anthology. Includes: Emilio Carballido, The Day They Let the Lions Loose; *Griselda Gambaro,*

The Camp; *Carlos Maggi,* The Library; *Enrique Buenaventura,* In the Right Hand of God the Father; *Luisa Josefina Hernández,* The Mulatto's Orgy; *Sergio Vodanović,* Viña: Three Beach Plays. Reviewed: Johnson, Harvey L.; Matas, Julio; Peden, Margaret; Rabkin, Gerald; Woodyard, George.

1569 Olivera, Otto. Review: "José Juan Arrom. *El teatro de Hispanoamérica en la época colonial.* La Habana: Anuario Bibliográfico Cubano, 1956." *Symposium*, 12, No. 2 (Fall 1958), 215-220. GEN

1570 Onetti, Jorge. "Uruguay, una visión dinámica," *Conjunto*, No. 6 (ene-mar 1968), 96-100. URUG

1571 Onís, Federico de. "Martí and the Caribbean Theatre," *The Caribbean: Its Culture*, Curtis Wilgus, ed. Gainesville: University of Florida Press, 1955, pp. 74-84. CUBA

1572 Onís, Juan de. "New Plays Chide Brazilian Regime," *New York Times* (25 April 1965), p. 26. BRAZ

On Opinião *and* Liberdade, Liberdade *directed by Flávio Rangel.*

1573 Ordaz, Luis. "Los autores de estos últimos treinta años," *Lyra*, XVII, No. 174-176 (1959). ARG

1574 ____. "*Barranca abajo*: el testimonio más importante del teatro rioplatense," *Revista de Estudios de Teatro* (Buenos Aires), 4, No. 11 (1970), 30-34. RIVER PLATE

1575 ____. *Breve historia del teatro argentino.* Buenos Aires: Editorial Universitaria de Buenos Aires, 1962-65. 8 Vols. ARG

Anthologies, with introductions on different epochs.

1576 ____. *El drama rural.* Buenos Aires: Hachette, "El pasado argentino," 1959. ARG

1577 ____. "La evolución del teatro en América Latina," *Literatura Contemporánea*, No. 20 (1970), 217-240. GEN

1578 ____. *Florencio Sánchez.* Buenos Aires: Centro Editor de América Latina, 1971. URUG

1579 Ordaz, Luis. *El hombre del campo en nuestro teatro.* Buenos Aires: Editorial Raigal, 1953. 351 p. ARG

Cuadernos de Arte Dramático, Suplementos de Estudio, Documentación, Investigación. Tomo II, No. 24-25.

1580 ____. "José González Castillo: Sainetero popular y dramaturgo," *Revista de Estudios de Teatro*, 2, No. 6 (1963), 32-35. ARG

1581 ____. "Luis Ambrosio Morante, hombre múltiple de la primera hora del teatro argentino," *Revista de Estudios de Teatro*, II, No. 4 (1962), 32-35. ARG

1582 ____. "Nuestro teatro en verso," *Lyra*, XVII, No. 174-176 (1959). ARG

1583 ____. *Siete sainetes porteños.* Buenos Aires: Ediciones Losange, 1958. ARG

Anthology with introduction. Contains: Nemesio Trejo, Los políticos; *Enrique de María,* Bohemia criolla; *José González Castillo,* La serenata; *Alberto Vacarezza,* Los escrushantes; *Carlos Mauricio Pacheco,* Barracas; *Armando y Enrique Santos Discépolo,* El organito; *Francisco Defilippis Novoa,* He visto a Dios.
Reviewed: Carella, Tulio.

1584 ____. "Teatro argentino, 1968," *Latin American Theatre Review*, 2/2 (Spring 1969), 69-72. ARG

1585 ____. *El teatro argentino.* Buenos Aires: Centro Editor de América Latina, 1971. 112 p. ARG

1586 ____. *El teatro en el Río de la Plata desde sus orígenes hasta nuestros días.* Buenos Aires: Editorial Futuro, 1945. 223 p. RIVER PLATE

Segunda edición, aumentada y corregida, Buenos Aires: Ediciones Leviatán, 1957. 347 p.

1587 ____. "Unamuno, Halac y DeQuinto," *Primer Acto*, No. 67 (1965), 53-54. ARG

1588 "Origen del teatro en Santa Fé de Bogotá, 1792-1796," *Revista del Archivo Nacional* (Bogotá), 6, No. 63/65 (jul-set 1944), 199-275. COL

1589 Oropeza Martínez, Roberto. "Introducción," *Sor Juana Inés de la Cruz. Obra poética; Los empeños de una casa.* México: Ateneo, 1962. MEX

1590 Orrillo, Winston. "Realidad del teatro en el Perú," *Conjunto*, 3, No. 8 (1969), 123-126. PERU

1591 Ortega, Julio. "El autor en los pasillos," *Textual* (Lima), No. 2 (set 1971), 17-18. GEN

1592 ____. "En busca del teatro peruano," *La Prensa* (Lima), 18 dic 1966, supl. dom., p. 44. PERU

1593 ____. "La noche de los asesinos," *Cuadernos Americanos*, CLXIV, No. 3 (mayo-jun 1969), 262-267. CUBA

On José Triana's La noche de los asesinos.

1594 Orthous, Pedro. "Misión de cultura del Teatro Experimental en el Norte," *Revista de Educación* (Santiago), 6, No. 40 (nov 1946), 393, 433-444. CHILE

1595 Ortiz, Fernando. *Los bailes y el teatro de los negros en el folklore de Cuba.* Prólogo de Alfonso Reyes. La Habana: 1951. 466 p. CUBA
Reviewed: Chase, Gilbert.

1596 Ortiz, Sergio Elías. "Notas sobre el teatro en el Nuevo Reyno de Granada," *Boletín de Historia y Antigüedades* (Bogotá), LVII, Nos. 669-671 (jul-set 1970), 411-424. COL

1597 Osorio, María Luisa. Review:"José Juan Arrom. *El teatro de Hispanoamérica en la época colonial.* La Habana: Anuario Bibliográfico Cubano, 1956." *Modern Language Journal*, XLI, No. 8 (Dec 1957), 402-403. GEN

1598 Otero, Leonardo. "José Agustín: monólogo e infinito," *Revista de la Universidad de México*, Suplemento, XXIV, No. 5-6 (ene-feb 1970), p. 11. MEX

On José Agustín's Abolición de la propiedad.

1599 Oursler, Anna Lovina. "El drama mexicano desde la Revolución de 1910 hasta el año 1940," *Memorias del Segundo Congreso Internacional de Catedráticos de Literatura Iberoamericana,* (agosto de 1940). Berkeley and Los Angeles: University of California Press, 1941, pp. 259-267. MEX

1600 Oviedo, José Miguel. "Sebastián Salazar Bondy en su teatro," *Revista Peruana de Cultura*, No. 7-8 (1966), 70-97. PERU

1601 Oyuela Cantos, José María. "El teatro de Francisco Tobar García," *Arco* (Bogotá), 9, No. 75 (ene 1967), 38-44. ECUAD

1602 Pabón, Luis Alberto. "Bosquejo para una historia del teatro paceño," in *La Paz en su IV Centenario, 1548-1948*. III. Buenos Aires: Edición del Comité Pro IV Centenario de la Fundación de La Paz, 1948, pp. 77-92. BOL

1603 Padrón, Carlos. "Cine con gente de verdad; Los primeros once años del Conjunto Dramático de Oriente," *Conjunto*, No. 14 (set-dic 1972), 102-110. CUBA

1604 "O Pagador de Promessas," *Anhembi*, XL, No. 118 (set 1960), 192-193. BRAZ

1605 Pagano, José León. "Recuerdos del *Facundo* de David Peña," *Boletín de Estudios de Teatro*, III, No. 10 (set 1945), 155-156. ARG

1606 Pagés Larraya, Antonio. "Belisario Roldán, los recuerdos olvidados en un poeta que realizó obra dramática," *Revista de Estudios de Teatro*, II, No. 6 (1963), 16-25. ARG

1607 Palant, Pablo T. "El joven Samuel Eichelbaum," *Davar*, No. 72 (set-oct 1957), 89-92. ARG

1608 Palazzolo, Octavio. "Mis experiencias como director," *Cuadernos de Cultura Teatral*, No. 10 (1940), 57-75. ARG

1609 Palls, Terry L. "Enajenación brechtiana en cuatro dramas de Luisa Josefina Hernández," *El Urogallo*, II, No. 7 (ene-feb 1971), 84-87. MEX

1610 ____. "The Theatre in Revolutionary Cuba, 1959-1969." Unpub. Ph.D. diss., Kansas, 1974. CUBA

1611 Panelo, Antonio and Isabel Herrera. "Hacia una

dramaturgia nacional y un teatro internacional," *Caimán Barbudo*, II, No. 34 (set 1969), 16-19. ARG CUBA

Report on activities of Argentine directors in Cuban National School of Art, 1962-1969.

1612 Panizza, Delio. "Martiniano Leguizamón: El hombre y su obra," *Cuadernos de Cultura Teatral*, No. 15 (1940), 25-64. ARG

1613 Panno, Hugo. "Los crisoles del teatro independiente," *Ensayos Argentinos*. Buenos Aires: Centro Editor de América Latina, 1971, pp. 92-102. [La Historia Popular, No. 68.] ARG

1614 "Panorama del teatro cubano," *Cuba en la UNESCO*, VI (feb 1965), 3-175. CUBA

Cuban theater, 1800-1850.

1615 "Para la historia o el recuerdo: Vida y cosas de teatro a través de las cartas," *Boletín de Estudios de Teatro* (Buenos Aires), 8, No. 28 (ene-mar 1950), 35-40. ARG

1616 Parajón, Mario. "El teatro que queremos para Cuba," *Islas* (Santa Clara), 2, No. 1 (set-dic 1959), 69-77. CUBA

1617 Parker, Alexander A. "The Calderonian Sources of *El divino Narciso* by Sor Juana Inés de la Cruz," *Romanistisches Jahrbuch* (Hamburg), XIX (1968), 257-274. MEX

1618 Parravicini, Florencio. "Mis experiencias como actor," *Cuadernos de Cultura Teatral*, No. 10 (1940), 81-95. ARG

1619 Parreño, Desiderio. "Havana Meets the Twentieth Century," *Theatre Arts* (New York), Aug 1947, 52-54. CUBA

1620 Partida Tayzán, Armando. "Ecos del Segundo Festival de Teatro Latinoamericano," *Revista de la Universidad de México*, XXVII, No. 1 (set 1972), 42-45. GEN

1621 ____. "¿Qué pasa con el teatro en México?" *Revista de la Universidad de México*, XXV, No. 2 (oct 1970), 42-45. GEN

A propos of Scorpio in mortante*; directing techniques of Jodorowsky, Julio Castillo and Gurrola.*

1622 Partida Tayzán, Armando. "Teatro Club: teatro comprometido," *Conjunto*, No. 11-12 (ene-abr 1972), 66-68. MEX

Reprinted from El Gallo Ilustrado*, No. 471.*

1623 Pasarell, Emilio J. "Guía para la producción dramática de Puerto Rico en el siglo XX," *Revista del Instituto de Cultura Puertorriqueña*, 8, No. 27 (abr-jun 1965), 50-60. PTO. RICO

1624 ____. *Orígenes y desarrollo de la afición teatral en Puerto Rico*. San Juan: Editorial del Departamento de Instrucción Pública del Estado Libre Asociado de Puerto Rico, 1970. 463 p. PTO. RICO

Reprinting of the 1951 and 1967 editions.

1625 ____. *Panorama teatral de Puerto Rico en el siglo XIX*. San Juan: Instituto de Cultura Puertorriqueña, 1960. PTO. RICO

Ciclo de conferencias sobre la literatura en Puerto Rico.

1626 Pascal, Mane. "Dramaturgos argentinos," *Cuadernos* (Paris), No. 98 (1965), 94-95. ARG

1627 Pasquariello, Anthony M. "The 'entremés' in Sixteenth-Century Spanish America," *The Hispanic American Historical Review*, 32, No. 1 (Feb 1952), 44-58. GEN

1628 ____. "The Evolution of the 'loa' in Spanish America," *Latin American Theatre Review*, 3/2 (Spring 1970), 5-19. GEN

1629 ____. Review: "Hymen Alpern and José Martel. *Teatro hispanoamericano*. New York: Odyssey Press, 1956." *Symposium*, 11, No. 1 (Spring 1957), 154-155. GEN

1630 ____. Review: "*Obras de Juan de Cueto y Mena*. Edición crítica con introducción y notas por Archer Woodford, prólogo de José Manuel Rivas Sacconi. Bogotá: Publicaciones del Instituto Caro y Cuervo, IX, 1952." *Hispanic Review*, XXII, No. 1 (Jan 1954), 84-86. COL

1631 Pasquariello, Anthony M. Review: "*Selección dramática de Cristóbal de Aguilar, autor de la Córdoba colonial.* Prólogo y notas por J. Luis Trenti Rocamora. Buenos Aires: Instituto Nacional de Estudios de Teatro, 1950." *Hispanic Review*, XX, No. 1 (Jan 1952), 80-81. ARG

1632 ____. "A Study of the 'Entremés' and the 'Sainete' in the Colonial Hispanic Theater, with a Consideration of the Social Customs Revealed in Them." Unpub. Ph.D. diss., Michigan, 1950. GEN

1633 ____. "Two Eighteenth-Century Peruvian Interludes, Pioneer Pieces in Local Color," *Symposium*, VI, No. 2 (Nov 1952), 385-390. PERU

1634 Patrick, Bert Edward. "Classical Mythology in Twentieth-Century Mexican Drama." Unpub. Ph.D. diss., Missouri, 1972. MEX

1635 Paulo, Rogério. *Notas de um Ator em Viagem, Cuba, 1970 e 1972.* Lisboa: Seara Nova, 1972?. CUBA

1636 ____. "Panorama teatral latinoamericano," *Conjunto*, No. 15 (ene-mar 1973), 128-132. GEN

1637 Pazos, Manuel R. "El teatro franciscano en Méjico durante el siglo XVI," *Archivo Ibero-Americano*, 2ª época, XI, No. 42 (abr-jun 1951), 129-189. MEX

1638 Pearce, T. M. "The New Mexican 'Shepherd's Play'," *Western Folklore*, No. 15 (Jan 1956), 77-88. U.S.

1639 Peden, Margaret S. "Emilio Carballido: curriculum operum," *Latin American Theatre Review*, 1/1 (Fall 1967), 38-49. MEX

1640 ____. "Emilio Carballido, Dramatic Author: His Work from 1948-1966." Unpub. Ph.D. diss., Missouri, 1966. MEX

1641 ____. *The Golden Thread and Other Plays.* Austin: University of Texas Press, 1970. MEX

Translation of Carballido plays: The Golden Thread, The Mirror, The Time and the Place, Theseus, The Intermediate Zone, *and the* Clockmaker from Córdoba.
Reviewed: Colecchia, Francesca; Lyday, Leon; Rabkin, Gerald; Skinner, Eugene.

1642 Peden, Margaret S. "Greek Myth in Contemporary Mexican Theatre," *Modern Drama*, XII, No. 3 (Dec 1969), 221-230. MEX

1643 ____. Review:"William I. Oliver. *Voices of Change in the Spanish American Theater*. Austin and London: University of Texas Press, 1971." *Latin American Theatre Review*, 6/1 (Fall 1972), 91. GEN

1644 ____. "Theory and Practice in Artaud and Carballido," *Modern Drama*, XI, (set 1968), 132-142. MEX

1645 ____. "Three Plays of Egon Wolff," *Latin American Theatre Review*, 3/1 (Fall 1969), 29-35. CHILE

1646 Peirano, Luis. "¿En qué consiste el teatro experimental?" *Textual* (Lima), No. 2 (set 1971), 31-34. GEN

1647 Peiser, Werner. "El barroco en la literatura mexicana," *Revista Iberoamericana*, No. 11 (Feb 1943), 77-93. MEX

Some reference to Sor Juana's autos.

1648 Peixoto, Fernando. "Problemas do Teatro no Brasil," *Revista Civilização Brasileira*, No. 15 (set 1967), 229-243. BRAZ

Also in Conjunto, *No. 9 (s.f.), 2-13.*

1649 ____. "Teatro no Brasil: Como transmitir sinais de dentro das chamas," *Latin American Theatre Review*, 7/1 (Fall 1973), 91-98. BRAZ

1650 Pelayo, Félix M. "César Iglesias Paz y su problemática de la clase media," *Revista de Estudios de Teatro*, III, No. 9 (1965), 54-63. ARG

1651 ____. "Miguel Faust Rocha," *Revista de Estudios de Teatro*, II, No. 6 (1963), 46-52. ARG

Argentine actor, 1898-1961, born Miguel Angel Faust.

1652 ____. "Tres corrientes formativas, tres autores," *Lyra*, XVII, No. 174-176 (1959). ARG

Siripo, Juan Moreira, *and* M'hijo el dotor; *Bernardo Canal Feijoo, Claudio Martínez Paiva, and Carlos Carlino.*

1653 Pellegrini, Aldo. *Teatro de la inestable realidad.* Buenos Aires: Ediciones del Carro de Tespia, 1964. 61 p. ARG

1654 Peñalosa Rueda, Juan. "El teatro de Colón," *Revista de las Indias* (Bogotá), XXXVII, No. 15 (set-oct 1950), 86-92. COL

1655 Peniche Vallado, Leopoldo. "José Antonio Cisneros, poeta, dramaturgo y hombre público," *Revista de la Universidad de Yucatán*, VIII, No. 45-46 (mayo-ago 1966), 45-68. MEX

1656 Pepe, Luz E. A. and María Luisa Punte. *La crítica teatral argentina (1880-1962).* Buenos Aires: Fondo Nacional de las Artes, 1966. 78 p. ARG

1657 Peraza, Fermín. "Bibliografía de José Antonio Ramos," *Revista Iberoamericana*, No. 24 (jun 1947), 335-400. CUBA

1658 Peraza, Luis. "El indio y el negro en nuestro teatro," *El Farol* (Caracas), mayo 1946, 2, 30. VEN

1659 ____. "Leopoldo Ayala Michelena y el teatro de Venezuela," *Boletín de Estudios de Teatro*, VIII, No. 31 (oct-dic 1950), 137-143. VEN

1660 Percas, Helena. Review: "José Juan Arrom. *El teatro de Hispanoamérica en la época colonial.* La Habana: Anuario Bibliográfico Cubano, 1956." *Revista Iberoamericana*, No. 44 (jul-dic 1957), 413-414. GEN

1661 Peredo Meza, Saúl. "Revelación de un nuevo manuscrito del Usca Paucar," *Literatura de la emancipación hispanoamericana y otros ensayos.* Lima: Universidad Nacional Mayor de San Marcos, Dirección Universitaria de Biblioteca y Publicaciones, 1972, pp. 297-301. PERU

1662 Pereira, José, ed. *Teatro e Cinema: Da Condenação do seu Desvirtuamento.* São Paulo: Exposição do Livro Editora, 1961. BRAZ

1663 Pereira, Teresinha Alves. "La estructura de *El último cargo*," *Latin American Theatre Review*, 8/1 (Fall 1974), 91-92. GUAT

On Manuel Galich's play.

1664 Pereira, Teresinha Alves. Review: "Héctor Azar. *Una proposición teatral: El espacio.* México: Universidad Nacional de México, 1972." *Latin American Theatre Review*, 6/2 (Spring 1973), 75-76. GEN

1665 ____. "II [i.e., Segundo] Festival de Teatro Latinoamericano, 1972: Depoimento," *Latin American Theatre Review*, 5/2 (Spring 1972), 63-66. GEN

1666 ____. "Sobre el tema de *María Soledad*," *Vida Universitaria* (Monterrey), 26 nov 1972, p. 11. PTO. RICO

On Francisco Arriví's María Soledad.

1667 ____. "Sobre un drama amoroso y político con Catulo y Lesbia," *Conjunto*, No. 15 (ene-mar 1973), 17-18. GUAT

On Manuel Galich's El pescado indigesto.

1668 ____. "Los temas permisibles en el teatro brasileño," *Conjunto*, No. 22 (oct-dic 1974), 83-85. BRAZ

1669 Pereira Salas, Eugenio. "El teatro en Santiago del Nuevo Extremo, 1709-1809," *Revista Chilena de Historia y Geografía*, XC, No. 98 (ene-jun 1941), 30-59. CHILE

Also as book, Santiago de Chile: Imprenta Universitaria, 1941. 56 p.
Reviewed: Jones, Willis Knapp.

1670 Pereyra Olazábal, Renée. *Casacuberta.* Buenos Aires: Kraft, 1956. 345 p. [Colección Vértice.] ARG

1671 Pérez Castro, Roberto. "El teatro independiente en la Argentina," *Boletín de Estudios de Teatro*, IV, No. 12 (mar 1946), 34-37. ARG

1672 Pérez Estrada, Francisco. *Teatro folklore nicaragüense.* Managua: Editorial Nuevos Horizontes, 1946. 177 p. NIC

1673 Pérez Vila, Manuel. "Polémicas sobre representaciones dramáticas: 1775-1829," *Revista Nacional de Cultura* (Caracas), 20, No. 127 (mar-abr 1958), 95-104. VEN

1674 ____. "El teatro en la Venezuela colonial," in

Venezuela 1498-1810. Caracas: Amigos del Museo de Bellas Artes de Caracas, 1965, pp. 69-92. VEN

1675 Perkins, Blasco. "Reseña del III Festival de Teatro Venezolano," *Zona Franca* (Caracas), 3, No. 42 (feb 1967), 38-39. VEN

1676 Pesante, Edgardo A. "Situación del autor teatral de la Argentina," *Universidad* (Santa Fe), No. 64 (abr-jun 1965), 217-237. ARG

1677 Petit, Magdalena. "The Little Theater in Chile," *Bulletin of the Pan American Union*, 82, No. 10 (Oct 1948), 560-565. CHILE

1678 Phillips, Jordan B. *Thirty Years of Puerto Rican Drama: 1938-1968*. Madrid: Ediciones Plaza Mayor, 1972. 220 p. PTO. RICO
Reviewed: Ceide-Echevarría, Gloria.

1679 Pianca, Marina and Domingo LoGiudice. "Primer festival internacional de teatro latinoamericano (San Francisco, California)," *Latin American Theatre Review*, 6/1 (Fall 1972), 77-85. GEN

1680 Piazza, Luis Guillermo, ed. *¿Qué pasa con el teatro en México?* México: Editorial Novaro, 1967. 204 p. MEX

A collection of essays by leading Mexican playwrights, directors and critics.

1681 Pichel, José. "Theater in the Americas," *Américas*, 11, No. 4 (Apr 1959), 22-27. GEN

1682 Pickenhayn, Jorge Oscar. "*La Salamanca* de Ricardo Rojas," *Nosotros*, 2ª época, XXII, No. 90 (set 1943), 307-310. ARG

1683 Piga T., Domingo. "Declaración de principios del Departamento de Teatro de la Universidad de Chile," *Conjunto*, 3, No. 7 (s.f.), 99-102. CHILE

1684 ____. "Experiencias teatrales de hoy, chilenas y latinoamericanas," *Revista de la Universidad de México*, XXVI, No. 6-7 (feb-mar 1972), 73-78. CHILE GEN

1685 ____. "Problemas del teatro popular," *Conjunto*, No. 14 (set-dic 1972), 8-13. GEN

1686 Pignataro, Jorge. *El teatro independiente uruguayo.* Montevideo: Arca, 1968. 134 p. URUG

1687 Pilditch, Charles. "La escena puertorriqueña--*Los soles truncos*," *Asomante*, XVII, No. 2 (1961), 51-58. PTO. RICO

On René Marqués's Los soles truncos.

1688 ____. "A Study of the Literary Works of René Marqués from 1948 to 1962." Unpub. Ph.D. diss., Rutgers, 1966. PTO. RICO

1689 Pimentel, A. Fonseca. *O Teatro de Nelson Rodrigues.* Rio de Janeiro: Edições Margem, 1951. 126 p. BRAZ

1690 Pineda, Rafael. "Pasado y presente del teatro en Venezuela," *El Farol* (Caracas), 15, No. 150 (feb 1954), 32-33. VEN

1691 Piñera, Virgilio. "Notas sobre el teatro cubano," *Unión*, VI, No. 2 (abr-jun 1967), 130-142. CUBA

1692 ____. "Notes sur le théâtre cubain," *Cahiers Renaud-Barrault*, No. 75 (1° trimestre 1971), 27-42. CUBA

1693 ____. "El teatro actual," *Casa de las Américas*, IV, No. 22-23 (ene-abr 1964), 95-107. CUBA

Round table, with participants Antón Arrufat, José Triana, Abelardo Estorino, José R. Brene, Nicolás Dorr.

1694 Pinto, Juan. "El inmigrante en nuestro teatro," *Universidad* (Santa Fe), No. 59 (ene-mar 1964), 41-62. ARG

1695 Pita Rodríguez, Félix. "Sobre *El último cargo*," *Conjunto*, No. 20 (abr-jun 1974), 81-82. GUAT

On Manuel Galich's play.

1696 Pizano y Saucedo, Carlos. "Centenario del Teatro Degollado de Guadalajara," *Historia Mexicana*, No. 16 (1966-67), 419-426. MEX

1697 Pla, Josefina. "En torno al personaje teatral contemporáneo," *Cuadernos Americanos*, XII, No. 4 (jul-ago 1953), 276-291. GEN

1698 Pla, Josefina. "Paraguay, su teatro actual," *Talía*, 5, No. 30 (1966), 13. PARA

1699 ____. "El teatro en Paraguay," *Escena* (Lima), 1, No. 2 (dic 1953), 20-21, 24. PARA

1700 ____. "El teatro en el Paraguay (1554-1870)," *Cuadernos Americanos*, XXIV, 141, No. 4 (jul-ago 1965), 201-222. PARA

1701 ____. *El teatro en el Paraguay. Primera parte: De la fundación a 1870*. Asunción: Escuela Salesiana, 1967. 92 p. PARA
Reviewed: Jones, Willis Knapp.

1702 ____. "El teatro paraguayo actual," *Alcor* (Asunción), No. 41 (1966), 21-23. PARA

1703 ____. "Teatro religioso medieval: su brote en Paraguay," *Cuadernos Hispanoamericanos*, No. 291 (set 1974), 666-680. PARA

1704 ____. "300 años de teatro paraguayo," *Comunidades* (Asunción), ene-abr 1965. PARA

1705 Podestá, Blanca. *Historia del Teatro Smart*. [Treinta años de una empresa argentina al servicio de la cultura, 1924-1954.] Buenos Aires: Kraft, 1953. 38 p. ARG

1706 Podestá, Bruno A. "Del T.U.C., su evolución y sus montajes," *Latin American Theatre Review*, 6/1 (Fall 1972), 87-90. PERU

Teatro de la Universidad Católica, Lima.

1707 ____. "Teatro Nacional Popular: Un teatro popular o la popularización del teatro?" *Latin American Theatre Review*, 7/1 (Fall 1973), 33-41. PERU

An interview with Alonso Alegría.

1708 Ponferrada, Juan Oscar. "Una experiencia nada inútil de teatro," *Dinámica social* (Buenos Aires), 8, No. 83/84 (nov 1957), 41-43. ARG

1709 ____. *Ezequiel Soria*. Buenos Aires: Ediciones Culturales Argentinas, Ministerio de Educación y Justicia, 1961. 55 p. ARG

1710 Ponferrada, Juan Oscar. "Orígenes y rumbos del teatro argentino," in *Argentina en Marcha*. Buenos Aires: Comisión Nacional de Cooperación Intelectual, 1947, I, 311-335. ARG

Also in Boletín de Estudios de Teatro *(Buenos Aires), 6, No. 20-21 (mar-jun 1948), 55-64.*

1711 ____. "Para una ubicación del costumbrismo criollo," *Lyra*, XVII, No. 174-176 (1959). ARG

1712 ____. "La sugestión telúrica en el teatro de Julio Sánchez Gardel," *Cuadernos de Cultura Teatral* (Buenos Aires), No. 22 (1947). Reviewed: Kurz, Harry. ARG

1713 Pontes, Joel. "Agora, Brasil, Teatro," *Caderno* [published with *O Tempo e o Modo*], No. 50 (jul-oct 1967), 142-147. BRAZ

1714 ____. "Dramaturgia Contemporânea no Brasil," *Luso-Brazilian Review*, III, No. 2 (Winter 1966), 25-42. BRAZ

1715 ____. *Machado de Assis e o Teatro*. Rio de Janeiro: Campanha Nacional de Teatro, Ministério de Educação e Cultura, 1960. 89 p. BRAZ

1716 ____. "Orígenes del teatro en Brasil," *Revista de la Universidad de México*, 20, No. 6 (feb 1966), 12-16. BRAZ

1717 ____. "Plínio Marcos, Dramaturgo da Violência," *Latin American Theatre Review*, 3/1 (Fall 1969), 17-27. BRAZ

1718 ____. "Os Primeiros Anos do Teatro no Brasil," in *El teatro en Iberoamérica* (Memoria del duodécimo congreso del Instituto Internacional de Literatura Iberoamericana.) México: IILI, 1966. BRAZ

1719 ____. "Recife: Um Centro de Renascimento Teatral no Brasil," *Comentário*, I (1961), 75-79. BRAZ

1720 ____. *O Teatro Moderno em Pernambuco*. São Paulo: Editôra São Paulo, 1966. 157 p. BRAZ

1721 ____. "O Teatro Sério de Artur Azevedo,"

Segundo Congresso Brasileiro, No. 37 (1964), 237-259. BRAZ

1722 Poore, Charles. "The Theatre in Mexico," *The International House Quarterly* (New York), 14, No. 4 (Autumn 1950), 235-238. MEX

1723 Porto, B. Marcel. "Existencia y dinamismo del teatro independiente," *Histonium* (Buenos Aires), 7, No. 77 (oct 1945), 695-698. ARG

1724 Portugal Catacora, José. "El teatro puñeno," *Escena* (Lima), 1, No. 2 (dic 1953), 12-13, 16, 26. PERU

1725 Portuondo, José Antonio. "El contenido político y social de las obras de José Antonio Ramos," *Revista Iberoamericana*, No. 24 (jun 1947), 215-250. CUBA

1726 ____ et al. *Panorama de la literatura cubana: conferencias*. La Habana: Universidad de La Habana, Centro de Estudios Cubanos, 1970. 239 p. [*Cuadernos Cubanos*, No. 12] CUBA

A series of lectures on Cuban literature. The last one, by Camila Henríquez Ureña, deals with the post-1959 period and emphasizes poetry and theater.

1727 Posada, Rafael. "Análisis tagmémico del idiolecto literario colombiano de Luis Enrique Osorio Morales: aplicación del análisis adverbial a seis obras dramáticas." Unpub. Ph. D. diss., Indiana, 1969. COL

1728 Potenze, Jaime. "Breve historia crítica del teatro argentino," *Cuadernos Hispanoamericanos*, No. 13 (ene-feb 1950), 99-111. ARG

Also in Lugones *(Córdoba), I, No. 1 (jul-set 1968), 99-118.*

1729 ____. "Del teatro del absurdo al teatro del optimismo," *Conjunto*, No. 13 (mayo-ago 1972), 98-105. GEN

1730 ____. "Encuesta sobre el teatro argentino," *Criterio* (Buenos Aires), 18 abr 1946, 354-356. ARG

1731 ____. "Influencia de Brecht en el teatro argentino," *Conjunto*, No. 19 (ene-mar 1974), 99-101. ARG

1732 Pottlitzer, Joanne. "Conformists in the Heart (An Interview with Richard Schechner)," *The Drama Review*, 14, No. 2 (Winter 1970), 39-42. GEN

1733 ____. "Theatre of a Forgotten Continent," *The Drama Review*, 14, No. 2 (Winter 1970), 34-38. GEN

1734 "El Premio Casa de las Américas 1973 y el autor premiado," *Conjunto*, No. 15 (ene-mar 1973), 2-3. CHILE

On Víctor Torres and his Una casa en Lota Alta.

1735 Presa Camino, Fernando de la. "Panorama actual del teatro peruano," *Fanal*, 16, No. 58 (1961), 26-31. PERU

1736 Preto-Rodas, Richard A. "Anchieta and Vieira: Drama as Sermon, Sermon as Drama," *Luso-Brazilian Review*, VII, No. 2 (Dec 1970), 96-103. BRAZ

1737 Prida Santacilia, Pablo. *Y se levanta el telón. Mi vida dentro del teatro*. México: Botas, 1960. 346 p. MEX

1738 "Primer festival de teatro nuevo de Latinoamérica," *Boletín* de la Comunidad Latinoamericana de Escritores (México), No. 2 (oct 1968), 34-35. GEN

1739 "Primer festival de verano," *Revista de Bellas Artes*, No. 11 (set-oct 1966), 105. MEX

1740 "Primera Reunión Nacional de Dramaturgos (20 al 24 de octubre de 1958)," *Anales de la Universidad de Chile*, 117, No. 115 (3er trimestre 1959), 114-135. CHILE

1741 Putnam, Samuel. Review: "Antonio Magaña Esquivel. *Imagen del teatro*. México: Ediciones Letras de México, 1940." *Books Abroad*, 15, No. 3 (Summer 1941), 329. MEX

1742 Quackenbush, L. H. "The 'auto' in Contemporary

Mexican Drama," *Kentucky Romance Quarterly*, XXI, No. 1 (1974), 15-30. MEX

1743 Quackenbush, L. H. "The 'auto' in the Contemporary Latin American Drama." Unpub. Ph.D. diss., Illinois, 1970. GEN

1744 ____. "The 'auto' Tradition in Brazilian Drama," *Latin American Theatre Review*, 5/2 (Spring 1972), 29-43. BRAZ

1745 ____. "Cuestión de vida y muerte: tres dramas existenciales," *Latin American Theatre Review*, 8/1 (Fall 1974), 49-56. MEX PAN

On El 9 *of Maruxa Vilalta, and* Juicio final *and* Enemigos *of José de Jesús Jiménez.*

1746 ____. "The Magian Kings Religious Drama in Latin American Theatre," *Latin American Literary Review*, II, No. 4 (Spring-Summer 1974), 139-148. GEN

1747 ____. "The Other *Pastorelas* of Spanish American Drama," *Latin American Theatre Review*, 6/2 (Spring 1973), 55-63. GEN

1748 Quintana, Marta. "Adecuación del espacio teatral," *Aisthesis*, No. 1 (1966), 63-75. CHILE

The theater houses of Santiago.

1749 Quintana, Raúl. "The Position of Rodolfo Usigli in the Mexican Theater." Unpub. Ph.D. diss., Southern California, 1972. MEX

1750 Quinto, José María de. "Primer informe americano," *Primer Acto*, No. 67 (1965), 12-21. GEN

The author's first impressions of Spanish American theater.

1751 ____. "Recuerdo emocional de Sebastián Salazar Bondy," *Primer Acto*, No. 69 (1965), 63-64. PERU

1752 ____. "Teatro cubano actual," *Insula*, No. 260-261 (1968), 3, 24-26. CUBA

1753 ____. "Teatro en América," *Insula*, No. 251 (1967), 14-15. GEN

1754 Quinto, José María de. "El teatro en Iberoamérica," *Insula*, No. 224-225 (1965), 25; No. 226, p. 13; No. 227, p. 28-29; No. 238 (1966), 14-15. GEN

Touring Spanish critic's comments on Spanish American theater.

1755 Quiroga, Carlos B. "Aparición y formación del teatro nacional; cómo deben presentarse sus características regionales," *Cuadernos de Cultura Teatral*, No. 17 (1942), 9-24. ARG

1756 Rabassa, Clementine C. "Demetrio Aguilera Malta and Epic Tradition." Unpub. Ph.D. diss., Columbia, 1971. ECUAD

1757 ____. "Prolegómeno al tema del negro en la obra de Demetrio Aguilera Malta," *Revista de la Comunidad Latinoamericana de Escritores* (México), No. 15 (1974), 22-25. ECUAD

1758 Rabell, Malkah. "Algunos ángulos del teatro en México," *Revista de la Universidad de México*, XXVI, No. 3 (nov 1971), 43-44. MEX

1759 ____. "Crisis, inquietudes, experimentaciones," *Revista de la Universidad de México*, XVII, No. 4 (dic 1972), 45-46. GEN

Discusses Shhhagrada *by Joel Novok and Marta Esviza;* Tu propiedad privada no es la mía *by Juan Carlos Uviedo;* Evangelios *by Julio Castillo.*

1760 ____. "Experimentos de espectáculo total: Ramos, Carbajal, Weisz," *Revista de la Universidad de México*, XXVI, No. 12 (ago 1972), 40-41. GEN

Adrián Ramos, Oceanic 13; *Roberto Carbajal,* Señora ascua del arcano naciente; *Gabriel Weisz,* Golem.

1761 ____. "*El juicio* y el caso de Aarón Hernán," *Revista de la Universidad de México*, XXVI, No. 9 (mayo 1972), 39-40. MEX

The actor Aarón Hernán in the Vicente Leñero play.

1762 Rabell, Malkah. "Lo actual en el Festival Latinoamericano," *Revista de la Universidad de México*, XXVI, No. 10 (jun 1972), 45-46. GEN

Concentrates on Osvaldo Dragún, Milagro en el mercado viejo; *Jorge Díaz*, Topografía de un desnudo; *Ivan García,* Fábula de los cinco caminantes.

1763 ____. "Un misterio: El teatro prehispánico," *Revista Mexicana de Cultura*, VI época, No. 60 (22 mar 1970), 1-2. GEN

1764 Rabkin, Gerald. "Rehearsing Latin American Drama," *Review 74* (New York), Winter [i.e., 1974], 62-71. GEN

A review essay on William Oliver's Voices of Change in the Spanish American Theatre, *George Woodyard's* The Modern Stage in Latin America: Six Plays, *Margaret Peden's translations of Emilio Carballido's* The Golden Thread and Other Plays *and Egon Wolff's* Paper Flowers, *and Derek Walcott's* Dream on Monkey Mountain.

1765 Radcliff-Umstead, Douglas. "Solórzano's Tormented Puppets," *Latin American Theatre Review*, 4/2 (Spring 1971), 5-11. GUAT

1766 Raeders, George. "Orígenes del teatro brasileño," *Revista de Estudios de Teatro*, No. 3 (1960), 58-60. BRAZ

1767 Rael, Juan B. "More Light on the Origin of *Los pastores*," *New Mexico Folklore Record*, No. 6 (1951-52), 1-6. U.S.

1768 ____. *The Sources and Diffusion of the Mexican Shepherds' Plays* (Origin and Development of the auto pastoril in Spain and Mexico). Guadalajara: La Joyita, 1965. 644 p. MEX

1769 Ragle, Gordon. "Rodolfo Usigli and his Mexican Scene," *Hispania*, XLVI, No. 2 (May 1963), 307-311. MEX

1770 Ramírez, Manuel D. "Florencio Sánchez and his Social Consciousness of the River Plate Region," *Journal of Inter-American Studies*, 8, No. 4 (1966), 585-594. RIVER PLATE

1771 Ramírez, Octavio. *Treinta años de teatro, 1925-1955*. Buenos Aires: Fondo Nacional de las Artes, 1963. 695 p. ARG

"Teatro rioplatense," pp. 3-162.

1772 Ramón y Rivera, Luis Felipe. "El teatro popular en Venezuela," *Boletín del Instituto de Folklore* (Caracas), 2, No. 8 (nov 1957), 261-266. VEN

1773 Ratcliff, Dillwyn F. "Folklore and Satire in a Brazilian Comedy," *Hispania*, XLIV, No. 2 (May 1961), 282-284. BRAZ

On Suassuna's Auto da Compadecida.

1774 ____. "Representative Plays of Northeastern Brazil," *Kentucky Foreign Language Quarterly*, IX, No. 2 (1962), 86-92. BRAZ

1775 Ratto Valerga, T. O. "El teatro en la cultura cubana," *Máscara* (Buenos Aires), 8, No. 94 (jul 1948), 12-14. CUBA

1776 Rau Alliende, Erwin. "Breve reseña histórica del teatro aficionado chileno," *Conjunto*, No. 13 (mayo-ago 1972), 86-89. CHILE

1777 Ravicz, Marilyn Ekdahl. *Early Colonial Religious Drama in Mexico: From Tzompantli to Golgotha*. Washington: Catholic University of America Press, 1970. 263 p. MEX
Reviewed: Huerta, Jorge A.

1778 Reedy, Daniel and Robert J. Morris. "The Lima Theatre, 1966-67," *Latin American Theatre Review*, 1/1 (Fall 1967), 26-38. PERU

1779 Reeve, Richard. "Sobre Carlos Fuentes, *Los reinos imaginarios: Todos los gatos son pardos* y *El tuerto es rey*," *Revista Iberoamericana*, No. 78 (ene-mar 1972), 170-173. MEX

1780 *References on Latin American music, the theatre and the dance*. Washington: Pan American Union, 1942. 9 leaves. GEN

1781 Reid, John T. "José Antonio Ramos y la literatura norteamericana," *Revista Iberoamericana*, No. 24 (jun 1947), 273-277. CUBA

1782 Rela, Walter. *Breve historia del teatro uruguayo. I, De la colonia al 900.* Buenos Aires: Editorial Universitaria de Buenos Aires, 1966. 138 p. URUG

Anthologizes: Bartolomé Hidalgo, Sentimiento de un patriota; *Víctor Pérez Petit,* Cobarde; *Florencio Sánchez,* En familia.

1783 ____. "Celebraciones teatrales y fiestas en el Paraguay colonial. Esquema histórico-bibliográfico," *Revista Iberoamericana de Literatura,* I, No. 1 (ago 1959), 65-88. PARA

Also in Revista de Estudios de Teatro, *3, No. 9 (1965), 64-82.*

1784 ____. "La colonia y la revolución, dos poetas en el teatro del Río de la Plata a comienzos del siglo XIX," *Revista de Estudios de Teatro,* II, No. 4 (1962), 42-54. RIVER PLATE

Among others, Juan Francisco Martínez and Bartolomé Hidalgo.

1785 ____. "Dramaturgia suramericana," *Idea: Artes y Letras* (Lima), 9, No. 37-38 (jun-dic 1958), 5; 10, No. 39-40 (ene-jun 1959), 4, 10. GEN

1786 ____. "Ernesto Herrera," *Revista de la Biblioteca Nacional,* I, No. 1 (1966), 233-234. URUG

1787 ____. *Florencio Sánchez, guía bibliográfica.* Montevideo: Editorial Ulises, 1967. 104 p. URUG

1788 ____. "Frecuencia del tema regional en el teatro sudamericano contemporáneo," *Anales de la Universidad de Chile,* CXVIII, No. 117 (1960), 195-201. GEN

1789 ____. *Historia del teatro uruguayo, 1808-1968.* Montevideo: Ediciones de la Banda Oriental, 1969. 187 p. URUG

1790 ____. "Literatura dramática suramericana contemporánea," *I. E. S.* (Montevideo), 1, No. 2 (ene-jun 1957), 104-124. GEN

Also in Universidad *(Santa Fe), No. 36 (dic 1957), 147-170.*

1791 ____. *El mito Santos Vega en el teatro del Río*

de la Plata. 3ª ed. Montevideo: Editorial Ciudad Vieja, 1966. 57 p. RIVER PLATE

1792 Rela, Walter. *El teatro brasileño.* Buenos Aires: Centro Editor de América Latina, 1969. 77 p. BRAZ

1793 ____. "Teatro brasileño; de las piezas de Padre Anchieta a la comedia costumbrista," *Revista Iberoamericana de Literatura* (Montevideo), IV, No. 4 (1962), 29-62. BRAZ

1794 ____. *Teatro completo de Ernesto Herrera.* Montevideo, 1965. [Prólogo y bibliografía.] URUG

1795 Retes Bisetti, Rogel. *El último mutis: Memorias de 58 años de teatro en Perú, Chile, Argentina, Uruguay y Bolivia.* Santiago: Talleres Gráficos, "La Nación," 1961. 280 p. GEN

1796 Revello, Edovico. "Apuntes para una historia del teatro uruguayo," *Comentario* (Buenos Aires), 12, No. 45 (nov-dic 1965), 67-75. URUG

1797 Revuelta, Vicente. "Un théâtre d'imprécation," *Cahiers Renaud-Barrault*, No. 75 (s.f.), 3-8. CUBA

1798 Rey, Luis. "Graves problemas afronta el teatro nacional," *Máscara* (Buenos Aires), 6, No. 70 (jul 1946), 27-28. ARG

1799 Reyes, Alfonso. "Los autos sacramentales en España y América," in his *Capítulos de literatura española.* 2ª serie. México: El Colegio de México, 1945, pp. 115-128. GEN

1800 ____. "El teatro criollo en el siglo XVI," in *Letras de la Nueva España.* México: Fondo de Cultura Económica, 1948. MEX

Reproduced in Obras completas de Alfonso Reyes, *Vol. XII. (Letras mexicanas.) México: Fondo de Cultura Económica, 1960.*

1801 Reyes, Carlos José. "Notas sobre la práctica teatral: la improvisación," *Conjunto*, No. 22 (oct-dic 1974), 43-53. COL

On the "creación colectiva" in theory, but with some reference to Colombia.

1802 ____. "Posibilidades y problemas del teatro

popular en Colombia," *Revista Casa de la Cultura*, No. 1 (jun-ago 1968), 19-25. COL

1803 Reyes, Carlos José. "Proyección del TEC en el teatro nacional," *Letras Nacionales* (Bogotá), II, No. 8 (mayo-jun 1966), 33-36. COL

1804 ____. "El teatro en Colombia en 1968," *Conjunto*, III, No. 8 (1969), 99-104. COL

1805 ____. "El teatro nacional, un reencuentro con la realidad," *Letras Nacionales* (Bogotá), I, No. 0 (feb 1965), 73-76. COL

1806 Reyes de la Maza, Luis. *Cien años de teatro en México (1810-1910)*. México: SepSetentas, 1972. MEX

1807 ____. "Francisco González Bocanegra, dramaturgo," *Anales del Instituto de Investigaciones Estéticas* (México), No.11 (1962), 79-88. MEX

1808 ____. "Poe volvió a morir," en "México en la cultura," Supl. de *Novedades* (13 mayo 1973), p. 5. ARG

Critique of Israfel *by Abelardo Castillo.*

1809 ____. *El teatro en México con Lerdo y Díaz, 1873-1879*. México: Instituto de Investigaciones Estéticas, UNAM, 1963. 345 p. MEX

1810 ____. *El teatro en México durante el Porfirismo*. 3 vol. México: Instituto de Investigaciones Estéticas, UNAM, 1964-1968. MEX

Vol. I, 1880-1887 (1964), 379 p.; Vol. 2, 1888-1899 (1965), 433 p.; Vol. 3, 1900-1910 (1968), 545 p.

1811 ____. *El teatro en México durante el Segundo Imperio (1862-1867)*. México: Instituto de Investigaciones Estéticas, UNAM, 1959. 238 p. MEX

1812 ____. *El teatro en México durante la independencia (1810-1839)*. México: Instituto de Investigaciones Estéticas, UNAM, 1969. 429 p. MEX

1813 ____. *El teatro en México en la época de Juárez (1868-1872)*. México: Instituto de Investigaciones Estéticas, UNAM, 1961. 249 p. MEX

1814 Reyes de la Maza, Luis. *El teatro en México en la época de Santa Ana.* Vol. I. México: Instituto de Investigaciones Estéticas, UNAM, 1972. MEX

1815 ____. *El teatro en México entre la Reforma y el Imperio (1858-1861).* México: Instituto de Investigaciones Estéticas, UNAM, 1958. 195 p. MEX

1816 ____. *El teatro en 1857 y sus antecedentes (1855-1856).* México: Instituto de Investigaciones Estéticas, UNAM, 1956. 430 p. MEX

1817 Reynolds, C. Russell. "The Santa María Egipciaca Motif in Modern Brazilian Letters," *Romance Notes*, XIII, No. 1 (Autumn 1971), 71-76. BRAZ

Includes commentary on Rachel de Queiroz's A Beata Maria de Egito.

1818 Rial Vázquez, José. "El dramaturgo Rodolfo Usigli y el teatro mexicano," *Tierra Firme* (Caracas), I, No. 6 (ago 1952), 23. MEX

1819 Ribeiro, Camila. "Novos caminhos do teatro universitário (O teatro universitário em marcha com o CPC)," *Revista Brasiliense,* No. 43 (1962), 188-190. BRAZ

1820 Ribeiro, Leo Gilson. "O Sol sôbre o Pantano: Nelson Rodrigues, um expressionista brasileiro," *Cadernos Brasileiros*, VI, No. 1 (jan-fev 1964), 50-65. BRAZ

1821 Rica, Carlos de la. "Anotaciones en torno a *O Pagador de Promessas*," *Revista de Cultura Brasileña*, No. 19 (dic 1966), 390-395. BRAZ

1822 ____. "*Morte y Vida Severina* (auto navideño pernambucano)," *Revista de Cultura Brasileña*, No. 23 (dic 1967), 351-357. BRAZ

1823 Richards, Stanley. "Brazilian Theatre," *Theatre Arts*, 47, No. 2 (Feb 1963), 64-65. BRAZ

1824 ____. "The New Brazilian Theatre," *Players*, XVI (Apr 1965), 172-173. BRAZ

1825 ____. "Theatre in Brazil," *Players*, XXXVII (Dec 1960), 57; XXXVIII (Nov 1961), 56. BRAZ

1826 Richardson, Ruth. "The Argentine Theater and Florencio Sánchez," in *Studies in Honor of Samuel Montefiore Waxman*, ed. by Herbert H. Golden. Boston: Boston University Press, 1969, pp. 232-240. RIVER PLATE

1827 Río, Amalia del. "Germán Luco Cruchaga, *La viuda de Apablaza;* Fernando Debesa, *Mamá Rosa;* Luis Alberto Heiremans, *Moscas sobre el mármol*," *Revista Hispánica Moderna*, XXVI, No. 3-4 (jul-oct 1960), 162. CHILE

1828 Río, Marcela del. "Alejandro Sieveking y el teatro en Chile," *Cuadernos de Bellas Artes*, 2, No. 4 (abr 1961), 31-36. CHILE

1829 ____. "La Argentina y el teatro de los 21," *Cuadernos de Bellas Artes*, 2, No. 12 (dic 1961), 19-28. ARG

Interview with Carlos Catania and other Argentine directors.

1830 ____. "*La noche de los asesinos* puesta por Juan José Gurrola," *Revista de Bellas Artes*, No. 18 (nov-dic 1967), 85-86. CUBA MEX

On Gurrola's production of the José Triana play.

1831 Ríos, Juan. "*Los invasores* de Egon Wolff," *Expreso* (Lima), 15 set 1965. CHILE

1832 Ripoll, Carlos and Andrés Valdespino. *Teatro hispanoamericano* (antología crítica). 2 vol. New York: Anaya Book Co., 1972-73. GEN

Prologues and bibliographies. Vol. I (Epoca colonial): Juan Pérez Ramírez, Desposorio espiritual entre el pastor Pedro y la iglesia mexicana; *Cristóbal de Llerena,* Entremés; *Fernán González de Eslava,* Coloquio séptimo; *Juan Ruiz de Alarcón,* La verdad sospechosa *and* Ganar amigos; *Juan del Valle y Caviedes,* El amor alcalde, Baile cantado del amor médico, *and* Coloquio entre la vieja y el Periquillo sobre una procesión celebrada en Lima; *Sor Juana Inés de la Cruz,* El Divino Narciso *and* Los empeños de una casa; *Juan de Espinosa Medrano,* Amar su propia muerte; *Pedro de Peralta Barnuevo,* Fin de fiesta de la comedia "Afectos vencen finezas" *and* El Mercurio galante; Ollanta; El amor de la estanciera. *Vol. II (Siglo XIX): Juan Cruz Varela,* Dido; *Manuel Eduardo de Gorostiza,* Contigo pan y cebolla; *Ignacio Rodríguez Galván,* Muñoz, visitador de México; *Gertrudis Gómez de Avellaneda,* La hija de las flores *and* Baltasar; *Manuel Ascensio Segura,* El sargento Canuto; *Ramón Méndez Quiñones,* Los jíbaros progresistas; *Florencio Sánchez,* La gringa, Barranca abajo, *and* Los muertos.

1833 Rivarola Matto, José María. "Julio Correa y el teatro guaraní," *Conjunto*, No. 11-12 (ene-abr 1972), 70-73. PARA

1834 Rivas, Esteban. *Carlos Solórzano y el teatro hispanoamericano.* México, 1970. 183 p. GUAT
Reviewed: Schoenbach, Peter J.

1835 Rivas, Osvaldo. "*Las bodas de Chivico y Pancha,*" *Revista de Estudios de Teatro*, IV, No. 10 (1966), 35-38. ARG

1836 Rivera de Alvarez, Josefina. "Génesis y desarrollo de la dramaturgia puertorriqueña hasta los umbrales de la generación del treinta," *Revista del Instituto de Cultura Puertorriqueña*, XIII, No. 49 (oct-dic 1970), 36-45. PTO. RICO

19th century to the 1930's.

1837 ____. "Orígenes del teatro puertorriqueño: *La juega de gallos o El negro bozal* de Ramón C. F. Caballero," *Revista del Instituto de Cultura Puertorriqueña*, II, No. 3 (abr-jun 1959), 20-25. PTO. RICO

1838 Robb, James Willis. "Alfonso Reyes, *Landrú* y el teatro," *El teatro en Iberoamérica* (Memoria del duodécimo congreso del Instituto Internacional de Literatura Iberoamericana). México: IILI (1966). MEX

1839 ____. "El *Landrú*, opereta póstuma de Alfonso Reyes," *Norte* (Amsterdam), VII, No. 1 (ene-feb 1966), 11-18. MEX

1840 ____. "El revés del calcetín: Alfonso Reyes, *Landrú* y el teatro," *La Palabra y el Hombre*, No. 37 (ene-mar 1966), 25-42. MEX

Also in Nivel *(México), No. 52 (abr 1967), 5-7, 10.*

1841 Robe, Stanley L., ed. *"Coloquio de pastores" from Jalisco, Mexico.* Berkeley and Los Angeles: University of California Folklore Studies, No. 4, 1954. MEX

1842 ____. "The Relationship of *Los pastores* to Other Spanish American Folk Drama," *Western Folklore*, No. 16 (Oct 1957), 281-287. MEX

1843 Robreño, Eduardo. *Historia del teatro popular cubano.* La Habana: Oficina del Historiador de la Ciudad de la Habana, 1961. 93 p. CUBA

1844 Rocha, Daniel. "Gastão Tojeiro," *Revista de Teatro* (Rio), No. 350 (mar-abr 1966), 9-17. BRAZ

1845 ____. "Literatura dramática brasileira; suas orígenes; período colonial," *Revista de Teatro*, No. 362 (mar-abr 1968), 15-16. BRAZ

1846 ____. "Oduvaldo Vianna," *Revista de Teatro*, No. 387 (maio-jun 1972), 7-8. BRAZ

1847 Rocha, Rubem. "A abolição no palco," *Cadernos Brasileiros*, 10, No. 47 (maio-jun 1968), 149-155. BRAZ

1848 ____. "Dois momentos praxis da dramaturgia brasileira," *Praxis* (São Paulo), No. 3 (1963), 65-73. BRAZ

1849 Rodrigues Cruz, Osmar. "Origem da Renovação no Teatro Brasileiro," *Revista Brasiliense*, No. 8 (nov-dez 1956), 106-122. BRAZ

1850 Rodríguez, Carlos. "¿Por qué los festivales anuales de teatro no rinden el fruto esperado?" *Cuadernos de Bellas Artes*, II, No. 2 (1961), 71-76. MEX

1851 Rodríguez, Roberto R. "La fantasía como técnica dramática en la obra seleccionada de Rodolfo Usigli." Unpub. Ph.D. diss., Louisiana State, 1974. MEX

1852 Rodríguez, Walfredo. *História do Teatro da*

Paraíba (Só a Saudade Perdura) 1831-1908. João Pessoa: Imprensa Oficial, 1960. 40 p. BRAZ

1853 Rodríguez Acasuso, Luis. "El teatro y la cultura en las provincias," *Boletín de Estudios de Teatro*, VII, No. 24-25 (ene-jun 1949), 19-21. ARG

1854 ____. "Tres actrices fundamentales de nuestro teatro: Blanca Podestá, Angelina Pagano, Camila Quiroga," *Lyra*, XVII, No. 174-176 (1959). ARG

1855 Rodríguez B., Orlando. "Antonio Acevedo Hernández, el hombre y el creador," in Antonio Acevedo Hernández, *El triángulo tiene cuatro lados*. Santiago: Imprenta Bolívar, 1963. CHILE

1856 ____. "Caminos nuevos en el cuarto festival nacional del teatro aficionado e independiente," *Apuntes*, No. 14 (ago 1961), 1-5. CHILE

1857 ____. "La dramaturgia chilena en los últimos veinte años," *Revista de Estudios de Teatro*, I, No. 3 (1960), 41-46. CHILE

1858 ____. "El significado de Bello en el teatro chileno: *Teresa*," *Mapocho*, IV, No. 12 (1965), 175-187. CHILE

1859 ____. "Síntesis de la evolución del teatro chileno," *Apuntes*, No. 10 (abr 1961), 5-30. CHILE

1860 ____. "El teatro chileno contemporáneo," *Apuntes*, No. 64 (nov-dic 1966), 1-41. CHILE

1861 ____ and Domingo Piga. *Teatro chileno del siglo XX*. Santiago: Universidad de Chile, Escuela de Teatro, 1964. 120 p. CHILE

1862 Rodríguez Bustamante, Norberto. "Una teoría teatral argentina," *Sur*, No. 227 (mar-abr 1954), 77-78. ARG

1863 Rodríguez Castelo, Hernán. "Teatro ecuatoriano," *Cuadernos Hispanoamericanos*, No. 172 (abr 1964), 81-119. ECUAD

1864 ____. "Tres microensayos: un siglo y medio de teatro ecuatoriano," *Letras Nacionales*, No. 8 (mayo-jun 1966), 80-87. ECUAD

1865 Rodríguez Larreta, Horacio. "El Festival de Teatro de Mar del Plata," *Ficción*, No. 7 (may-jun 1957), 112-115. ARG

1866 Rodríguez Monegal, Emir. *Literatura uruguaya del medio siglo*. Montevideo: Editorial Alfa, 1966. 436 p. URUG

Includes sections on Florencio Sánchez, pp. 313-332; Antonio Larreta, pp. 332-345; Carlos Maggi, pp. 346-366.

1867 Rodríguez Rouanet, Francisco. "Notas sobre una representación actual del *Rabinal Achí* o *Baile del Tun*," *Guatemala Indígena*, II, No. 1 (1962), 25-55. GUAT

1868 Rodríguez Sardiñas, Orlando. "Carlos Solórzano," *Chasqui*, No. 1 (ene-feb 1972), 12-19. GUAT

1869 ____. "Fiel y balanza del teatro hispanoamericano contemporáneo," *Exilio* (New York), 6, No. 3 (otoño 1972), 65-80. GEN

1870 ____. Review: "Carlos H. Monsanto. *La protesta social en la dramaturgia de Acevedo Hernández*. México: B. Costa-Amic, 1971." *Latin American Theatre Review*, 6/1 (Fall 1972), 95-97. CHILE

1871 ____ and Carlos Miguel Suárez Radillo. *Teatro selecto contemporáneo hispanoamericano*. 3 vol. Madrid: Escelicer, 1971. GEN

Prologues and bibliographies. Anthology includes: Vol. I: Juan Pérez Carmona, Piedra libre; *Matías Montes Huidobro,* La sal de los muertos; *Roberto A. Menéndez,* La ira del cordero; *Carlos Solórzano,* El hechicero; *José de Jesús Jiménez,* Enemigos; *Francisco Arriví,* Coctel de don Nadie. *Vol. II: Jorge Rozsa,* Hambre; *María Clara Machado,* Pluft, el fantasmita; *Samuel Rovinski,* Gobierno de alcoba; *Rolando Steiner,* La trilogía del matrimonio; *Iván García Guerra,* Don Quijote de todo el mundo; *Mauricio Rosencof,* Los caballos; *César Rengifo,* Las torres y el viento. *Vol. III: Carlos José Reyes,* Metamorfosis; *Egon Wolff,* Flores de papel; *José Martínez Queirolo,* Los unos vs. los otros; *Andrés Morris,* Oficio de hombres; *Maruxa Vilalta,* Cuestión de narices; *Josefina*

Pla, Historia de un número; *Gregor Díaz,* Los del cuatro.

1872 Rodríguez-Seda, Asela Concepción. "George Bernard Shaw in the Hispanic World: His Reception and Influence." Unpub. Ph.D. diss., Illinois, 1973. GEN

1872a ____. "Shaw and the Hispanic World: A Bibliography," *Modern Drama*, XIV, No. 3 (Dec 1971), 335-339. GEN

1873 ____. "Las últimas obras de Usigli: efebocracia o gerontocracia?" *Latin American Theatre Review*, 8/1 (Fall 1974), 45-48. MEX

1874 Roitman, Bernardo. "Apuros de un director mendocino," in *Teatro y universidad*. Tucumán: Facultad de Filosofía y Letras, Universidad Nacional, 1960, pp. 177-189. ARG

1875 Rojas, Arístides. "Orígenes del teatro en Caracas," *Crónica de Caracas*, 4, No. 19 (ago-dic 1954), 575-587. VEN

Also in Cuaderno *(Caracas), No. 1 (jun 1966), 13-24.*

1876 Rojas, Hernán. "El primer festival nacional de teatro aficionado," *Anales de la Universidad de Chile*, No. 101 (1956), 191-195. CHILE

1877 Rojas, María Angélica. "El público asistente a los circos hasta la aparición de *Juan Moreira*," *Revista de Estudios de Teatro*, No. 3 (1960), 50-57. ARG

1878 Rojas, Nerio. "El verdadero Juan Moreira," *Boletín de Estudios de Teatro*, I, No. 2 (jun 1943), 5-13. ARG

1879 Rojas, Ricardo. "El indio en el teatro," *Revista de las Indias* (Bogotá), VIII, No. 25 (ene 1941), 185-192. GEN

1880 Rojas Garcidueñas, José. "Piezas teatrales y representaciones en Nueva España en el siglo XVI," *Revista de Literatura Mexicana*, I, No. 1 (jul-set 1940), 148-154. MEX

A listing only; no critical analysis.

1881 Rojas Garcidueñas, José. "El primer siglo de teatro en México," *Artes de México*, 16, No. 123 (1969). MEX

1882 ____. *El teatro de Nueva España en el siglo XVI.* México: SepSetentas, 1973. (First edition, 1935) 191 p. MEX

1883 Rojas Paz, Pablo. "Payró y su tiempo," *Nosotros*, 2ª época, VII, No. 17 (jun 1942), 217-236. ARG

1884 ____. "El teatro y las ideas," *Cuadernos de Cultura Teatral*, No. 9 (1940), 63-81. GEN

1885 Rojo de la Rosa, Grínor. "Estado actual de las investigaciones sobre teatro hispanoamericano contemporáneo," *Revista Chilena de Literatura*, 2, No. 3 (1970), 133-161. GEN

1886 ____. *Orígenes del teatro hispanoamericano contemporáneo.* (La generación de dramaturgos de 1927: Dos direcciones.) Valparaíso: Ediciones Universitarias de Valparaíso, 1972. 227 p. GEN

1887 Romero Lozano, Bernardo. "Reflexiones sobre teatro nacional," *Revista de América* (Bogotá), VII, No. 20 (ago 1946), 225-229. COL

1888 Romero Peláez, Celso. "El teatro en Venezuela: problemas y soluciones," *Cultura Universitaria* (Caracas), No. 57 (set-oct 1956), 112-115. VEN

1889 Rosa-Nieves, Cesáreo. "Notas para los orígenes de las representaciones dramáticas en Puerto Rico," *Asomante*, VI, No. 1 (ene-mar 1950), 63-77. PTO. RICO

Also in Boletín de la Academia de Artes y Ciencias de Puerto Rico*, 4, No. 2 (abr-jun 1968), 419-423.*

1890 Rosbaco, José M. "El teatro independiente en Argentina," *Pro Arte* (Santiago de Chile), 4, No. 139 (9 ago 1951), 6, 8. ARG

1891 Rose, Gonzalo. "Teatro contemporáneo del Perú," *Humanismo* (México), 4, No. 17-18 (ene-feb 1954), 83-87. PERU

1892 Rosenberg, Donald Louis. "The Dramatic Theory of

Rodolfo Usigli. The Poetry of Selective Realism." Unpub. Ph.D. diss., Iowa, 1962. MEX

1893 Rosenfeld, Anatol. "Héroes y Coringas," *Conjunto*, No. 9 (s.f.), 29-45. BRAZ

Aspects of dramatic theory in present-day Brazil. Translated by Manuel Galich. Reprinted from Teoría e Prática, *No.* 2.

1894 ____. "Jorge Andrade," *Palco + Platêia*, No. 3 (1970), 48-50. BRAZ

1895 ____. "A Obra de Dias Gomes," in *Teatro de Dias Gomes*. 2 vol. Rio de Janeiro: Editôra Civilização Brasileira, 1972, I, xi-xliii. BRAZ

1896 ____. "Teatro em 70: São Paulo," *Palco + Platêia*, No. 7 (s.f.), 10-12. BRAZ

1897 Rosenstein, Cynthia. "El papel de la comicidad en el teatro de Fernán González de Eslava," *La Palabra y el Hombre*, No. 39 (jul-set 1966), 405-412. MEX

1898 Rubertino, María Luisa. "Planteos en nuestro teatro de hoy: autor y público," *Revista de Estudios de Teatro*, V, No. 12 (1972), 9-13. ARG

1899 Rudni, Silvia. "Jorge Lavelli: El triunfo de la sensibilidad," *Conjunto*, No. 10 (s.f.), 87-89. ARG

1900 Ruiz Castañeda, María del Carmen. "Ignacio Rodríguez Galván," *Cuadernos de Bellas Artes*, No. 9 (mayo-jun 1966), 5-20. MEX

1901 Ruiz Regalado, Margarita. "El comienzo de la ira," *Conjunto*, No. 15 (ene-mar 1973), 59-60. MEX

On Emilio Carballido's Un pequeño día de ira.

1902 ____. "Cuatro obras de Carlos Solórzano," *Conjunto*, No. 17 (jul-set 1973), 107-109. GUAT

1903 Ruz Menéndez, Rodolfo. "La obra dramática de don Manuel Barbachano y Tarrazo," *Revista de la Universidad de Yucatán*, XI, No. 61 (ene-feb 1969), 56-69. MEX

1904 Ryan, Paul Ryder. "The Living Theatre in Brazil,"

The Drama Review, 15, No. 3a [T-51], (Summer 1971), 21-30. BRAZ

1905 Saavedra Molina, Julio. "Rubén Darío y Sarah Bernhardt," *Anales de la Universidad de Chile*, No. 41 (1941), 17-45. NIC

1906 Sabat Pebet, Juan Carlos. "Aportes para una biografía: Sobre el origen y la carrera de Juan Aurelio Casacuberta," *Boletín de Estudios de Teatro*, VIII, No. 31 (oct-dic 1950), 129-136. ARG

1907 ____. "Sobre los orígenes teatrales montevideanos," *Boletín de Estudios de Teatro*, III, No. 11 (1945), 232-243. URUG

1908 ____. *El teatro dramático italiano en el Uruguay*. Montevideo: Instituto Italiano de Cultura, 1962. URUG

Reprint from Diálogo, *No. 15-18 (mayo-ago 1962).*

1909 Sada, Concepción. "El teatro en México," *Rueca* (México), No. 18 (verano 1948), 50-54. MEX

1910 Sáenz, Gerardo, ed. *Ecos teatrales*, by Luis G. Urbina. México: Instituto Nacional de Bellas Artes, 1963. 256 p. MEX

Prologue, selection, notes and bibliography.

1911 Sáez, Antonia. "El teatro en Puerto Rico; desde sus comienzos hasta el 1900," *Revista del Instituto de Cultura Puertorriqueña*, 4, No. 12 (jul-set 1961), 12-16. PTO. RICO

1912 ____. *El teatro en Puerto Rico (notas para su historia)*. San Juan: Editorial Universitaria, 1950. 185 p. PTO. RICO

1913 Salas, Carlos. *Historia del teatro en Caracas*. Caracas: Ediciones de la Secretaría General, Cuatricentenario de Caracas, 1967. 383 p. VEN

1914 Salazar S., Edgar. "Teatro en Manizales," *Boletín Cultural y Bibliográfico*, XII, No. 12 (1969), 44-47. GEN

First and second Festival Latinoamericano de Teatro Universitario in Manizales, 1968 and 1969.

1915 Salceda, Alberto G. "Cronología del teatro de Sor Juana," *Abside* (México), XVII, No. 3 (jul-set 1953), 333-358. MEX

1916 Saldarriaga Vélez, Alberto. "*Calle tal, número tal* por Regina Mejía de Gaviria," *Universidad de Antioquia* (Medellín), No. 169 (abr-jun 1968), 919-926. COL

1917 Saldías, José Antonio. "Grandeza y decadencia de un teatro recién nacido," *Anales del Instituto Popular de Conferencias*, No. 27 (1942), 116-128. ARG

1918 ____. "Grandeza y decadencia del teatro argentino," *Oriente y Occidente*, No. 29 (set 1941), 54-59. ARG

1919 ____. "Itinerario de Roberto Casaux," *Cuadernos de Cultura Teatral*, No. 21 (1945), 9-42. ARG

1920 ____. "Mariano Galé, benemérito del teatro argentino," *Cuadernos de Cultura Teatral* (Buenos Aires), No. 22 (1947). ARG
Reviewed: Kurz, Harry.

1921 Salvador, Francisco. "Del teatro en Honduras," *Honduras Rotaria* (Tegucigalpa), 17, No. 174 (set 1957), 15, 28-31; 17, No. 175 (oct 1957), 16. HOND

1922 ____. "El teatro en Honduras," *Revista de la Universidad* (Tegucigalpa), 1, No. 1 (jul-set 1960), 103-122. HOND

1923 San Martín, Hebrero. "La Compañía Argentina de Comedias se presenta en Madrid," *La Estafeta Literaria*, No. 175 (15 ago 1959), 14. ARG

1924 Sánchez, Everardo. "El teatro en la evangelización de Méjico," *Alvernia* (México), XX, No. 39 (1960), 49-61. MEX

1925 Sánchez, Luis Alberto. "El drama de Centro América," *Revista de América*, 1, No. 2 (feb 1945), 216-221. CENTR AM

1926 Sánchez, Luis Alberto. *El señor Segura, hombre de teatro; biografía y crítica.* Lima: Editorial P. T.C.M., 1947. PERU

1927 Sánchez, Luis Rafael. "El teatro de Emilio S. Belaval," *Sin Nombre* (San Juan), IV, No. 4 (abr-jun 1974), 54-61. PTO. RICO

1928 Sánchez Garrido, Amelia. "La 'disponibilidad' adolescente en el nuevo teatro mexicano," *Revista de Estudios de Teatro* (Buenos Aires), II, No. 6 (1963), 26-31. MEX

Cantón's Malditos, *Mendoza's* Las cosas simples, *Ibargüengoitia's* Susana y los jóvenes.

1929 ____. "Documentación de peculiaridades lingüísticas rioplatenses en el teatro gauchesco primitivo," *Revista de Humanidades* (Buenos Aires), 1, No. 1 (set 1961), 193-208. RIVER PLATE

1930 ____. *Indagación de lo argentino.* Buenos Aires: Ediciones Culturales Argentinas, Ministerio de Educación y Justicia, 1962. 190 p. ARG

Includes four chapters on theater.

1931 ____. "Situación del teatro gauchesco en la historia del teatro argentino. I. Antecedentes. II. El drama rural," *Revista de la Universidad* (La Plata), No. 14 (mayo-ago 1961), 9-27; No. 15 (set-dic 1961), 29-44. ARG

1932 ____. "El teatro de la revolución (1810-1823)," *Revista de Estudios de Teatro* (Buenos Aires), II, No. 4 (1962), 5-19. ARG

1933 Sánchez Trincado, J. L. "Estudios sobre teatro; el intérprete," *Boletín de Estudios de Teatro*, III, No. 9 (jun 1945), 118-120. GEN

Published earlier in El Universal *(Caracas), 12 dic 1944.*

1934 Santa Cruz, Abel. "El teatro y sus problemas," *Talía*, I, No. 9 (jul-ago 1954), 14. ARG

1935 Santiago, Haroldo. "Teatro e Nacionalismo," *Revista Brasiliense*, No. 27 (jan-fev 1960), 186-189. GEN

1936 Santiago, Haroldo. "Teatro Nacional Popular," *Revista Brasiliense*, No. 26 (nov-dez 1959), 198-201. BRAZ

The TBC and in support of the Teatro de Arena.

1937 Santiago, José Alberto. "El teatro universitario en la Argentina," *Primer Acto*, No. 67 (1965), 50-52. ARG

1938 Santiago, Silviano. "*A Moratória* em Processo," *PMLA*, 83, No. 2 (May 1968), 332-339. BRAZ

1939 Santos, José de Oliveira. "*A Revolução na América do Sul* de Augusto Boal," *Revista Brasiliense*, No. 32 (nov-dez 1960), 158-164. BRAZ

1940 ____. "Solano Trindade e o Teatro Popular Brasileiro," *Revista Brasiliense* (São Paulo), No. 33 (jan-fev 1961), 170-172. BRAZ

1941 ____. "O Teatro Experimental do Serviço Social da Industria," *Revista Brasiliense*, No. 33 (1961), 174-177. BRAZ

1942 ____. "Uma Temporada Positiva para o Teatro Paulista," *Anhembi*, XLV (1962), 378-380. BRAZ

1943 ____. "A União Paulista da Classe Teatral," *Revista Brasiliense*, No. 34 (1961), 170-173. BRAZ

1944 Santos, Romualdo. "Tres menciones: teatro latinoamericano de agitación," *Conjunto*, No. 13 (mayo-ago 1972), 20-23. GEN

Commentary on El asesinato de X, *(Creación Colectiva); Augusto Boal's* Torquemada; *Julio Mauricio's* Un despido corriente. *See #1945.*

1945 Sastre, Alfonso. "Teatro latinoamericano de agitación: tres menciones," *Conjunto*, No. 13 (mayo-ago 1972), 18-19. GEN

The prologue to Teatro latinoamericano de agitación. *La Habana: Casa de las Américas, 1972.*

1946 Satz, Asa. "Antropología, arte y teatro," *Cuadernos Americanos*, X, No. 1 (ene-feb 1951), 101-121. GEN

1947 Saunders, John F. "The Literary Works of Miguel N. Lira." Unpub. Ph.D. diss., Missouri, 1965. MEX

1948 Savage, R. Vance. "The 'Mexican' Theater of Rodolfo Usigli: Theory and Practice." Unpub. Ph. D. diss., Oregon, 1969. MEX

1949 ____. "Rodolfo Usigli's Idea of Mexican Theatre," *Latin American Theatre Review*, 4/2 (Spring 1971), 13-20. MEX

1950 Saz Sánchez, Agustín del. *Sor Juana Inés de la Cruz* (Vidas de mujeres ilustres). Barcelona: Seix y Barral, 1954. MEX

1951 ____. *Teatro hispanoamericano*. 2 vol. Barcelona: Editorial Vergara, 1963-64. 313,385 p. GEN

1952 ____. *Teatro social hispanoamericano*. Barcelona: Editorial Labor, 1967. 177 p. GEN

1953 Scarabótolo, Hélio Alberto. "Evolución de la dramaturgia brasileña," *Revista de Estudios de Teatro*, 2, No. 5 (1962), 40-51. BRAZ

Also in Universidad *(Santa Fe), No. 53 (jul-set 1962), 259-278.*

1954 ____. "El teatro brasileño de nuestros días," *Ficción*, No. 39 (set-oct 1962), 43-50. BRAZ

1955 Schaeffer Gallo, Carlos. "El acervo regional en el teatro vernáculo," *Revista de Estudios de Teatro*, I, No. 2 (1959), 25-30. ARG

1956 ____. "Florencio Parravicini," *Cuadernos de Cultura Teatral*, No. 21 (1945), 47-87. ARG

1957 ____. "Joaquín de Vedia," *Boletín de Estudios de Teatro*, IV, No. 14 (set 1946), 153-155. ARG

1958 ____. "Retratos en movimiento," *Lyra*, XVII, No. 174-176 (1959). ARG

About Orfilia Rico, Roberto Casaux, Florencio Parravicini.

1959 ____. "Retratos en movimiento: César Iglesias Paz," *Boletín de Estudios de Teatro*, IV, No. 12 (mar 1946). ARG

1960 Schaeffer Gallo, Carlos. "Retratos en movimiento: Enrique García Velloso," *Boletín de Estudios de Teatro*, III, No. 10 (set 1945), 157-159. ARG

1961 ____. *El revés de la máscara: Añoranzas y recuerdos teatrales rioplatenses*. Buenos Aires: Editorial Huemul, 1965. 195 p. RIVER PLATE

1962 ____ et al. "Homenaje a Florencio Sánchez," *Revista de Estudios de Teatro*, 1, No. 3 (1960), 15-24. URUG

1963 Schanzer, George O. "Ernesto Herrera, dramaturgo uruguayo." Unpub. Ph.D. diss., Iowa, 1950. URUG

1964 ____. "Génesis y re-interpretación de *La moral de Misia Paca* de Ernesto Herrera," *Sexto Congreso del Instituto Internacional de Literatura Iberoamericana*. México: IILI, 1954, pp. 197-204. URUG

1965 ____. "A Great National Drama of Uruguay," *Modern Language Journal*, XXXVIII, No. 5 (1954), 220-223. URUG

On Ernesto Herrera's El león ciego.

1966 ____. "The Mexican Stage in the Fall of 1971," *Latin American Theatre Review*, 5/2 (Spring 1972), 45-49. MEX

1967 ____. "El teatro hispanoamericano de post mortem," *Latin American Theatre Review*, 7/2 (Spring 1974), 5-16. GEN

1968 ____. "La vida errante de Ernesto Herrera," *Revista Nacional* (Montevideo), VI, No. 207 (1961), 77-88; No. 208 (1961), 195-218. URUG

1969 Schilling, Hildburg. *Teatro profano en la Nueva España* (Fines del siglo XVI a mediados del siglo XVIII). México: Centro de Estudios Literarios, Imprenta Universitaria, 1958. 290 p. Reviewed: Lamb, Ruth. MEX

1970 Schlicher, Allaire. "The Theater of Armando Moock." Unpub. Ph.D. diss., Michigan State, 1974. CHILE

1971 Schmidt, Donald L. "El teatro de Osvaldo Dragún,"

Latin American Theatre Review, 2/2 (Spring 1969), 3-20. ARG

1972 Schneider, Luis Mario. "José Gorostiza, escritor de teatro," *Revista de la Universidad de México*, XXV, No. 5 (ene 1971), 34-35. MEX

1973 Schneider de Cabrera, Ana. "Elementos teatrales en el folklore nacional," *Cuadernos de Cultura Teatral*, No. 9 (1940), 45-57. ARG

1974 Schoenbach, Peter J. "La libertad en *Las manos de Dios*," *Latin American Theatre Review*, 3/2 (Spring 1970), 21-29. GUAT

1975 ____. "Modern Brazilian Social Theatre: Art and Social Document." Unpub. Ph.D. diss., Rutgers, 1972. BRAZ

1976 ____. Review: "Esteban Rivas. *Carlos Solórzano y el teatro hispanoamericano*. México, 1970." *Latin American Theatre Review*, 4/2 (Spring 1971), 87-89. GUAT

1977 ____. "Rio and São Paulo Theatres in 1970: Foreign Dramaturgy," *Latin American Theatre Review*, 5/1 (Fall 1971), 69-80. BRAZ

1978 ____. "Rio and São Paulo Theatres in 1970: National Dramaturgy," *Latin American Theatre Review*, 5/2 (Spring 1972), 67-80. BRAZ

1979 Schons, Dorothy. "The Mexican Background of Alarcón," *PMLA*, 57, No. 1 (Mar 1942), 89-104. MEX

Article divided into two parts: "The Tradition of the Drama in Mexico in the Sixteenth Century," pp. 89-97; "New World Reminiscences in Alarcón," pp. 97-104.

1980 Schwartz, Kessel. "Francisco Tobar García and *Un hombre de provecho*," *Romance Notes*, XIV, No. 2 (Winter 1972), 252-257. ECUAD

1981 ____. "*La gringa* and *The Cherry Orchard*," *Hispania*, XLI, No. 1 (Mar 1958), 51-55. URUG

1982 ____. "Life and Art in a Drama by Jacobo Langsner," *Romance Notes*, XIII, No. 3 (Spring 1972), 441-444. URUG

About Los artistas, 1954.

1983 Scoseria, Cyro. *Un panorama del teatro uruguayo.* Montevideo: Publicaciones AGADU, 1963. 34 p. URUG

1984 ____. "El teatro en el Uruguay," *Revista Nacional*, Nos. 213-214 (jul-dic 1962), 182-213. URUG

1985 Scott, Wilder P. "A Critical Study of the Life and Dramatic Works of Rodolfo Usigli." Unpub. Ph.D. diss., Georgia, 1968. MEX

1986 ____. "French Literature and the Theater of Rodolfo Usigli," *Romance Notes*, XVI, No. 1 (Autumn 1974), 228-231. MEX

1987 ____. "A Note on Rodolfo Usigli and the Nickname 'Visconde'," *Romance Notes*, XIV, No. 3 (Spring 1973), 484-485. MEX

1988 ____. "Rodolfo Usigli and Contemporary Dramatic Theory," *Romance Notes*, XI, No. 3 (Spring 1970), 526-530. MEX

1989 ____. "Toward an Usigli Bibliography (1931-1971)," *Latin American Theatre Review*, 6/1 (Fall 1972), 53-63. MEX

1990 Seixas Sobrinho, José. *O Teatro em Sabará, da Colônia à República.* Belo Horizonte: Alvares, 1961. 194 p. BRAZ

1991 Serrador, Esteban. "El teatro y sus problemas," *Talía*, II, No. 10 (abr 1955), 10. GEN

1992 "VI [i.e., Sexto] festival de teatro latinoamericano," *Casa de las Américas*, VII, No. 40 (ene-feb 1967), 152-153. GEN

1993 Shank, Theodore. "A Return to Mayan and Aztec Roots," *The Drama Review*, 18, No. 4 (Dec 1974), 56-70. MEX

Comments on Chicano and Latin American theater festival in Mexico City, June-July, 1974.

1994 Shaw, Donald L. "A propos of Ricardo Rojas' *Ollantay*," *Latin American Theatre Review*, 4/1 (Fall 1970), 13-21. ARG

1995 ____. "A propósito de *Funeral Home* de Walter

Beneke," *Cuadernos Hispanoamericanos*, No. 211 (1967), 168-174. EL SAL

1996 Shaw, Donald L. "Pasión y verdad en el teatro de Villaurrutia," *Revista Iberoamericana*, No. 54 (1962), 337-346. MEX

1997 ____. "René Marqués' *La muerte no entrará en palacio:* An analysis," *Latin American Theatre Review*, 2/1 (Fall 1968), 31-38. PTO. RICO

1998 Shedd, Karl E. "Thirty Years of Criticism of the Works of Florencio Sánchez," *Kentucky Foreign Language Quarterly*, III, No. 1 (1956), 29-39. URUG

1999 Sheridan, Rev. Gerard J. "'Lo mexicano' in the Theater of Rodolfo Usigli." Unpub. Ph.D. diss., St. John's, 1968. MEX

2000 Sibirsky, Saúl. "La obra teatral de Sor Juana Inés de la Cruz," *Romance Notes*, VII, No. 1 (1965), 21-24. MEX

2001 Siemens, William L. "Assault on the Schizoid Wasteland: René Marqués' *El apartamiento*," *Latin American Theatre Review*, 7/2 (Spring 1974), 17-23. PTO. RICO

2002 "Siete autores en busca de un teatro," *Conjunto*, 3, No. 6 (ene-mar 1968), 7-23. GEN

Includes Rodolfo Walsh, Francisco Urondo, Hiber Conteris, Aimé Césaire, Manuel Galich, Alvaro Menén Desleal, and Alfonso Sastre.

2003 Silva, Ahtayde Ribeiro da. "História contemporânea do teatro brasileiro," *2004* (Rio), II, No. 1 (1961), 50-52. BRAZ

2004 Silva, Eurico. "Oduvaldo Vianna," *Revista de Teatro*, No. 387 (maio-jun 1972), 8. BRAZ

2005 Silva, Mario Norberto. "Pioneer Theatre: the Buenos Aires Independents," *Américas*, 14, No. 11 (1962), 32-36. ARG

2006 Silva Cáceres, Raúl. *La dramaturgia de Armando Moock: un ensayo de interpretación.* Santiago: Editorial Universitaria, Sociedad de Escritores de Chile, 1964. 110 p. CHILE

2007 Silva Castro, Raúl. *Panorama literario de Chile.* Santiago: Editorial Universitaria, 1961. CHILE

Theater, pp. 394-432.

2008 Silverio Boj (pseud. of Walter G. Wéyland). *Roberto J. Payró.* Buenos Aires: Ediciones Culturales Argentinas, Ministerio de Educación y Justicia, 1962. 152 p. ARG

2009 Simmonds, Adolfo H. "La formación del teatro ecuatoriano; fragmentos de una conferencia," *Revista del Colegio Nacional Vicente Rocafuerte* (Guayaquil), No. 53 (ene-set 1941), 7-14. ECUAD

2010 Simon, Sara. "The Trashumante Theatre," *Latin American Theatre Review*, 6/1 (Fall 1972), 27-33. MEX

An ambulatory theater experience in Monterrey, Mexico.

2011 Sisto, David T. "The Gaucho-Criollo Honor Code in the Theater of Florencio Sánchez," *Hispania*, XXXVIII, No. 4 (Dec 1955), 451-455. URUG

2012 Skármeta, Antonio. "El motivo de oposición entre aldea y ciudad en dos dramas chilenos," *Revista Chilena de Literatura*, No. 1 (otoño 1970), 31-41. CHILE

On Pueblecito *by Armando Moock and* La canción rota *by Antonio Acevedo Hernández.*

2013 Skinner, Eugene R. "Carballido: Temática y forma de tres autos," *Latin American Theatre Review*, 3/1 (Fall 1969), 37-47. MEX

Also in Textos *(Manizales), 1, No. 4 (s.f.), 2-3.*

2014 ____. Review: "Margaret S. Peden. *The Golden Thread and Other Plays.* Austin: University of Texas Press, 1970." *Latin American Theatre Review*, 4/2 (Spring 1971), 86-87. MEX

2015 Smith, John David. "Humor in the Short Stories and Plays of Rafael Solana." Unpub. Ph.D. diss., Southern California, 1965. MEX

2016 Smith, Robert J. Review: "Errol Hill. *The*

Trinidad Carnival: Mandate for a National Theatre. Austin and London: University of Texas Press, 1972." *Latin American Theatre Review*, 5/2 (Spring 1972), 80-82. TRI

2017 Snaidas, Adolfo. "Las dos mulatas de Xavier Villaurrutia," *Revista de la Universidad de México*, XXVII, No. 2 (oct 1972), I. MEX

La mulata de Córdoba, *screenplay (1945) and opera (1948).*

2018 ____. "*El solterón* de Xavier Villaurrutia," *Revista de la Universidad de México*, XXVII, No. 5 (ene 1973), 4-6. MEX

2019 ____. *El teatro de Xavier Villaurrutia.* México: SepSetentas, 1973. 206 p. MEX

2020 Sola, René de. "Reflexiones sobre el teatro," *Arco* (Bogotá), II, No. 6 (ene-feb 1960), 7-15. GEN

2021 Solana, Rafael. *Noches de estreno.* (Presentación de Francisco Monterde). México: Ediciones Oasis, 1963. 358 p. MEX

2022 Solari Swayne, Manuel. "Año teatral positivo," *El Comercio* (Lima), 1 ene 1967, p. 19. PERU

2023 ____. "El TUC: cinco años de hermosa labor cultural," *El Comercio* (Lima), 22 jun 1966, p. 2. PERU

2024 Soler-Tossas, José. "Estudio y análisis de cuatro obras teatrales de René Marqués." Unpub. Ph.D. diss., Southern California, 1972. PTO. RICO

2025 Solórzano, Carlos. "Algunas ideas sobresalientes de América hispánica expresadas en el teatro del siglo XX," *El teatro en Iberoamérica* (Memoria del duodécimo congreso del Instituto Internacional de Literatura Iberoamericana). México: IILI (1966). GEN

2026 ____. "Algunos paralelismos entre la novela y el teatro hispanoamericano de este siglo," in *Memoria* (XIII congreso del Instituto Internacional de Literatura Iberoamericana (Caracas), 1968, pp. 43-50. GEN

Also in Actas *del Tercer Congreso Internacional de Hispanistas (México), Carlos Magis, ed. (1970), pp. 853-859.*

2027 Solórzano, Carlos. "The Contemporary Latin American Theatre," *Prairie Schooner*, XXXIX, No. 2 (Summer 1965), 118-125. GEN

Translated by Rafael Sánchez.

2028 ____. "Méjico: Una escena permanente de América Latina," *Primer Acto*, No. 105 (feb 1969), 60-66. MEX

2029 ____. "Miguel Angel Asturias y el teatro," *Revista Iberoamericana*, No. 67 (ene-abr 1969), 101-104. GUAT

2030 ____. "Primer Festival de Teatro Nuevo de Latinoamérica," *Latin American Theatre Review*, 2/2 (Spring 1969), 60-68. MEX

Also in El Libro y el Pueblo, *No. 56 (1969), 35-37.*

2031 ____. *El teatro actual latinoamericano*. México: Ediciones de Andrea, 1972. 338 p. GEN

Prólogo, pp. 5-14. Includes: Carlos Gorostiza, El pan de la locura; *Guillermo Francovich,* Un puñal en la noche; *Oduvaldo Viana,* Cuatro cuadras de tierra; *Enrique Buenaventura,* El menú; *Daniel Gallegos,* La colina; *Antón Arrufat,* La repetición; *Isidora Aguirre,* Los papeleros; *Demetrio Aguilera Malta,* Infierno negro.

2032 ____. *Teatro breve hispanoamericano*. Madrid: Aguilar, 1970. 362 p. GEN

"Prólogo." Anthology contains: Osvaldo Dragún, Historia del hombre que se convirtió en perro; *Carlos Maggi,* El apuntador; *Josefina Pla,* Historia de un número; *Julio Ortega,* La campana; *Francisco Tobar García,* Las sobras para el gusano; *Ramón Chalbaud,* Las pinzas; *Gustavo Andrade Rivera,* Remington 22; *Virgilio Piñera,* Estudio en blanco y negro; *Francisco Arriví,* Un cuento de hadas; *Iván García,* Fábula de los cinco caminantes; *José de Jesús Martínez,* Segundo asalto; *Alberto Cañas,* Algo más que dos sueños; *Alberto Icaza,* Ancestral 66; *Alvaro Menén Desleal,* El circo y otras piezas falsas;

Carlos Solórzano, Los fantoches; *Elena Garro,* La señora en su balcón.
Reviewed: Barrera, Ernesto; Matas, Julio.

2033 Solórzano, Carlos. "El teatro de la posguerra en México," *Hispania,* XLVII, No. 4 (Dec 1964), 693-697. MEX

Also in Artes de México, *16, No. 123 (1969).*

2034 ____. "El teatro hispanoamericano contemporáneo," *Cuadernos del Congreso por la Libertad de la Cultura* (Paris), No. 100 (1965), 44-48. GEN

2035 ____. *El teatro hispanoamericano contemporáneo.* México: Fondo de Cultura Económica, 1964. 2 vol. GEN

Prologue. Anthology contains: Vol. I: Agustín Cuzzani, Sempronio; *Mario Benedetti,* Ida y vuelta; *Egon Wolff,* Los invasores; *Sebastián Salazar Bondy,* El fabricante de deudas; *Enrique Buenaventura,* En la diestra de Dios Padre; *René Marqués,* La muerte no entrará en palacio. *Vol. II: Demetrio Aguilera Malta,* El tigre; *César Rengifo,* Lo que dejó la tempestad; *Abelardo Estorino,* El robo del cochino; *Franklin Domínguez,* El último instante; *José de Jesús Martínez,* Juicio final; *Pablo Antonio Cuadra,* Por los caminos van los campesinos...; *Walter Béneke,* Funeral Home; *Carlos Solórzano,* Las manos de Dios.
Reviewed: Anderson-Imbert, Enrique; Dauster, Frank.

2036 ____. *Teatro latinoamericano del siglo XX.* Buenos Aires: Editorial Nueva Visión, 1961. 104 p. GEN

2037 ____. *El teatro latinoamericano en el siglo XX.* México: Editorial Pormaca, 1964. 200 p. GEN
Reviewed: Arrom, José J.

2038 ____. "El teatro mexicano contemporáneo," *Casa de las Américas,* 5, No. 28-29 (ene-abr 1965), 99-104. MEX

2039 ____. "Teatro mexicano de hoy," *Primer Acto,* No. 83 (1967), 52-56. MEX

2040 ____. "Los teatros universitarios de México," *Revista Interamericana de Bibliografía,* XV, No. 1 (ene-mar 1965), 29-34. MEX

2041 Solórzano, Carlos. *Testimonios teatrales de México*. México: Universidad Nacional Autónoma de México, 1973. 240 p. MEX

2042 Sordelli, Virgilio O. "Lola Membrives," *Lyra*, XI, No. 131-133 (1954). ARG

2043 Sorenson, Thora. "Recent Developments in the Argentine Theater," *Hispania*, XXXIX, No. 4 (Dec 1956), 446-449. ARG

2044 Soto Venegas, Rodolfo. "Experiencias de un autor de teatro de masas," *Aisthesis* (Santiago), No. 1 (1966), 141-147. GEN

2045 Sotoconil, Rubén. *Teatro escolar* (manual y antología). Santiago: Editora Austral, 1965. GEN CHILE

Manual, pp. 7-87, followed by an anthology of nine "piezas fáciles."

2046 Sousa, José Galante de. *O Teatro no Brasil*. 2 Vol. Rio de Janeiro: Ministerio da Educação e Cultura, Instituto Nacional do Livro, 1960. 457, 581 p. BRAZ

Vol. I reprinted in Rio de Janeiro: Editôra do Ouro, 1968. 398 p.

2047 Souza, Alfonso Ruy de. *História do Teatro na Bahia*. Bahia: Livraria Progresso, 1959. BRAZ

2048 Spell, Jefferson Rea. "Sidelights on Manuel Eduardo de Gorostiza from his Archive," in *Homage to Charles Blaise Quaglia*. Lubbock: Texas Tech Press, 1962. MEX

2049 ____. "The Theater in New Spain in the Early Eighteenth Century," *Hispanic Review*, XV, No. 1 (Jan 1947), 137-164. MEX

2050 Spell, Lota M. "Para la biografía de Gorostiza," *Historia Mexicana*, VIII, No. 2 (oct-dic 1958), 230-235. MEX

On Manuel Eduardo de Gorostiza.

2051 Spencer, L. Anne M. "Aztec Elements in Twentieth Century Mexican Drama." Unpub. Ph.D. diss., Kansas, 1974. MEX

2052 Speratti Piñero, Emma Susana. "Dos aspectos de la literatura mexicana del siglo XIX. I. Lo histórico y lo antihistórico en *Muñoz, visitador de México*, de Ignacio Rodríguez Galván. II. El teatro neoclásico en la literatura mexicana: *Indulgencia para todos*, de Manuel Eduardo de Gorostiza," *Revista Iberoamericana*, No. 38 (abr-set 1954), 321-332. MEX

2053 Staif, Kive. "Consideraciones sobre la crítica teatral," *Revista de Estudios de Teatro*, II, No. 6 (1963), 39-43. GEN

2054 Stanchina, Camilo F. "La crisis del teatro nacional," *Nosotros*, 2ª época, VI, 15, No. 69 (dic 1941), 307-313. ARG

2055 Sten, María. "Juglares del pueblo: el teatro campesino como factor de liberación," in "Diorama," Supl. de *Excelsior* (17 jun 1973), p. 13. MEX

2056 ____. *Vida y muerte del teatro nahuatl: El Olimpo sin Prometeo*. México: SepSetentas, 1974. 214 p. MEX

2057 Stevanovitch, Emilio A. "Esbozo para un origen del teatro argentino," *Vigencia* (Buenos Aires), 1, No. 1 (set-oct 1968), 25-26. ARG

2058 Stimson, Frederick S. "Spanish Themes in Early American Literature in the Novel, Drama, and Verse." Unpub. Ph.D. diss., Michigan, 1952. GEN

2059 Storni, Eduardo Raúl. *Ficción y realidad humana en el teatro contemporáneo*. Santa Fe: Librería y Editorial Castellví, 1956. 43 p. ARG

2060 ____. "Notas sobre el teatro argentino, 1810-1960," *Estudios Americanos* (Sevilla), 20, No. 103 (jul-ago 1960), 61-71. ARG

2061 Stowell, Christopher. "Theatrical Regulations in Mexico from Colonial Times." Unpub. Ph.D. diss., Southern California, 1968. MEX

2062 Suárez, Gilma. "Un artista llamado Santiago García," *Letras Nacionales*, No. 24 (mayo-jun 1974), 78-81. COL

2063 Suárez Radillo, Carlos Miguel. "El aporte popular

a la cultura: el Teatro de los Barrios," *Imagen*, No. 7 (3 jul 1971). VEN

2064 Suárez Radillo, Carlos Miguel. "Apuntes incompletos para una historia del teatro cubano en el siglo XX," *Revista Guadalupe* (Madrid), No. 6 (1958), 3-7. CUBA

2065 ____. "Cinco años de teatro hispanoamericano en Madrid," *Mundo Hispánico* (Madrid), 16, No. 185 (ago 1963), 43-47. GEN

2066 ____. "Comentario y consideraciones en torno al 'Proyecto para el Fomento de las Artes Teatrales en Puerto Rico'," *Revista del Instituto de Cultura Puertorriqueña*, VIII, No. 26 (ene-mar 1965), 14-19. PTO. RICO

2067 ____. "Cuando los títeres toman conciencia," *Fundateatros* (Caracas), No. 2 (1970), 18-20. GEN

Also in Revista de Revistas, *No. 3291 (18 oct 1970), 11-15.*

2068 ____. "Dos generaciones de violencia en el teatro colombiano contemporáneo," *Alero* (Guatemala), No. 2, 3ª época (set-oct 1973), 18-28. COL

Also in Anales de Literatura Hispanoamericana *(Madrid), No. 2-3 (1973-74), 111-135.*

2069 ____. "José Gabriel Núñez: una nueva expresión de la violencia en el teatro venezolano actual," *Revista Nacional de Cultura* (Caracas), No. 199 (1971), 102-107. VEN

On El largo camino del Edén.

2070 ____. "Mayoría de edad del teatro independiente argentino," *Cuadernos Hispanoamericanos*, No. 272 (feb 1973), 187-200. ARG

2071 ____. "Un medio a ensayar para la creación de un teatro auténticamente popular en Hispanoamérica," *Anales de Literatura Hispanoamericana* (Madrid), No. 1 (1972), 127-142. GEN

2072 ____. "Un medio a ensayar para la creación de un teatro popular," *Jornada* (San José), 2, No. 14 (1971). GEN

2073 Suárez Radillo, Carlos Miguel. "El negro y su encuentro de sí mismo a través del teatro," *Cuadernos Hispanoamericanos*, No. 271 (ene 1973), 34-49. GEN

2074 ____. "Notas sobre mi puesta en escena de *Historias para ser contadas* de Osvaldo Dragún," *Primer Acto*, No. 35 (jun-jul 1962), 10-13. ARG

2075 ____. "Poesía y realidad social en el teatro peruano contemporáneo," *Cuadernos Hispanoamericanos*, No. 269 (nov 1972), 254-270. PERU

2076 ____. "Prólogo," in Alfredo Sancho, *Las tres carátulas*. México: Finisterre, 1970. COSTA RICA

2077 ____. "El pueblo, protagonista y espectador teatral en Ecuador," *Tertulia* (San José), No. 3 (ene-mar 1972), 6-13. ECUAD

2078 ____. "Renace el teatro hispanoamericano en Madrid," *Mundo Hispánico*, No. 316 (jul 1974), 32-33. GEN

Productions by the Teatro Experimental Hispanoamericano, a Venezuelan theater group under the direction of Germana Quintana, of works by Maruxa Vilalta (Mexico) and José Martínez Queirolo (Ecuador).

2079 ____. "Responsabilidad social y estética del teatro para niños," *Fundateatros* (Caracas), No. 3 (1970), 8-12. GEN

2080 ____. "San Miguelito, Panamá: de cómo el teatro transformó un barrio," *Imagen*, No. 33 (15 feb 1972), 12-13. PAN

2081 ____. "Síntesis panorámica del teatro ecuatoriano de hoy, y Estudio crítico sobre José Martínez Queirolo (con su pieza *Q.E.P.D.*)," *Fundateatros* (Caracas), No. 4 (1971), 1-11. ECUAD

2082 ____. "Lo social en el teatro iberoamericano actual," *Imagen*, No. 83 (15 oct 1970), 45-47. GEN

Also in Revista de Revistas, *No. 3302 (3 ene 1971), 89-98.*

2083 ____. "El teatro boliviano: de lo histórico a lo

humano contemporáneo," *Cuadernos Hispanoamericanos*, No. 263-264 (mayo-jun 1972), 339-354. BOL

2084 Suárez Radillo, Carlos Miguel. "El teatro chileno actual y las universidades como sus principales fuerzas propulsoras," *Revista Interamericana de Bibliografía*, XXII, No. 1 (ene-mar 1972), 18-29. CHILE

2085 ____. "El teatro iberoamericano actual: de la realidad a la escena," *Fundateatros* (Caracas), No. 1 (1970), 25-28. GEN

2086 ____. "El teatro infantil en España e Hispanoamérica," *Cultura* (San Salvador), No. 36 (abr-jun 1965), 138-144. GEN

2087 ____. "El teatro venezolano en busca de autenticidad," *Imagen*, No. 94-95 (abr 1971), 13-18. VEN

2088 ____. "Tema y problema en el teatro hispanoamericano contemporáneo," *Cuadernos Hispanoamericanos*, No. 138 (jun 1961), 394-400. GEN

Also in Cultura *(San Salvador), No. 37 (jul-set 1965), 94-101.*

2089 ____. "Temática y problemática en el teatro hispanoamericano actual," *Aconcagua* (Madrid), 2, No. 1 (1966), 25-33. GEN

2090 ____. *13* [i.e., *Trece*] *autores del nuevo teatro venezolano.* Caracas: Monte Avila Editores, 1971. 540 p. VEN

"Prólogo," pp. 11-16. Anthology contains: Ricardo Acosta, Agua linda; *José Ignacio Cabrujas,* Fiésole; *Román Chalbaud,* Los ángeles terribles; *Isaac Chocrón,* Tric Trac; *Alejandro Lasser,* Catón y Pilato; *Elisa Lerner,* En el vasto silencio de Manhattan; *José Gabriel Núñez,* Los peces del acuario; *Gilberto Pinto,* El hombre de la rata; *Lucía Quintero,* 1 x 1 = 1, pero 1 + 1 = 2; *César Rengifo,* La esquina del miedo; *Rodolfo Santana,* La muerte de Alfredo Gris; *Elizabeth Schön,* Intervalo; *Paul Williams,* Las tijeras.
Reviewed: Barrera, Ernesto; Dauster, Frank; Matas, Julio.

2091 ____. "Vigencia de la realidad venezolana en el

teatro de César Rengifo," *Latin American Theatre Review*, 5/2 (Spring 1972), 51-61. VEN

2092 Suárez Radillo, Carlos Miguel. "Visión de la problemática social en el teatro hispanoamericano," *Norte* (Amsterdam), No. 5 (nov 1963), 65-67. GEN

2093 Suassuna, Ariano. "Folk Theater in Northeastern Brazil," *Américas*, XVI, No. 11 (nov 1964), 18-23. BRAZ

2094 ____. "Genealogia Nobiliárquica do Teatro Brasileiro," *Américas*, XVI, No. 12 (dez 1964), 18-23. BRAZ

2095 ____. "Teatro, região, e tradição," in *Gilberto Freyre: Sua ciência, sua filosofia, sua arte* (Ensaios sôbre o autor de *Casa grande e senzala* e sua influência na moderna cultura do Brasil comemorativos do 25° aniversário da publicação desse seu livro). Rio de Janeiro: José Olympio, 1962, pp. 474-483. BRAZ

2096 Sumel, Humberto. "Teatro cubano," *Policía* (La Habana), (nov 1942), 30-33, 63. CUBA

2097 Swigger, Nancy Duncan. "Gonçalves Dias as a Dramatist." Unpub. Ph.D. diss., Indiana, 1970. BRAZ

2098 Tamayo Vargas, Augusto. "Obras menores en el teatro de Peralta," *Letras* (Universidad de San Marcos), No. 72-73 (1964), 70-85. PERU

Also in Revista Histórica *(Lima), No. 27 (1964), 82-95.*

2099 ____. "La Perricholi fue limeña," *Estudios de Teatro Peruano* (Lima), VI, No. 18 (1954). PERU

2100 ____. "Peruvian Literature in 1961," *Books Abroad*, 36, No. 3 (Summer 1962). PERU

"Theater," pp. 267-269.

2101 Tatum, Charles M. "[Review of Leñero's *El juicio*]," *Chasqui*, 2, No. 1 (nov 1972), 55-57. MEX

2102 "Teatro," *Guía Quincenal de la Actividad Intelectual y Artística Argentina* (Buenos Aires), 1947-1950. ARG

2103 "El teatro actual," *Casa de las Américas*, IV, No. 22-23 (ene-abr 1964), 95-107. GEN

2104 *El teatro actual latinoamericano.* Prólogo y selección de Carlos Solórzano. México: Ediciones de Andrea, 1972. GEN

For listing of contents, see Solórzano, Carlos.

2105 "Teatro argentino, 1966. Encuesta," *Primer Acto*, No. 77 (1966), 4-8. ARG

2106 *Teatro argentino contemporáneo.* Prólogo y selección de Arturo Berenguer Carisomo. Madrid: Aguilar, 1962. 475 p. ARG

Anthology. Includes: A. Malfatti and N. Llanderas, Así es la vida; *Conrado Nalé Roxlo,* La cola de la sirena; *Juan Oscar Ponferrada,* El carnaval del diablo; *José León Pagano,* El secreto; *Pedro E. Pico,* Agua en las manos; *Samuel Eichelbaum,* Dos brasas.

2107 "Teatro brasileño," *Primer Acto*, No. 75 (1966). BRAZ

Number devoted to Brazil, with essays by Angel Crespo and Walmir Ayala and translations of O Pagador de Promessas *and* Morte e Vida Severina.

2108 *Teatro breve hispanoamericano.* Selección y prólogo de Carlos Solórzano. Madrid: Aguilar, 1970. 362 p. GEN

For listing of contents, see Solórzano, Carlos.

2109 *Teatro chileno actual.* Santiago: Zig-Zag, 1966. 307 p. CHILE

Anthology, with comments by the authors, "Sobre mi teatro." Includes: José Ricardo Morales, Hay una nube en su futuro; *Isidora Aguirre,* Carolina; *Fernando Debesa,* Persona y perro; *Gabriela Roepke,* Una mariposa blanca; *Enrique Molleto,* El sótano; *Sergio Vodanović,* Las exiladas; *Egon Wolff,* Mansión de lechuzas; *Luis Alberto Heiremans,* Sigue la estrella; *Alejandro Sieveking,* Mi hermano Cristián; *Jorge Díaz,* El génesis fue

mañana.
Reviewed: Lyday, Leon.

2110 *Teatro chileno contemporáneo*. Selección y prólogo de Julio Durán Cerda. Madrid: Aguilar, 1970. 498 p. CHILE

Anthology includes: María Asunción Requena, Ayayema; *Egon Wolff,* Los invasores; *Luis Alberto Heiremans,* El abanderado; *Sergio Vodanović,* Viña; *Alejandro Sieveking,* Animas de día claro; *Jorge Díaz,* El cepillo de dientes. Reviewed: Luzuriaga, Gerardo.

2111 *Teatro cubano contemporáneo*. 2d. ed. Selection by Dolores Martí de Cid, prologue by José Cid Pérez. Madrid: Aguilar, 1962. 448 p. CUBA

Anthology includes: Luis A. Baralt, Tragedia indiana; *José Cid Pérez,* Hombres de dos mundos; *Carlos Felipe,* El travieso Jimmy; *Renée Potts,* Imagíname infinita; *José Antonio Ramos,* Tembladera; *Marcelo Salinas,* Alma guajira.

2112 "Teatro e Realidade Brasileira," *Revista Civilização Brasileira,* IV, Caderno Especial No. 2 (jul 1968), 286 p. BRAZ

For index, see Latin American Theatre Review, *2/2 (Spring 1969), 82.*

2113 "Teatro: El creador de la Comedia Nacional," *Primera Plana* (Buenos Aires), IV, No. 182 (27 jun 1966), 66-70. ARG

2114 *El teatro en Iberoamérica* (Memoria del duodécimo congreso del Instituto Internacional de Literatura Iberoamericana, 1966). México: Editorial Cultura, 1967. 192 p. GEN

Individual essays listed by author.

2115 "El teatro en Latinoamérica," *Máscara* (Buenos Aires), 7, No. 88-89 (ene-feb 1948), 12-14; 7, No. 90 (mar 1948), 24-25. GEN

2116 "El teatro en México," *Artes de México*, 16, No. 123 (1969), 106 p. MEX

Includes: Alfonso Caso, "El uso de las máscaras entre los antiguos mexicanos"; José Rojas Garcidueñas, "El primer siglo de teatro en

México"; Francisco Monterde, "Don Juan Ruiz de Alarcón y el teatro"; Sergio Fernández, "La metáfora en el teatro de Sor Juana"; Armando de Maria y Campos, "El teatro mexicano entre dos siglos"; Salvador Novo, "La metamorfosis de Ulises"; Carlos Solórzano, "El teatro de la posguerra en México."

2117 *El teatro en México*. México: Instituto Nacional de Bellas Artes, 1958-1964. 2 vol. MEX

An annual discontinued after two years. Vol. I covers 1922-1957; Vol. II covers 1958-1964.

2118 *Teatro Experimental do Negro. Testemunhos*. Rio de Janeiro: Edições GRD, 1966. 170 p. BRAZ

2119 *Teatro guatemalteco contemporáneo*. Selección y prólogo de Carlos Solórzano. Madrid: Aguilar, 1964. 327 p. GUAT

Anthology includes: Rafael Arévalo Martínez, Los duques de Endor; *Miguel Angel Asturias,* Soluna; *Miguel Marsicovetere y Durán,* El espectro acróbata; *Manuel Galich,* Entre cuatro paredes; *Carlos Solórzano,* Doña Beatriz (la sin ventura).

2120 *Teatro hispanoamericano*. Hymen Alpern and José Martel, eds. New York: The Odyssey Press, 1956. GEN

For listing of contents, see Alpern, Hymen, and José Martel.

2121 *Teatro hispanoamericano* (antología crítica). Carlos Ripoll and Andrés Valdespino, eds. 2 vol. New York: Anaya Book Co., 1972-73. GEN

For listing of contents, see Ripoll, Carlos, and Andrés Valdespino.

2122 *Teatro hispanoamericano contemporáneo*. Carlos Solórzano, ed. México: Fondo de Cultura Económica, 1964. 2 vol. GEN

For listing of contents, see Solórzano, Carlos.

2123 "El teatro latinoamericano," *El Gallo Ilustrado*, supl. dom. de *El Día* (México), No. 170 (26 sep 1965). GEN

2124 *Teatro libre de Buenos Aires, esencia y función.* Buenos Aires: Ediciones del Teatro Libre de Buenos Aires, 1946. 30 p. ARG

Cuadernillos de Extensión Cultural.

2125 *Teatro mexicano contemporáneo.* Selección y prólogo de Antonio Espina. Madrid: Aguilar, 1962. 514 p. MEX

Anthology includes: Xavier Villaurrutia, ¿En qué piensas?, Parece mentira, *and* Sea Ud. breve; *Celestino Gorostiza,* El color de nuestra piel; *Rodolfo Usigli,* El gesticulador; *Luis G. Basurto,* Cada quien su vida; *Jorge Ibargüengoitia,* Susana y los jóvenes; *Luisa Josefina Hernández,* Los frutos caídos.

2126 *Teatro mexicano del siglo XIX.* Selección, prólogo y notas de Antonio Magaña Esquivel. México: Fondo de Cultura Económica, 1972. 572 p. MEX

Anthology includes: José Joaquín Fernández de Lizardi, Todos contra el Payo y el Payo contra todos o La visita del Payo en el Hospital de Locos; *Manuel Eduardo de Gorostiza,* Contigo pan y cebolla; *Fernando Calderón,* A ninguna de las tres; *Ignacio Rodríguez Galván,* Muñoz, visitador de México; *Francisco González Bocanegra,* Vasco Núñez de Balboa; *José Antonio Cisneros,* Diego el mulato.

2127 *Teatro mexicano del siglo XX.* 3 vol. México: Fondo de Cultura Económica, 1956. MEX

Vol. I (Letras mexicanas, 25), selección, prólogo y notas de Francisco Monterde. Anthology includes: Manuel José Othón, El último capítulo; *Marcelino Dávalos,* Así pasan; *Federico Gamboa,* La venganza de la gleba; *José Joaquín Gamboa,* Vía Crucis; *Carlos Noriega Hope,* La señorita Voluntad; *Víctor Manuel Díez Barroso,* Véncete a ti mismo; *Ricardo Parada León,* Hacia la meta; *Lázaro y Carlos Lozano García,* Al fin mujer; *María Luisa Ocampo,* Al otro día; *Julio Jiménez Rueda,* La silueta de humo; *Carlos Díaz Dufóo,* Padre mercader.
Vol. II (Letras mexicanas, 26), selección, prólogo y notas de Antonio Magaña Esquivel. Anthology includes: Francisco Monterde, Proteo; *Juan Bustillo Oro,* San Miguel de las Espinas; *Mauricio Magdaleno,* Pánuco 137; *Celestino Gorostiza,* El

color de nuestra piel; *Xavier Villaurrutia,* El yerro candente; *Alfonso Reyes,* Ifigenia cruel; *Rodolfo Usigli,* El gesticulador; *Concepción Sada,* Un mundo para mí; *Miguel N. Lira,* Vuelta a la tierra; *Luis G. Basurto,* Cada quien su vida; *Edmundo Báez,* Un alfiler en los ojos.
Vol. III (Letras mexicanas, 27), selección, prólogo y notas de Celestino Gorostiza. Anthology includes: Salvador Novo, La culta dama; *Agustín Lazo,* El caso de don Juan Manuel; *Emilio Carballido,* La danza que sueña la tortuga; *Sergio Magaña,* Los signos de Zodíaco; *Federico Schroeder Inclán,* Hoy invita la Güera; *Luisa Josefina Hernández,* Los frutos caídos; *Rafael Solana,* Debiera haber obispas; *Héctor Mendoza,* Las cosas simples; *Ignacio Retes,* Una ciudad para vivir; *Jorge Ibargüengoitia,* Clotilde en su casa.
Reviewed: Dauster, Frank.

2128 *Teatro mexicano del siglo XX.* Selección, prólogo y notas de Antonio Magaña Esquivel. México: Fondo de Cultura Económica, 1970. 2 vol. MEX

Vol. I (Letras mexicanas, 98). Anthology includes: Federico S. Inclán, La última noche con Laura; *Luisa Josefina Hernández,* Los huéspedes reales; *J. Humberto Robles,* Los desarraigados; *Fernando Sánchez Mayans,* Las alas del pez; *Salvador Novo,* Cuauhtémoc; *Antonio Magaña Esquivel,* Semilla del aire; *Rodolfo Usigli,* Corona de luz; *Celestino Gorostiza,* La Malinche; *Sergio Magaña,* El pequeño caso de Jorge Lívido; *Juan García Ponce,* Doce y una, trece.
Vol. II (Letras mexicanas, 99). Anthology includes: Octavio Paz, La hija de Rappaccini; *Elena Garro,* La señora en su balcón; *Antonio González Caballero,* Señoritas a disgusto; *Héctor Azar,* La appassionata; *Maruxa Vilalta,* Cuestión de narices; *Emilio Carballido,* Yo también hablo de la rosa; *Margarita Urueta,* El señor perro; *Hugo Argüelles,* La ronda de la hechizada; *Vicente Leñero,* Los albañiles.

2129 "El teatro mexicano era así y sigue así," *Hoy* (México), 28 feb 1948, pp. 51-61. MEX

2130 *Teatro mexicano, 1963.* Selección y prólogo de

Antonio Magaña Esquivel. México: Aguilar, 1965. 324 p. MEX

Anthology includes: Salvador Novo, La guerra de las gordas; *Emilio Carballido,* ¡Silencio, pollos pelones, ya les van a echar su maíz!; *Rafael Solana,* Ensalada de Nochebuena; *Luisa Josefina Hernández,* Los duendes.

2131 *Teatro mexicano, 1964.* Selección y prólogo de Antonio Magaña Esquivel. México: Aguilar, 1967. 302 p. MEX

Anthology includes: Antonio González Caballero, El medio pelo; *Héctor Azar,* Olímpica; *Maruxa Vilalta,* Un país feliz; *Margarita Urueta,* El hombre y su máscara.

2132 "El Teatro Nacional Popular de Bolivia," *Conjunto*, No. 2 (1964), 15-16, 57-58. BOL

2133 "El Teatro Nacional y algo de su historia (entrevista con Alberto Calvo)," *Lotería* (Panamá), 3, No. 35 (oct 1958), 57-67. PAN

2134 "Un teatro nuevo popular: desde Arica a Puerto Montt," *Conjunto*, No. 16 (abr-jun 1973), 4-7. CHILE

2135 "O Teatro Paulista em 1972," *Anuario das Artes - 1972.* São Paulo: Asociação Paulista de Críticos de Artes, 1973. BRAZ

Reviews collected from various newspapers and periodicals of the 1972 São Paulo theater season.

2136 *Teatro peruano contemporáneo.* Prólogo de Aurelio Miró Quesada. Lima: Editorial Huascarán, 1948. 324 p. PERU

Anthology includes: Juan Ríos, Don Quijote; *Percy Gibson Parra,* Esa luna que empieza; *Sebastián Salazar Bondy,* Amor, gran laberinto.

2137 *Teatro peruano contemporáneo.* Prologue by José Hesse Murga. Madrid: Aguilar, 1959. 399 p. PERU

Anthology includes: Percy Gibson Parra, Esa luna que empieza; *Juan Ríos,* Ayar Manko; *Bernardo Roca Rey,* La muerte de Atahualpa; *Sebastián Salazar Bondy,* No hay isla feliz; *Enrique Solari Swayne,* Collacocha.

2138 "Teatro popular de México," *Cuadernos de Bellas Artes*, IV, No. 12 (dic 1963), 21-24. MEX

Celestino Gorostiza's inauguration address.

2139 *Teatro puertorriqueño* [Primer Festival, 1958]. Introduction. San Juan: Instituto de Cultura Puertorriqueña, 1959. 460 p. PTO. RICO

Anthology includes: Manuel Méndez Ballester, Encrucijada; *Emilio S. Belaval,* La hacienda de los cuatro vientos; *Francisco Arriví,* Vejigantes; *René Marqués,* Los soles truncos. Reviewed: Dauster, Frank.

2140 *Teatro puertorriqueño* [Segundo Festival, 1959]. Prologue by Francisco Arriví. San Juan: Instituto de Cultura Puertorriqueña, 1960. 403 p. PTO. RICO

Anthology includes: Luis Rechani Agrait, Mi señoría; *Enrique A. Laguerre,* La resentida; *Fernando Sierra Berdecía,* Esta noche juega el jóker.

2141 *Teatro puertorriqueño* [Tercer Festival, 1960]. Prologue by Francisco Arriví. San Juan: Instituto de Cultura Puertorriqueña, 1961. 613 p. PTO. RICO

Anthology includes: René Marqués, Un niño azul para esa sombra; *Piri Fernández,* De tanto caminar; *Myrna Casas,* Roto en el tiempo; *Emilio S. Belaval,* Cielo caído; *Gerard Paul Marín,* En el principio la noche era serena.

2142 *Teatro puertorriqueño* [Cuarto Festival, 1961]. Prologue by Francisco Arriví. San Juan: Instituto de Cultura Puertorriqueña, 1962. 802 p. PTO. RICO

Anthology includes: Francisco Arriví, María Soledad; *Salvador Brau,* La vuelta al hogar; *René Marqués,* La carreta; *Luis Rafael Sánchez,* Los ángeles se han fatigado *and* La hiel nuestra de cada día; *Manuel Méndez Ballester,* El milagro.

2143 *Teatro puertorriqueño* [Quinto Festival, 1962]. Prologue by Francisco Arriví. San Juan: Instituto de Cultura Puertorriqueña, 1963. 392 p. PTO. RICO

Anthology includes: Manuel Méndez Ballester, Tiempo muerto; *Emilio S. Belaval,* Circe o el amor; *César Andreu Iglesias,* El inciso hache.

2144 *Teatro puertorriqueño* [Sexto Festival, 1963]. Prologue by Francisco Arriví. San Juan: Instituto de Cultura Puertorriqueña, 1964. 357 p. PTO. RICO

Anthology includes: Manuel Méndez Ballester, La feria o el mono con la lata en el rabo; *Edmundo Rivera Alvarez,* El cielo se rindió al amanecer; *Emilio S. Belaval,* La vida.

2145 *Teatro puertorriqueño* [Séptimo Festival, 1964]. Prologue by Francisco Arriví. San Juan: Instituto de Cultura Puertorriqueña, 1965. 638 p. PTO. RICO

Anthology includes: Luis Rechani Agrait, Todos los ruiseñores cantan; *René Marqués,* El apartamiento; *Luis Rafael Sánchez,* ... O casi el alma; *Francisco Arriví,* Coctel de don Nadie.

2146 *Teatro puertorriqueño* [Octavo Festival, 1965]. Prologue by Francisco Arriví. San Juan: Instituto de Cultura Puertorriqueña, 1966. 728 p. PTO. RICO

Anthology includes: Luis Rechani Agrait, ¿Cómo se llama esta flor?; *Manuel Méndez Ballester,* Bienvenido don Goyito; *Ana Inés Bonnin Armstrong,* La difícil esperanza; *René Marqués,* Mariana o el alba.

2147 *Teatro puertorriqueño* [Noveno Festival, 1966]. Prologue. San Juan: Instituto de Cultura Puertorriqueña, 1968. 445 p. PTO. RICO

Anthology includes: René Marqués, Los soles truncos; *Luis Rechani Agrait,* Mi señoría; *Francisco Arriví,* Vejigantes; *Manuel Méndez Ballester,* Bienvenido don Goyito.

2148 *Teatro puertorriqueño* [Décimo Festival, 1967]. Prologue by Francisco Arriví. San Juan: Instituto de Cultura Puertorriqueña, 1969. PTO. RICO

Anthology includes: Gerard Paul Marín, El retablo y guiñol de Juan Canelo; *Roberto Rodríguez Suárez,* Las ventanas; *Alejandro Tapia y Rivera,* La cuarterona.

2149 *Teatro puertorriqueño* [Undécimo Festival, 1968]. Prologue by Francisco Arriví. San Juan: Instituto de Cultura Puertorriqueña, 1970. PTO. RICO

Anthology includes: Roberto Rodríguez Suárez, El casorio; *Manuel Méndez Ballester,* Arriba las mujeres; *Julio Marrero Núñez,* El hombre terrible del 87; *Luis Rafael Sánchez,* La pasión según Antígona Pérez; *Ballets de San Juan.*

2150 "El teatro retorna al pueblo," *Conjunto*, No. 16 (abr-jun 1973), 2-4. GEN

2151 *Teatro selecto contemporáneo hispanoamericano.* Orlando Rodríguez Sardiñas and Carlos Miguel Suárez Radillo, eds. 3 vol. Madrid: Escelicer, 1971. GEN

For listing of contents, see Rodríguez Sardiñas, Orlando, and Carlos Miguel Suárez Radillo.

2152 *Teatro uruguayo contemporáneo.* Selección y prólogo de Fernán Silva Valdés. Madrid: Aguilar, 1960. 556 p. URUG

Anthology includes: Florencio Sánchez, Barranca abajo; *Ernesto Herrera,* El león ciego; *Vicente Martínez Cuitiño,* Servidumbre; *José Pedro Bellán,* ¡Dios te salve!; *Fernán Silva Valdés,* El burlador de la pampa; *Yamandú Rodríguez,* 1810.

2153 "Teatro venezolano 1967," *Expediente* (Caracas), No. 1 (s.f.), 13-23. VEN

Comments stemming from Third Festival prize awards.

2154 *Teatro y universidad.* Tucumán: Universidad Nacional, Facultad de Filosofía y Letras, 1960. ARG

Individual essays listed by author.

2155 "III Festival de Teatro," *Revista Nacional de Cultura* (Caracas), XXVIII, No. 177 (set-oct 1966), 175. VEN

2156 *Tercer festival del teatro venezolano: 1967.* Caracas: Centro de Investigación y Desarrollo del Teatro, 1967. [Cuaderno, 5.] VEN

A collection of reviews of the plays.

2157 Terrán, Jaime. "Teatro de arte popular en Bogotá," *Mundo Hispánico* (Madrid), 18, No. 213 (dic 1965), 36-37. COL

2158 Tessen, Howard W. "Manuel Ascensio Segura." Unpub. Ph.D. diss., Yale, 1947. CHILE

2159 Tessier, Domingo. "El Teatro Experimental de la Universidad de Chile," *Revista de la Universidad de México*, XI, No. 3 (nov 1956), 15-19. CHILE

2160 Teurbe Tolón, Edwin, and Jorge Antonio González. *Historia del teatro en La Habana*. I. Santa Clara: Dirección de Publicaciones, Universidad Central de las Villas, 1961. 165 p. CUBA
Reviewed: Campos, Jorge; Casey, Calvert.

2161 "The theatre in Argentina during 1944," *Argentine News* (Buenos Aires), No. 73 (Apr 1945), 26-28. ARG

2162 "Un théâtre national populaire à Quito," *World Theater*, 16, No. 5-6 (set-dec 1967), 538-541. ECUAD

2163 "Theatrical activity in Argentina during 1945," *Argentine News* (Buenos Aires), No. 79 (oct-dic 1945), 30-31. ARG

2164 Thomas, Earl W. "Protest in the Novel and Theater," *Brazil in the Sixties*. Nashville: Vanderbilt University Press, 1972, pp. 397-421. BRAZ

2165 Tiempo, César (seud. de Israel Zeitlin). *Máscaras y caras*. Buenos Aires: Editorial Arrayán, 1943. 502 p. RIVER PLATE

Elías Alippi, Francisco Alvarez, Enrique Amorim, Eduardo Aparicio, Luis Arata, etc.

2166 ____. "Rápida presencia de Muiño y Alippi," *Lyra*, XVII, No. 174-176 (1959). ARG

2167 ____. *La vida romántica y pintoresca de Berta Singerman*. Buenos Aires: Editorial Sopena, 1941. 156 p. ARG

2168 Tilles, Solomon H. "An Experimental Approach to the Spanish American Theatre," *Modern Language Journal*, LVI, No. 5 (May 1972), 304-305. GEN

Method of teaching a play, editing text, vocabulary lists, based on Emilio Carballido's Rosalba y los Llaveros.

2169 ____. "Rodolfo Usigli's Concept of Dramatic Art," *Latin American Theatre Review*, 3/2 (Spring 1970), 31-38. MEX

2170 Tirri, Néstor. *Realismo y teatro argentino.* Buenos Aires: Ediciones La Bastilla, 1973. ARG

2171 Tobar García, Francisco. "La noche no es para dormir," *Arco* (Bogotá), II, 8-9 (mayo-ago 1960), 253-254. ECUAD

A self-interview.

2172 ____. "Nuestro teatro en la segunda mitad del siglo XIX," *Carteles* (La Habana), 2 ene 1949, pp. 40-41. CUBA

2173 ____. "El teatro vernáculo cubano," *Carteles* (La Habana), 31, No. 43 (22 oct 1950), 52-53; 31, No. 49 (3 dic 1950), 50-51; 31, No. 53 (31 dic 1950), 74-75. CUBA

2174 ____. "La vida teatral de la Habana de 1790 a 1846," *Carteles* (La Habana), 1 feb 1948, pp. 30-31. CUBA

2175 Torre Revello, José. "El teatro," in his *Crónicas del Buenos Aires colonial.* Buenos Aires: Editorial Bajel, 1943. ARG

2176 ____. "Los teatros en el Buenos Aires del siglo XVIII," *Revista de Filología Hispánica,* VII (1945), 23-42. ARG

2177 Torres Fierro, Danubio. "Los caminos de la dramaturgia uruguaya," *Conjunto,* No. 13 (mayo-ago 1972), 93-97. URUG

2178 Torres León, Fernán. "La cultura en Colombia, 1964 ... El teatro," *Boletín Cultural y Bibliográfico,* VII, No. 7 (1964), 1275-1277. COL

2179 Torres Ríoseco, Arturo. *Ensayos sobre literatura latinoamericana.* México: Fondo de Cultura Económica, 1953. MEX

Includes: "Teatro indígena de México," pp. 7-25; "Tres dramaturgos mexicanos del período colonial: Eslava, Alarcón, Sor Juana," pp. 26-56.

2180 ____. "El primer dramaturgo americano--Fernán González de Eslava," *Hispania,* XXIV, No. 2 (May 1941), 161-170. MEX

2181 Torres Varela, Hilda. "¿Existe un teatro sudamericano?" *Cuadernos*, No. 19 (jul-ago 1956), 204-210. GEN

2182 ____. "Hacia una conjetura en el porvenir del teatro," *Cuadernos* (Paris), No. 53 (oct 1961), 128-134. GEN

2183 Tosta García, F. "Teatro de Maderero," *Crónica de Caracas*, 4, No. 19 (ago-dic 1954), 618-620. VEN

2184 Tovar, Juan. "*Inventando que sueño* de José Agustín," *Revista de Bellas Artes*, No. 22 (jul-ago 1968), 59-60. MEX

2185 *13 autores del nuevo teatro venezolano.* Carlos Miguel Suárez Radillo, ed. Caracas: Monte Avila Editores, 1971. 540 p. VEN

For listing of contents, see Suárez Radillo, Carlos M.

2186 Trenti Rocamora, José Luis. "Documentos para la historia del teatro porteño existentes en la Biblioteca Nacional," *Boletín de Estudios de Teatro*, Nos. 18-19 (set-dic 1947), 135-139. ARG

Colonial and nineteenth century.

2187 ____. "Espíritu de la censura teatral en tiempos de la Independencia," *Boletín de Estudios de Teatro*, VIII, No. 28 (ene-mar 1950), 25-28. ARG

2188 ____. "Gente de teatro del Buenos Aires colonial," *Boletín de Estudios de Teatro* (Buenos Aires), 5, No. 17 (jun 1947), 69-83. ARG

2189 ____. "Un impreso de interés para la historia del teatro colonial porteño," *Universidad* (Santa Fe), XXI (1949), 289-297. ARG

2190 ____. "El primer teatro porteño," *Boletín de Estudios de Teatro* (Buenos Aires), 5, No. 16 (mar 1947), 22-24. ARG

2191 ____. "La primera pieza teatral argentina," *Boletín de Estudios de Teatro* (Buenos Aires), 4, No. 15 (dic 1946), 224-234. ARG

A loa *presented in 1717 during the reign of Felipe V. Text follows.*

2192 Trenti Rocamora, José Luis. "El repertorio de la dramática colonial hispanoamericana," *Boletín de Estudios de Teatro*, VII, No. 26 (jul-set 1949), 104-125. GEN

2193 ____. *El repertorio de la dramática colonial hispanoamericana*. Buenos Aires: Talleres Gráficos ALEA, 1950. 110 p. GEN

2194 ____. *Selección dramática de Cristóbal de Aguilar, autor de la Córdoba colonial*. Prólogo y notas. Buenos Aires: Instituto Nacional de Estudios de Teatro, 1950. 144 p. ARG
Reviewed: Pasquariello, Anthony M.

2195 ____. *El teatro en la América colonial*. Buenos Aires: Huarpes, 1947. 534 p. GEN
Reviewed: Johnson, Harvey L.; Leonard, Irving.

2196 ____. "El teatro porteño durante el período hispánico," *Estudios*, LXXVIII, No. 425 (dic 1947), 408-434. ARG

2197 ____. "El teatro y la jura de Carlos IV en Arequipa," *Mar del Sur*, II, No. 5 (mayo-jun 1949), 28-35. PERU

2198 ____, ed. *Promoción y defensa del teatro nacional*. Buenos Aires: Ediciones del Carro de Tespis, 1962. 143 p. ARG

Documents by the "Secretario de Cultura y Acción Social de la Municipalidad de la ciudad de Buenos Aires," describing various theatrical groups.

2199 *3 obras de teatro nuevo*. Managua: Academia Nicaragüense de la Lengua, 1957. 225 p. NIC

Anthology with introduction. Includes: Joaquín Pasos and José Coronel Urtecho, Chinfonía burguesa; *Pablo Antonio Cuadra,* Por los caminos van los campesinos; *Rolando Steiner,* Judit.

2200 Triana y Antorveza, Humberto. "La temporada teatral de 1833 en Santa Fe de Bogotá," *Boletín Cultural y Bibliográfico* (Bogotá), VII, No. 9 (1964), 1629-1631. COL

2201 Trífilo, S. Samuel. "Celestino Gorostiza and the Contemporary Mexican Theater," *Drama and Theatre*, 9, No. 3 (Spring 1971), 147-150. MEX

2202 Trífilo, S. Samuel. "The Contemporary Theater in Mexico," *Modern Language Journal*, 46, No. 4 (Apr 1962), 153-157. MEX

2203 ____. "Mexican Theater Goes to Paris ... and a Polemic," *Hispania*, XLVII, No. 2 (May 1964), 335-337. MEX

2204 ____. "The Theater of Wilberto Cantón," *Hispania*, 54, No. 4 (Dec 1971), 869-875. MEX

2205 ____. "Wilberto Cantón: Mexican Dramatist," *Drama and Theatre*, 10, No. 3 (Spring 1972), 137-138. MEX

2206 Troiano, James J. "Pirandellism in the Theatre of Roberto Arlt," *Latin American Theatre Review*, 8/1 (Fall 1974), 37-44. ARG

2207 Trumper, Bernardo. "Experiencias de un escenógrafo," *Aisthesis* (Santiago), No. 1 (1966), 125-132. GEN

2208 Tschudi, Lilian. *Teatro argentino actual*. Buenos Aires: Fernando García Gambeiro, 1974. ARG

2209 Tull, John F. "Life and Works of Nalé Roxlo." Unpub. Ph.D. diss., Yale, 1958. ARG

2210 ____. "La mujer en el teatro de Nalé Roxlo," *Duquesne Hispanic Review*, III, No. 3 (Invierno 1964), 133-137. ARG

2211 ____. "El mundo teatral de Wilberto Cantón," *Duquesne Hispanic Review*, VI, No. 2 (Fall 1967), 1-7. MEX

2212 ____. "Poesía y humorismo en la obra de Nalé Roxlo," *Hispanófila*, No. 14 (1962), 41-44. ARG

2213 ____. "Shifting Dramatic Perspectives in Nalé Roxlo's *Judith y las rosas*," *Hispania*, 55, No. 1 (Mar 1972), 55-59. ARG

2214 ____. "A Source of the Doubling of Characters in *Judith y las rosas*," *Romance Notes*, II, No. 1 (Fall 1960), 21-22. ARG

2215 ____. "El teatro breve de Nalé Roxlo," *Duquesne Hispanic Review*, VI, No. 1 (1969), 37-40. ARG

2216 Tull, John F. "Unamuno y el teatro de Nalé Roxlo," *Estudios Americanos* (Sevilla), XXI (1961), 45-50. ARG

2217 ____. "Unifying Characteristics in Nalé Roxlo's Theater," *Hispania*, 44, No. 4 (1961), 643-646. ARG

2218 Tunberg, Karl A. "The New Cuban Theatre: A Report," *The Drama Review*, 14, No. 2 (Winter 1970), 43-55. CUBA

2219 Ugarte, Mario. "La posición de Federico Schroeder Inclán en el teatro mexicano contemporáneo." Unpub. Ph.D. diss., Southern California, 1971. MEX

2220 Ugarte Chamorro, Guillermo. "La actividad teatral en Lima," *Revista Peruana de Cultura*, No. 1 (mar-jun 1963), 169-174. PERU

Also in Boletín Cultural Peruano, *7, No. 15 (ene-jun 1964), 20-21, 23.*

2221 ____. "Los amores de Lope y un actor del Perú colonial," *Estudios de Teatro Peruano*, IV, No. 34 (1965), 4 p. PERU

2222 ____. "Antiguas vinculaciones de los teatros peruano y chileno," *Correo* (Lima), 16 nov 1965. PERU CHILE

2223 ____. "Ausencia de Ricardo Villarán, autor teatral peruano," *Estudios de Teatro Peruano*, IV, No. 12 (1965), 3 p. PERU

2224 ____. "Un conflicto del teatro limeño de 1834," *Estudios de Teatro Peruano*, IV, No. 25 (1962), 4 p. PERU

2225 ____. "Discurso...," *Apuntes* (Chile), No. 12 (jun 1961), 11-33. PERU CHILE

Relations between Chilean and Peruvian theater.

2226 ____. "Don Benjamín Vicuña MacKenna y el teatro peruano en la emancipación," *Estudios de Teatro Peruano*, IV, No. 18 (1961), 2 p. PERU

2227 ____. "Don Manuel Moncloa y Covarrubias, ilustre

hombre de teatro," *Letras* (Universidad de San Marcos, Lima), No. 62-63 (1959), 44-57. PERU

2228 Ugarte Chamorro, Guillermo. "La Escuela Nacional de Arte Escénico celebró su octavo aniversario," *Escena* (Lima), 1, No. 3 (mar 1954), 3-7. PERU

2229 ____. "Hima Sumac, drama de Clorinda Matto de Turner," *Estudios de Teatro Peruano*, IV, No. 1 (oct 1959), 1-3. PERU

2230 ____. "Homenaje de la ENAE a Manuel A. Segura en el 150 aniversario de su nacimiento," *Escena* (Lima), 3, No. 6 (set 1955), 3-11. PERU

2231 ____. "Joaquín Gantier, biógrafo de 'Santa Juana de América'," *Estudios de Teatro Latinoamericano*, V, No. 15 (oct 1964), 1-3. BOL

2232 ____. "Labor de la ENAE en 1954," *Escena* (Lima), 2, No. 5 (mayo 1955), 4-8, 28. PERU

Escuela Nacional de Arte Escénico.

2233 ____. "*Los patriotas de Lima en la noche feliz;* la primera comedia del Perú independiente," *Estudios de Teatro Peruano*, IV, No. 10 (ago 1960), 1-5. PERU

2234 ____. "El Perú y el teatro en la obra de Fray Camilo Henríquez," *Estudios de Teatro Latinoamericano*, V, No. 10 (sep 1961), 2 p. PERU ARG

2235 ____. "La primera loa teatral del Perú independiente," *Estudios de Teatro Peruano*, IV, No. 7 (1960), 1-5. PERU

2236 ____. "Ricardo Palma y Carlos Augusto Salaverry, autor teatral," *Estudios de Teatro Peruano*, IV, No. 40 (1965), 1-3. PERU

Also in Correo *(Lima), 27 nov 1965.*

2237 ____. "El teatro de la independencia del Perú," in *Literatura de la emancipación hispanoamericana y otros ensayos*. Lima: Universidad Nacional Mayor de San Marcos, Dirección Universitaria de Biblioteca y Publicaciones, 1972, pp. 27-39. PERU

2238 ____. "El teatro de Lima y un glorioso episodio

de la independencia del Perú," *Estudios de Teatro Peruano*, IV, No. 2 (nov 1959), 1-4. PERU

2239 Ugarte Chamorro, Guillermo. "El teatro en Arequipa durante el conflicto con España (1864-1866)," *Letras* (Universidad de San Marcos, Lima), No. 76-77 (1966), 126-137. PERU

2240 ____. "El teatro en el epistolario de don Ricardo Palma," *Estudios de Teatro Peruano*, IV, No. 3 (ene 1960), 1-4. PERU

2241 ____. "El teatro en la Biblioteca peruana de don Mariano Felipe Paz Soldán," *Boletín Bibliográfico* (Lima), 29, No. 1-4 (dic 1959), 34-37. PERU

2242 ____. "El teatro en la Biblioteca peruana de Gabriel René Moreno," *Boletín de la Sociedad Geográfica e Histórica* (Sucre), 48, No. 450 (1965), 353-367. PERU

Also in Estudios de Teatro Peruano, *IV, No. 37 (1965), 11 p.*

2243 ____. "El teatro en la obra poética de José Joaquín Olmedo," *Estudios de Teatro Peruano*, IV, No. 14 (1961), 1-5. ECUAD

2244 ____. "El teatro y Riva Agüero, presidente del Depto. de Lima," *Estudios de Teatro Peruano*, IV, No. 37 (1965), 1-3. PERU

2245 ____. "El telón del teatro de Lima y la independencia del Perú," *El Comercio* (Lima), 8 mar 1965. PERU

2246 Ulive, Ugo. "El Galpón," *Conjunto*, No. 3 (s.f.). URUG

2247 ____. "Mito y verdad de Florencio Sánchez," *Conjunto*, No. 1 (1964), 14-16, 49-50. URUG

2248 Ulles, Mário. *A Vida Intima do Teatro Brasileiro; 50 Anos do Teatro: 1903-1953.* Rio de Janeiro, 1954. BRAZ

2249 Ulloa Zamora, Alfonso. *El teatro nacional* (Apuntes para la biografía de un Coliseo). San José: Editorial Costa Rica, 1972. COSTA RICA

2250 Uría-Santos, María R. "El simbolismo de *Doña*

Beatriz: Primera obra de Carlos Solórzano," *Revista de Estudios Hispánicos*, VI, No. 1 (ene 1972), 63-70. GUAT

2251 Uribe Echevarría, Juan. "El teatro costumbrista," in *Tipos y costumbres de Chile*, Pedro Ruiz Aldea, ed. Santiago: Zig-Zag, 1947, pp. xlvi-lii. CHILE

2252 Urquiza, Juan José de. *El Cervantes en la historia del teatro argentino*. Buenos Aires: Ediciones Culturales Argentinas, 1968. 131 p. ARG

2253 ____. "Del teatro de otros tiempos: El estreno de *Jesús Nazareno*," *Boletín de Estudios de Teatro*, VIII, No. 28 (ene-mar 1950), 41-45. ARG

Recollections of the "estreno" of the Enrique García Velloso play.

2254 ____. "Evocación de Nicolás Granada," *Revista de Estudios de Teatro*, III, No. 9 (1965), 17-26. ARG

2255 Urtizberea, Raúl. "Presente y futuro de nuestro teatro," *Estudios* (Buenos Aires), L, No. 530 (dic 1961), 831-836. ARG

2256 Usigli, Rodolfo. *Anatomía del teatro*. México: Ecuador 0° 0' 0", 1967. 38 p. MEX

2257 ____. "Dos conversaciones con George Bernard Shaw y algunas cartas," *Cuadernos Americanos*, V, XXX, No. 6 (nov-dic 1946), 249-275; VI, XXXI, No. 1 (ene-feb 1947), 227-250. MEX

2258 ____. *Ideas sobre el teatro*. México: Instituto Mexicano de Cultura, 1969. GEN

2259 ____. *Itinerario del autor dramático*. México: La Casa de España en México, 1940. GEN

2260 ____. "Position and problems of the contemporary Mexican playwrights," *Proceedings of the Conference on Latin American Fine Arts* (June 14-17, 1951; cosponsored by the College of Fine Arts and the Institute of Latin American Studies, The University of Texas). Austin: University of Texas Press, 1952, pp. 58-70. MEX

2261 ____. "Primer ensayo hacia una tragedia mexicana,"

Cuadernos Americanos, Año IX, LII, No. 4 (jul-ago 1950), 102-125. MEX

2262 Usigli, Rodolfo. "El teatro de propaganda," *Panoramas* (México), 3, No. 13 (ene-feb 1965), 137-142. MEX

2263 Valdés, Isidro Fernán. "El teatro y sus problemas," *Talía*, II, 1, No. 10 (abr 1955), 11. GEN

2264 Valdés Rodríguez, J. M. "Algo sobre el teatro en Cuba," *Universidad de la Habana*, 28, No. 170 (nov-dic 1964), 47-63. CUBA

2265 Valdés Vivó, Raúl. "Azahares en la selva," *Conjunto*, No. 11-12 (ene-abr 1972), 13-14. CUBA

On the background of this author's play, Naranjas en Saigon.

2266 Valdez, Luis. "Notes sur le théâtre chicano," *Travail Théâtral* (Paris), No. 7 (avr-juin 1972), 71-74. U.S.

Les Actos, *pp. 75-77.*

2267 Valencia, Gerardo. "Reflexiones en torno al teatro colombiano," *Universidad Nacional de Colombia*, I, No. 2 (mar-mayo 1945), 63-70. COL

2268 ____. "Los temas nacionales en el teatro colombiano," *Boletín de la Academia Colombiana*, XIX, No. 80 (1969), 473-486. COL

2269 Valera y Alcalá Galiano, Juan. "El teatro en Chile," *Cartas americanas*. Madrid: Aguilar, 1942. CHILE

2270 Valldeperes, Manuel. "Un teatro americano con conflicto y humana preocupación," *La Torre* (San Juan), 15, No. 57 (jul-set 1967), 167-179. GEN

2271 Valle, Rafael Heliodoro. Review: "Armando de Maria y Campos. *El teatro está siempre en crisis...* (crónicas de 1946 a 1950). México: Ediciones Arriba el Telón, 1954." *Revista*

Interamericana de Bibliografía, V, No. 3 (jul-set 1955), 197. GEN

2272 Vallejo, Santiago. "El teatro en Trujillo," *Escena* (Lima), 2, No. 5 (mayo 1955), 11-12, 22. PERU

2273 VanLiew, Lucille, and Karen Getty. "Del Narciso secular al divino Narciso," *Etcaêtera* (Guadalajara), 2ª época, III, No. 8-10 (jul 1968), 61-70. MEX

On the works of Calderón and Sor Juana Inés de la Cruz.

2274 Vargas Ugarte, Rubén. "Introducción," in *Amar su propia muerte;* comedia del Dr. Juan de Espinosa Medrano. Lima: Biblioteca Histórica Peruana, 14, 1943. PERU

2275 ____. "Prólogo," in *De nuestro antiguo teatro.* Lima: Compañía de Impresores y Publicidad, 1943. PERU

Collection of plays from the 16th, 17th and 18th centuries with introduction and notes by Vargas Ugarte.

2276 Vázquez, Miguel Angel. "La farsa dentro de la vida. *Requiem por un girasol* del chileno Jorge Díaz," *Alero* (Guatemala), 4, No. 2 (1971), 61. CHILE

2277 Vázquez-Amaral, Mary. "*Yo también hablo de la rosa* de Emilio Carballido: un estudio crítico," *Revista de la Universidad de México*, XXVII, No. 5 (ene 1973), 25-29. MEX

2278 Vázquez Pérez, Eduardo. "La audacia colectiva frente a los mitos y la colonización cultural," *Conjunto*, No. 18 (oct-dic 1973), 17-22. COL GEN

2279 ____. "En dos Chiles muy distintos," *Conjunto*, No. 21 (jul-set 1974), 59-60. CHILE

2280 ____. "Una experiencia de creación colectiva en Ecuador," *Conjunto*, No. 22 (oct-dic 1974), 54-58. ECUAD

2281 ____. "El teatro argentino, Julio Mauricio y los retratos," *Conjunto*, No. 16 (abr-jun 1973), 86-94. ARG

2282 Vázquez Pérez, Eduardo. "Tendremos un teatro nacional o no tendremos teatro," *Conjunto*, No. 14 (set-dic 1972), 38-42. GEN

2283 ____. "*Túpac Amaru*, afirmación revolucionaria," *Conjunto*, No. 15 (ene-mar 1973), 15-16. ARG

On Osvaldo Dragún's Túpac Amaru.

2284 Vedia, Leónidas de. "La comedia argentina," *Lyra*, XVII, No. 174-176 (1959). ARG

2285 Vega, Carlos. "Danzas en el teatro de antaño," *Revista de Estudios de Teatro*, II, No. 4 (1962), 55-58. ARG

2286 Veiga Fialho, A. "Teatro em 1964: Um Balanço," *Revista Civilização Brasileira*, No. 1 (mar 1965), 218-221. BRAZ

2287 Velasco, Margot. "Del drama épico a la dramaturgia de documento," in "El gallo ilustrado," Supl. de *El Día* (18 mar 1973), p. 12. GEN

2288 ____. "Dos obras, dos puestas en escena, dos momentos en la historia de México, dos actitudes ante la función teatral," in "El gallo ilustrado," Supl. de *El Día* (13 mayo 1973), p. 15. MEX

Critique of Examentlatelolco *and Willebaldo López's* Yo soy Juárez.

2289 ____. "Realidad y magia en el teatro de Solórzano," in "El gallo ilustrado," Supl. de *El Día* (3 jun 1973), p.14. GUAT

2290 ____. "Rictus memorables en la agonía del drama: Un libro de Osvaldo Dragún," in "El gallo ilustrado," Supl. de *El Día* (6 mayo 1973), p. 14. ARG

Critique of Dragún's Y nos dijeron que éramos inmortales.

2291 Velásquez, Francisco. "¿Hacia dónde va el teatro universitario?" *Revista Teatro* (Medellín), No. 4 (1970-71), 31-33. GEN

2292 ____. "Segundo festival latinoamericano de teatro," *Conjunto*, No. 9 (s.f.), 121-125. GEN

Segundo festival de Teatro Universitario, Manizales, 1969.

2293 Vélez, Joseph F. "Una entrevista con Emilio Carballido," *Latin American Theatre Review*, 7/1 (Fall 1973), 17-24. MEX

2294 ____. "Tres aspectos de *El relojero de Córdoba* de Emilio Carballido," *Explicación de Textos Literarios*, 1-2 (1973), 151-159. MEX

2295 Ventura Agudiez, Juan. "Armando Moock y el sainete argentino," *Duquesne Hispanic Review*, III, No. 3 (Invierno 1964), 139-164. ARG CHILE

2296 ____. "El concepto costumbrista de Armando Moock," *Revista Hispánica Moderna*, 29, No. 2 (1963), 148-157. CHILE

2297 Vergara, Pilar. "Tres opiniones sobre el teatro chileno," *Cuadernos del Sur* (Buenos Aires), 4, No. 35 (jun 1967), 474-476. CHILE

2298 Vergara de Bietti, Noemí. "Los tres Payró," *Cursos y Conferencias* (Buenos Aires), IL, No. 274 (set 1956), 314-331. ARG

2299 "*Vestido de Noiva*," *Anhembi*, XXXI, No. 92 (1958), 401-404. BRAZ

On Nelson Rodrigues's play.

2300 Vetancurt, Agustín de. *Teatro mexicano; descripción breve de los sucesos exemplares de la Nueva-España en el Nuevo Mundo Occidental de las Indias*. Madrid: J. Porrúa Turanzas, 1960-61. MEX

Subsequent version: Vetancurt, Agustín de. Teatro mexicano; *descripción breve de los sucesos ejemplares, históricos y religiosos del Nuevo Mundo de las Indias. Crónica de la Provincia del Santo Evangelio de México. Menologio franciscano de los varones más señalados, que con sus vidas ejemplares, perfección religiosa, ciencia, predicación evangélica en su vida, ilustraron la Provincia del Santo Evangelio de México. 1 ed. facsimilar. México: Editorial Porrúa, 1971.*

2301 Viale Paz, Julio César. "50 años de teatro argentino: el panorama de la escena nacional desde el estreno de *La piedra de escándalo* hasta nuestros días," *Continente* (Buenos Aires), No. 72 (mar 1953), 67-81. ARG

2302 Viale Paz, Julio César. "Lucio V. Mansilla, autor teatral," *Revista de Estudios de Teatro*, 4, No. 11 (1970), 3-6. ARG

2303 ____. "Semblanza de Francisco de Ducasse," *Cuadernos de Cultura Teatral* (Buenos Aires), No. 22 (1947), 65-89. ARG
Reviewed: Kurz, Harry.

2304 Vianna Filho, Oduvaldo. "O meu *Corpo a Corpo*," *Revista de Teatro* (Rio), No. 387 (maio-jun 1972), 29-30. BRAZ

Commentary, followed by text of play.

2305 Vidal, Hernán. "*Esa luna que empieza* y Maeterlinck: La contemporaneidad modernista," *Latin American Theatre Review*, 6/2 (Spring 1973), 5-11. PERU

A study involving Percy Gibson Parra's play.

2306 Vidal, Jacqueline, and Enrique Buenaventura. "Apuntes para un método de creación colectiva," *Revista Teatro* (Medellín), No. 9 (1972), 45-96. COL

The TEC of Cali, Colombia.

2307 Vieta, Ezequiel. "Dramaturgia y revolución," *Universidad de la Habana*, XXXI, No. 186-188 (jul-dic 1967), 59-70. CUBA

Also as: "Cuba: Dramaturgia y revolución," Primer Acto, *No. 108 (1969), 22-30.*

2308 Vilalta, Maruxa. "El teatro del Granero en 1963," *Cuadernos de Bellas Artes*, V, No. 5 (mayo 1964), 21-25. MEX

2309 Villacis Molina, Rodrigo. "El teatro en Quito," *Letras del Ecuador*, XVI, No. 120 (ene-feb 1961), 12-21. ECUAD

2310 Villafañe, Javier. "El mundo de los títeres," *Cuadernos de Cultura Teatral* (Buenos Aires), No. 20 (1944), 71-84. GEN

2311 Villagómez, Alberto. "Prolegómenos para una sociología del teatro," in *Literatura de la emancipación hispanoamericana y otros ensayos.* Lima: Universidad Nacional Mayor de San Marcos, Dirección Universitaria de Biblioteca y Publicaciones, 1972, pp. 293-296. GEN

2312 Villaurrutia, Xavier. "Mexican Painters and the Theatre," *World Theatre*, 1, No. 3 (1951), 36-40. MEX

2313 ____. "Un nuevo autor dramático," in his *Textos y pretextos: literatura--drama--pintura.* México: La Casa de España en México, s.f., 177-182. MEX

About Celestino Gorostiza.

2314 ____. "El teatro es así," in his *Textos y pretextos: literatura--drama--pintura.* México: La Casa de España en México, s.f., 183-190. MEX

On the status of the recent Mexican theater.

2315 ____. "Teatro y cinematógrafo: convergencias y divergencias," *Cuadernos Americanos*, VI, No. 3 (mayo-jun 1947), 221-236. GEN

2316 ____. "Textos," *Revista de Bellas Artes*, No. 7 (ene-feb 1966). MEX

"El teatro: recuerdos y figuras," pp. 8-15.

2317 Viñas, David. *Del apogeo de la oligarquía a la crisis de la ciudad liberal: Laferrère.* Buenos Aires: Editorial Jorge Alvarez, 1967. 157 p. ARG

2318 Vodanović, Sergio. "Experiencias de un autor," *Aisthesis* (Santiago), No. 1 (1966), 103-110. CHILE

2319 ____. "El Grupo Aleph," *Latin American Theatre Review*, 4/2 (Spring 1971), 61-64. CHILE

2320 Wagner, Fernando. "Perfil del teatro mexicano moderno," *Annali Instituto Universitario Orientale, Sezione Romanza* (Napoli), VII (1965), 255-260. MEX

2321 Waiss, Oscar. "El drama de América Latina," *Tri S*, No. 5 (1962), 47-55. GEN

2322 Ward, James W., III. "A Tentative Inventory of Young Puerto Rican Writers," *Hispania*, 54, No. 4 (Dec 1971), 924-930. PTO. RICO

Among others, Luis Rafael Sánchez.

2323 Warren, Virgil A. "Status of Modern Cuban Theater," *Hispania*, XXIV, No. 2 (May 1941), 205-210. CUBA

2324 Weber de Kurlat, Frida. *Lo cómico en el teatro de Fernán González de Eslava*. Buenos Aires: Universidad de Buenos Aires, Facultad de Filosofía y Letras, 1963. 253 p. MEX

2325 ____. "Estructuras cómicas en los coloquios de Fernán González de Eslava," *Revista Iberoamericana*, No. 41-42 (ene-dic 1956), 393-407. MEX

2326 ____. "Formas del sayagués en los 'Coloquios espirituales y sacramentales' de Fernán González de Eslava, México, 1610," *Filología* (Buenos Aires), V, No. 3 (1959), 248-262. MEX

2327 Weinburg, María Beatrix de. "Revisión crítica de una interpretación de ciertas formas lingüísticas del primitivo teatro gauchesco," in *Sextas jornadas de historia y literatura norteamericana y rioplatense*. 2 vol. Buenos Aires: Asociación Argentina de Estudios Americanos. s.f. ARG

2328 Weisinger, Nina Lee. Review: "Arturo Mori. *Treinta años de teatro hispanoamericano*. Prólogo de José Elizondo. México: Editorial Moderna, 1941." *Hispania*, XXV, No. 1 (Feb 1942), 122. GEN

2329 Weller, Hubert P. "La obra teatral de Antonio Acevedo Hernández: dramaturgo chileno (1886-1962)." Unpub. Ph.D. diss., Indiana, 1964. CHILE

2330 Wéyland, Walter G. *Roberto J. Payró*. Buenos Aires: Ediciones Culturales Argentinas, Ministerio de Educación y Justicia, 1962. 152 p. ARG

2331 Williams, E. Eugene. "Abnormal Psychology in

Some of Usigli's Works," *Specialia* (Carbondale, Illinois), No. 1 (1969). MEX

2332 Williams, E. Eugene. "Character and Characterization in the Plays of Rodolfo Usigli." Unpub. Ph.D. diss., Georgia, 1971. MEX

2333 Wilson Marín, Carlos. "Teatro chileno: La compañía profesional de la Universidad Católica," *Insula*, XVI, No. 176-177 (1961?), 23. CHILE

2334 Wogan, Daniel and Américo Barabino. "Los americanismos de Florencio Sánchez," *Revista Iberoamericana*, No. 27 (jun 1948), 145-197. URUG

2335 Wolff, Federico. "Síntesis del movimiento teatral uruguayo," *Conjunto*, No. 5 (oct-dic 1967), 89-92. URUG

2336 Woodford, Archer. *Obras de Juan de Cueto y Mena*. Edición crítica con introducción y notas. Prólogo de José Manuel Rivas Sacconi. Bogotá: Publicaciones del Instituto Caro y Cuervo, IX, 1952. 314 p. COL
Reviewed: Pasquariello, Anthony M.

2337 Woodyard, George. "A Metaphor for Repression: Two Portuguese Inquisition Plays," *Luso-Brazilian Review*, X, No. 1 (Jun 1973), 68-75. BRAZ

Includes Dias Gomes's O Santo Inquérito.

2338 ____. *The Modern Stage in Latin America: Six Plays*. New York: Dutton, 1971. 331 p. GEN

Anthology includes: René Marquês, The Fanlights; *Alfredo Dias Gomes,* Payment as Pledged; *Osvaldo Dragún,* And They Told Us We Were Immortal; *Jorge Díaz,* The Place Where the Mammals Die; *José Triana,* The Criminals; *Emilio Carballido,* I Too Speak of the Rose.
Reviewed: Matas, Julio; Rabkin, Gerald.

2339 ____. Review: "Antonio Magaña Esquivel, ed. *Teatro mexicano del siglo XX*. México: Fondo de Cultura Económica, 1970." *Hispania*, 54, No. 2 (May 1971), 403. MEX

2340 ____. Review: "*Tres obras de teatro*. La Habana: Casa de las Américas, 1970." *Hispania*, 56, No. 1

(Mar 1973), 182. GEN

Review of Roberto Cossa, Germán Rozenmacher, Carlos Somigliani and Ricardo Talesnik, El avión negro; *Egon Wolff,* Flores de papel; *Eduardo Pavlovsky,* La mueca.

2341 Woodyard, George. Review: "William I. Oliver. *Voices of Change in the Spanish American Theater.* Austin and London: University of Texas Press, 1971." *Revista Interamericana de Bibliografía,* XXIII, No. 3 (jul-set 1973), 341-342. GEN

2342 ____. "The Search for Identity: A Comparative Study in Contemporary Latin American Drama." Unpub. Ph.D. diss., Illinois, 1966. GEN

2343 ____. "The Theatre of the Absurd in Spanish America," *Comparative Drama,* III, No. 3 (Fall 1969), 183-192. GEN

Principally Jorge Díaz, Elena Garro, Virgilio Piñera, Griselda Gambaro.

2344 ____. "Toward a Radical Theatre in Spanish America," in *Contemporary Spanish American Literature.* Houston: University of Houston, 1973, pp. 93-102. GEN

Focuses on Luis Rafael Sánchez and Vicente Leñero.

2345 Wyatt, James Larkin. "La obra dramática de Rodolfo Usigli." Diss., Universidad Nacional Autónoma de México, 1950. MEX

2346 Xammar, Luis Fabio. "Juan de Arona, romántico del Perú," *Revista Iberoamericana,* No. 12 (May 1943), 455-478. PERU

Pseudonym of Peruvian Pedro Paz Soldán y Unanue.

2347 ____. "Virgilio y Juan de Arona," *Revista "3",* No. 9 (s.f.), 42-47. PERU

2348 "Y pasaron veinte años," *Apuntes* (Santiago), No. 12 (jun 1961), 7-10. CHILE

20th anniversary of founding of Teatro Experimental of the University of Chile.

2349 Yáñez, Rubén, and Carlos Martínez Moreno. *El teatro actual*. Buenos Aires: Centro Editor de América Latina, 1968, pp. 481-496. URUG

2350 Yáñez Silva, Nathanael. *Memorias de un hombre de teatro*. Santiago de Chile: Zig-Zag, 1966. CHILE

2351 Ybarra-Frausto, Tomás, and Luis Valdez. "Teatro chicano: Two Reports," *Latin American Theatre Review*, 4/2 (Spring 1971), 51-55. U.S.

2352 Yépez Miranda, Alfredo. "La incanidad del *Ollantay*," *Revista del Instituto Americano de Arte* (Cuzco), VII, No. 2 (1954), 157-170. PERU

2353 ____. "Testimonio de una civilización," *Revista de Estudios de Teatro*, No. 2 (1959), 49-60. PERU

On Ollantay.

2354 Young, Howard T. Review: "Willis Knapp Jones. *Breve historia del teatro latinoamericano*. México: Studium, 1956." *Hispania*, XL, No. 3 (Sept 1957), 391. GEN

2355 Yunque, Alvaro. *Presencia, vacilación y esperanza del teatro argentino*. Buenos Aires: Anteo, 1946. 29 p. ARG

Teatro del partido comunista.

2356 Zampa, Giorgio. "Il *Murieta* de Neruda e il *Toller* de Dorst," *Dramma*, 46, No. V (1971), 58-64. CHILE

2357 Zapata Olivella, Manuel. "Comparsas y teatro callejero en los carnavales colombianos," *Boletín Cultural y Bibliográfico* (Bogotá), VI, No. 11 (1963), 1763-1765. COL

2358 Zavala Muñiz, Justino. *20 años de Comedia Nacional*.

Montevideo: Comisión de Teatros Municipales, 1967. URUG

2359 Zavalía, Alberto de. *Presente y porvenir del teatro*. Buenos Aires: Dirección General de Cultura, 1957. 44 p. GEN

2360 "Ze Vicente: pela estrada afora," *Palco + Platéia*, No. 12 (s.f.), 10-13. BRAZ

On playwright José Vicente.

INDEX

In addition to the index of names, the following subject categories are also included:

(A) denotes Actor/Actress
(D) denotes Director

Index